"With wisdom and eloquence, *The Place of Us* is a heartfelt, brutally honest account of great loss and even greater love. Thank you for giving words to the raw, desperate feelings of grief I too felt after the sudden death of my disabled son. Brilliant illustration of the competition in our hearts between grief and love, lightness and dark black." —Patti Saylor, disability rights advocate and mother of the late Ethan Saylor

"Advocating for his right to live in this world was her gift to him. An ethereal goodbye was his gift to her. *The Place of Us* is a mother's story of the wonderful, panicked, joyful, relentless, upside down, victorious, anguished, miraculous life of loving a child who has not come to stay. A story everyone should hear but no parent should have to tell. Telling it is Karen's gift to us." —Nancy Stephan, author of *The Truth about Butterflies: A Memoir*

"Karen Draper shares personal details as a parent who must fight for her child to have what every other child has: friends, daily routines, community acceptance, and appreciation for their gifts and talents. This book tells the tale of perseverance, love, and community, as she and her family break barriers of prejudice. Whether you have a disabled child or not, every family should read this." —Carol Quirk, Ed.D., CEO Maryland Coalition for Inclusive Education

"In the struggles of Karen, her husband Sam, and most vitally, her son Preston, we see vividly the strength it requires to take part in miracles. And to endure them. The Drapers redefine courage and in so doing, discover a singular grace in living that most of us miss. Read this book. Take a vicarious journey to the world of the Drapers. You'll be better for it." —Paul Daugherty, author of *An Uncomplicated Life* and father of an adult daughter with Down Syndrome

The Place of Us

The Place of Us

a memoir of love, loss & courage

Karen Draper

E. L. Marker
Salt Lake City

E. L. Marker, an imprint of WiDo Publishing
Salt Lake City, Utah
widopublishing.com

Cover design by Steven Novak
Book design by Marny K. Parkin
Hummingbird icon by macrovector_official from freepik.com

ISBN 978-1-947966-24-6
Printed in the United States of America

In loving memory of Preston Edward Draper
July 19, 1983–December 20, 2006

And to my beloveds here on earth—Sam and Samantha

Contents

It began on the inside
where all things pivot and ponder.
Where fear is buried and courage grown.

Then it rose up from the earth of me
to sit and breathe
on the high ground of skin and bone,
where it simmered until the lightness
burned all the bad things off of me.

And love began again

Author's Note

To aid me in remembering twenty-three years worth of living, I relied on my journal notes, writing notebook, school communication books and records, as well as hospital records and my own memory. I initially interviewed teachers, principals and peer buddies to make sure that my perception of Preston was at least close to theirs and during the interviews I learned of things I never knew. Some names have been changed for various reasons. This book was driven by the teachable pivotal moments in Preston's life and anyone who was in that moment was then brought into the storyline.

Preface

I HAD NO REAL VISION OF WHAT HE WOULD LOOK LIKE. I didn't even know he was a *he*. Instead, my thoughts lay in the realm of supposed things—like feeding and diapering, rocking him to sleep and sleepless nights. I supposed Sam and I would be wandering around the farmhouse at three a.m., our bare feet skimming over the cracks in the old pine flooring. Intersecting each other long enough to hand off the little bundle in our arms like weary soldiers changing guard. His birth on Tuesday ensured he would be home for the first of many lazy Sunday mornings spent snuggled in bed. I supposed the newspaper and magazines would be spread about as we watched him sleep in between us while an old movie played like white noise. That's what our brand new family was supposed to look like.

Family.

A word I dreamt of. From this omnipotent moment on we would no longer be just Sam and Karen. We were now Mom and Dad and firstborn baby—a real honest to goodness family. A supposedly typical reading the Sunday paper in bed family. Somehow, long ago and faraway, Preston chose us as his parents. And our definition of life, of what defined "typical," or "supposed" or "easy," changed overnight.

Growing a life is never easy. I don't think anything worthwhile ever is. When you stop to think about it, all new life begins in darkness and stretches toward some form of lightness. Ours isn't a fairy tale. It is a life tale—a history of how we arrived at the place of us. This is how we grew a life from darkness into lightness. It began like this.

"We had a healthy baby boy last night! What happened?" Sam's voice sounded like he had already hung up the phone. One minute we were floating happily along and the next minute a great riptide pulled us out—away from all we knew. The trouble with riptides is the more you try to swim the way you know to swim, the further it pulls you out and down. Eventually, through much trial and error, we adapted by figuring out a new way that at first didn't make sense to our logical brains. Up to this point our world had been logical and chronological, just the way we planned, in the order we planned. Our life made sense the way logical is literally implanted in the word chronological. Typical had come to sit comfortably in our brains. Why we got pulled out to sea didn't matter. It was an irrevocable fact. It only mattered that we found a new uncommon way to keep our heads above water.

Overnight we were transformed from what we thought we were supposed to be to who and what we grew into.

We were supposed to be a typical mother and father about to have our first child. Then we could officially become the typical American family. I could see our future. It held all the typical extraordinary events. My life list told me so.

We would vacation at the beach in August, craft Halloween costumes and parade around the neighborhood with our 2.0 children, stay up all night wrapping and assembling Christmas presents so we could bask in the ten-minute glow on our children's faces, sit at the kitchen table helping with homework while listening to after school tales, cheer like idiots at sporting events. And eventually, at major milestone celebrations like graduations and weddings, after having raised obviously brilliant children, moisture would slip quickly over our eyes the way the years had slipped quickly by—both incapable of being caught. Yes. Our family scrapbook would look similar to that of our friends.

We were all supposed to be typical in our own right so we could share commonalities around the campfire as easily as we passed marshmallows back and forth.

We're not meant to suppose things into being. Yet we do. We are born to stretch and bend beyond what is imaginable to our knowing soul, to dream ourselves into a great unknowing—one realization after another.

Each realization: so intrinsic to the organs necessary for loving and breathing between the skin and bone of life, empowering us to become who we are meant to be.

Step by step we learned that all the supposed things—the dreamed of feared of things—existed only in the crystal ball of our mind. And over the course of time each one would be uniquely brought to life, purely, by the oxygen of lived moments—our first realization.

Now we were different, beautifully different in our own right. This is who we were meant to be.

I think everyone has a higher being that knows who and what you're meant to be. Some beings speak to us in code that requires translation from an expert. Some whisper. Some yell excitedly—they're the lucky ones who knew straight from the womb what they wanted to be. Some beings (like mine) take years before their mission can be achieved. No matter how or when you become the person you're meant to be, it only matters that you listen to the silence of your knowing soul.

That very thing carries the sound of happiness and enlightenment.

I didn't set out to write a spiritual book. But as this book began telling me what it was meant to be, as I wrote and rewrote more of it, I realized it was very spiritual. How can the telling of a life, the breathing in and out of pain and joy, not be spiritual? No matter what you believe, sharing a life with other human beings filled with laughter and tears, and above all, love, is spiritual.

Our story began in a hospital room in Pennsylvania in 1983. Weeks after our son was born, I wrote my first note to him. I wrote from my heart, from a place of love I've never before known. It was penned as a hello/good-bye letter due to his ominous beginnings.

I believe he came to me to cause me to write and think in a new uncommon way. After all, he was an uncommon boy. I had everything I needed from that point on. My heart, my truth, and a piece of paper and pen by which to share them both. At least that's what I thought. It would be miles and miles later. With scraps of paper scattered about my life like crumbs on a messy wayward trail that would eventually lead me back to who I was meant to be. Thirty years to be exact. Thirty years of collecting scraps of my truth before I would sit down to face my fear head on in the center of my internal universe.

Why is it that truth, our greatest gift, is often scary as hell? In my case I needed to attend a life classroom before I was afforded the vantage point from which I could clearly see the portal to my path. I had to step back, way, way back, to a place of unknowing in order to take in the entirety of its message.

This is who I was meant to be: a spirited woman, friend and lover to my husband, mother of a differently gifted boy, mother of a wise and witty girl. Advocate. And now, writer. Reporter of courage and fear, of love and loss. Storyteller of unexplainable things.

I am here, this infinitely whole and broken person to tell Preston's story, because he allowed me to touch the recesses of my spirit, my soul, and most importantly, my mother's heart.

This is my fingerprint of our family's uncommon lifestyle. How I inhaled it, then blew it onto paper in long and short exaggerated breaths until I had no air left inside of me.

This book is a love song to my husband and children. It is a declaration of rights for children with disabilities and the parents who love and care for them. A testament to the power of one and the collective voice of many. An acknowledgement of a wondrously diverse community we were blessed to know. A consideration of humankind. And from a mother's perspective—a grief anthem.

This is my manifesto on how to celebrate a life.

When life defies definition and the words you typically live by can't be found; you change the definitions and make up a few words of your own.

miracle /mirek(e)l/ ~

a surprising and welcome event that is not explicable by natural or scientific laws and is therefore considered to be the work of a divine agency

Origin ~

Middle English: via Old French from Latin miraculum 'object of wonder,' from mirari "to wonder at, marvel, be astonished," from mirus "wonderful, astonishing, amazing"

miracle ~

a newborn baby

grass growing

laughter, breathing, walking, talking

a sunrise,

anything . . . everything

Chapter 1a

On the Cusp of Heaven and Hell: Part One

*I*NTUITION OR PREMONITION?

The August sun was already busy making heat. I sat on my lavender paisley bedspread writing my fourth-grade shopping list before my annual back to school physical at noon. My mother checked in at the receptionist window while simultaneously motioning with her eyes the way moms do, for me to sit down and not stare. The dark paneled walls of the doctor's office made the mother and baby appear more vivid than I wanted. It was just the four of us.

The mother held him across her lap to accommodate the big thick block of sponge her baby's huge head was resting on. His head filled the entirety of the sponge. I didn't listen to my mother. I stared. I couldn't help notice the million blue veins frantically racing all over his head like they didn't know where to go. Then there was the way the mother looked at him as though he was the most beautiful baby on earth. Her eyes never left his. My nine-year-old brain didn't understand why she looked so proud.

Some memories are visceral. They're put in our way for a reason. The memory of the mother and baby never left me. It visited in my memory place more times than I can count. And when I became pregnant, it lived with me.

Two businessmen in dark monochromatic suits stood like carved figures under the Sycamore lined street watching my burgeoning belly and me bent inches over the sidewalk, breathing through a contraction. With their shiny black shoes in my peripheral, I stared at the sidewalk's machine-made ridges wondering if they were meant to hold things or let them go. In the cement were variations of gray I'd never noticed before. I suppose with great intimacy all things reveal themselves in time. Was this variation of labor, unlike what I'd imagined, revealing a new truth to me? In this weird unexpected moment as my good-sized pain was made evident to onlooking strangers; along with our son—a process, conscious or otherwise, was born that saved me and my husband, Sam, on most days. It wasn't anything we strategized over or even contemplated. Preston and his challenges came at us too quick for that. It was more like a soft but firm whisper that somehow kept us from going mad or worse yet, from floating away separately.

A process employed of a life's worth of endings that were really great and small beginnings in disguise, where we found the delicacy and strength of beginning again. It was there, organically in the air, reminding us:

Before we become busy with knowing. Let us unknow. Before we end what could have been. Let us begin again.

I should have known right then by the irreconcilable colors as he arrived against the sharp silence of nothingness. His shock of red hair delighted us. Skin the color of milk. His blueness of eyes fought the intensity of red hair. *She* knew but couldn't say. Not yet. My introvert brain needed to receive him in layers, dark and light layers that at first didn't make sense. Yet there was something in the layering that did.

Was the pallor of our son's skin due to his Irish heritage or the long labor? I wondered. An unnerving quiet overwhelmed our ears. Not the long-awaited sound we dreamed of, where a tiny cry burst from brand new lungs. The expected cry. The one that was supposed to grow louder with every second he was in this world without us.

From the delivery room table, white knuckled grip in his, I watched Sam's face transform into a question mark. The tiled labor room walls seemed to push the already muffled sounds down to an inaudible level. Our ears painfully cognizant of just how insistent silence can be. Sam and I remained hostage to the quiet bustle of doctors and nurses with loud looks in their eyes. We watched helplessly as the nurse administered oxygen. Silence overtook the room like a freight train roaring toward us. *Come on*, Sam whispered, as if willing life into our soundless baby boy. I now understood why it's called The Miracle of Life. It felt however miracles feel when the world comes alive again. When you burst from the realm that feels thick and unyielding. The elation, as you vow never to ask God for anything again. After what felt like forever in this cautious place where we forgot to breathe, we heard the faint but miraculous cry of our newborn son.

I'd never witnessed a miracle, at least not that I was aware of. I couldn't help but imagine how many unseen miracles happen in the span of our lives. How many had I already missed? The delivery nurse walked toward us cradling our son, now wondrously crying and breathing with life.

While I beheld Preston's perfectly made body I realized that, now, I was aware. The miraculous timing of every molecule knitting together in an unbroken chain of organs, bones, tissue and blood, with a casing of downy skin to cover the humanness of his inner workings brought me to tears as I looked into the eyes of our tiny baby boy who was staring directly into my soul.

I wasn't prepared to fall this much in love. What human being is ever ready to experience a love so instantaneous and exquisite as this precise moment, when your tears meet your smile, all orchestrated by a new little heart now beating outside of yours.

I awoke the next morning groggy but still a new mother anxious to hold Preston in my arms. The mom across the hall was already nursing her baby. I grew impatient watching the clock on the wall ticking away another fifteen minutes of my baby's life I was missing. Yesterday's minutes were mere dashes telling me when I needed to be somewhere or how much time was left before dinner was done. But now they were tangible and irrevocable. Overnight our son had become our second hand and we were now the guardians of time. This responsibility came with a heaviness I hadn't expected. Patience was not a gift I currently possessed, not in the careful way I would need it now

I sat tethered to my IV thinking, practicing my yoga breath, trying to quell this strange new presence.

I sarcastically wished there was a Buffet of Life ripped of calories but loaded with portions of virtues needed for the day—an appetizer ripe with courage, an entrée heaped with patience, a side order of kindness for an unkind day, a whopping bowl of humor, and a tall glass of hope for when my glass feels half empty.

An air of indifference wafted in beside Nurse Tate who nonchalantly proceeded to check my vitals, looking toward me instead of at me. "Could you please bring my son to me so I can nurse him?" I asked. Her voice was void of emotion. She explained they were warming him up because he was cold. "Who better to warm him than me!" I retorted. I had quickly gone from being impatient to feeling confused and angry. My hospital room was quiet. A private cocoon encapsulated from the chaos in the nursery down the hall. My only thoughts were that of annoyance with indifferent nurses and taking Preston home to his newly decorated nursery. The first room we'd painstakingly finished in the farmhouse we were renovating. Powder blue wallpaper with beige upside-down teardrops covered the walls and worn out pine floors had been refinished to a warm brown that glowed in the morning light. The Jenny Lind crib with the blue and yellow plaid blanket draped over the railing, the changing table with baby powder, lotion, diapers and the oak rocker were first baby fresh and ready to soak up his delicious newborn smell.

My mother's intuition, like our newborn son, hadn't been sufficiently caressed. It didn't know how to function in this world yet. I hadn't lived in it long enough for it to permeate my being, my brand new *Mothers Being*.

My heart and soul was now simultaneously linked to my child's without prior thought or effort. An unexplainable connectivity of heart and mind had begun inside a space in me I wasn't aware of. That's what the hard lump in my throat was as I watched Nurse Tate trying to camouflage any trace of emotion on her face. I kept telling myself it was purely first time mother's jitters but this new connectivity wouldn't easily be denied. My heart had instantaneously transformed into a capacity and might of which I've never known. From this moment on, feelings that had been birthed into the world alongside my son would flourish with his every breath. Making a baby had made another heart in me.

After what seemed like hours, Dr. Baer appeared. The urgent look on his face stopped me from airing my complaints. Barely two feet into my room he started to explain, his hand already scratching his head. "Sorry to keep you waiting, but I've been busy with your son." He tentatively sat on the side of my bed placing his hand on my knee like a father about to deliver bad news. I felt my heart racing, no doubt trying to run from what it was about to hear. Our mechanism for dealing with trauma hadn't been established. I was in full panic mode, not knowing what to do or feel. This was supposed to be one of the happiest days in our lives. I'd married my best friend just three years ago. Sam and I were so in love at twenty-five and ready to begin the life we had supposed into being.

My hands squeezed the corner of the starchy white sheet into a tight ball to keep them from shaking. Words shot from his mouth like hand grenades tearing into my heart as my ears received them. Each one worse than the last. In ten horrible minutes the afterglow of having our beautiful little human being was left in ruins. Dr. Baer quickly left to care for him and prepare transportation to a NICU hospital an hour away. I picked up the phone to call Sam. My hands shook uncontrollably in time with my voice. Shock. Yes. This is what being in shock must feel like. I went numb. My presence slipped hastily into some other dimension. I half pinched myself to make sure it was real. It was. I became another person hearing myself use words I couldn't grasp—seizures, apnea, hydrocephalus.

This can't be happening swirled wildly in my head as I waited for Sam to arrive and tell me that Preston would be all right.

Our son had been at the NICU hospital for two and a half days. Sixty hours, twenty minutes and eleven seconds that I hadn't been able to hold, kiss, or bask in his luscious powdery cake smell. I chanted his name repeatedly hoping he would feel my energy through the universe while my eyes labored hard to remember every inch of him. I tried with all my new Mothers Being might, but I could not recall his smell, it's like a wind that flew by too quickly to inhale. Instead I breathed in vacant hospital air. This un-motherly feeling that's no feeling at all greatly disturbed my Mothers Being.

It flitted around like a frantic bird caught inside a room with no windows.

Time felt redefined, unjust as if it were playing a cruel joke on us. We were living a life and death scenario only known to us from movies. The same carefree summer sky that ushered us into the hospital now looked dismally gray and unwelcoming from my bed. Our naïve hearts struggled with the realization that time seemed to contradict itself. We entertained a different knowing; that a blossoming July canopy no longer foretold of a happy, worry-free day. We were quickly growing up.

I had confidence that the staff of the NICU was doing everything possible to help Preston, that he felt Sam's presence, and that that alone strengthened him. Still, a puzzling disquiet entered out of nowhere. It felt curious the way it took over my being as if it was there all along; waiting until the birth of our son. Our dream of having our first child had been driven into some dark alley and parked. The shocking, seemingly random moments of the last three days, opposite of what I thought was supposed to happen, gave me a new realization beyond what I could understand right now. Sam and I were frightfully scared. We hurt somewhere deep down inside where we've never hurt before. Not even my newfound Mothers Being could protect me. Perhaps it was her who was causing me to hurt so I could grow from this point forward. For now, she existed in my innermost recesses where I hadn't yet learned to reach.

My arms physically ached to hold Preston. From my hospital bed I watched the mom across the hall bond with her new baby. I existed in a perpetual Bermuda Triangle of sorts.

This day that was supposed to be, that no longer was, had eaten up all the logic in my brain. People chatting in the hallway, laughter and babies crying now roared like a thundercloud around my lonely triangle of photo— bed—phone. I stared numbly at the Polaroid picture of Preston: pale, tiny, his head slightly enlarged, lying amid a tangle of IV's and tubes that encompassed him like a hungry octopus, then at the mute black phone, then back out the window at the sad, almost blue sky. Across the hall, I heard family members sharing their childbirth stories. The sweet sound of new baby joy overflowed from their room, encroaching the doorway of my empty room.

The next day was hard. I made my laps within the close proximity of the phone, stepping outside my room by a few yards. I watched the mother across the hall lay a knitted pink blanket on her bed. She looked the way I imagined I would have looked, with her eyes nervous and joyful at once as she smoothed out the handmade blanket with the precision of a surgeon. Her husband then handed their baby girl to her. The healthy pink of her skin against a lacy white dress and bonnet stopped me in my tracks. She turned to look at me, both of our eyes telling silent, disparate stories. Her mouth opened like she was taking in a quick breath of air, as if duty-bound (mother to mother). Thinking better of it, her mouth closed half shut. I looked down at the floor then turned to go back to my room.

This was supposed to be our moment, too. Instead, our little guy lay in an incubator hooked up to a ventilator wearing nothing but a clear medical diaper with swabs of amber colored betadine around it, his going home pastel yellow outfit still in my bag.

How many ways had I already changed before even leaving the hospital? How many molecules had been rearranged to create such a vast difference in the way everything looked and felt? My Mothers Being knew from the moment he was born that our world would never be the same. She called out in whispers that, for now, sat softly on my shoulder until I was strong enough to withstand more weight. *One day you'll understand*, she murmured. *One day*. Our buffet of life was being changed with no input from our souls. Right now I sat miles away from understanding.

Over time, we crafted a new definition for "all right": he is still alive. Hours grew into days, days into weeks, and weeks turned into months the way an innocuous sore throat turns into pneumonia; quickly and slowly all at once. Questions and answers became our new way of life.

Alive? Yes. Doing well? No. Doing okay? Maybe. Doing horribly? Yes. Alive? Yes. Critical? Yes. Going to live? Maybe. Stable? No. Critical? Yes. Going to live? No.

The next few months consisted of transports to two other hospitals by ambulance. An unwelcome diagnosis of congestive heart failure met us at the first NICU door. We felt overwhelmed at another health problem. We tried to be positive, but the universe felt unreasonable.

While his potential heart problem was monitored and medications administered, Sam needed to get back to work. Employers only understood *emergency* for so long.

My parents had come to offer their comfort while Sam was away. Dad got out of their blue station wagon wearing the usual plaid shirt, coordinating pants, straw hat and pipe in hand; the only thing missing was his constant cup of coffee. He walked to the back of the car, motioning for me to follow. He spoke with a curious tenderness unfamiliar to me, "I made a little something for the boy." My father: the fixer, the thinker. His idle hands needed something to do with the immense worry they held so they carved a rocking horse lamp for his acutely sick grandson. Made from a walnut tree on their land, the palomino colored horse stood complete with a handmade leather saddle. He brought it to Pennsylvania as a symbol of hope, not only for his grandson, but for his daughter and son-in-law too. He was trying to ignite our hope that felt severed from the universe. I was overcome with love when I saw my father holding the cardboard box in his big hands, like a fragile egg filled with his homemade offering for Preston. He looked at me apologetically as if to say, "Sorry I can't make him better, babe, but I made this lamp as an assurance that he'll be alright." With an Irish heart of gold and busy hands, my dad was doing all that he knew to do.

He told the universe his grandson would need a light.

We'd been sent with sirens blazing for emergency shunt surgery at the next hospital. Arriving too freshly scarred to know the ropes.

We trusted everyone to first do no harm. Preston was taken into a ward where five beds lined each side of the room. This precious being of ours, weighing a scant five pounds, was placed next to a five-year-old boy who was hooked up to a clear machine that contained his bowel drainage. His sad, lonely eyes and gaunt appearance registered the number of hospital days that were no longer counted. A team of residents came around asking the usual case history questions. My eyes deliberately searched the room looking for a reason our new baby was amongst all this. Sam grew more frustrated with each question. "You do realize we were sent here on an emergency basis to be seen by Dr. Rolex, don't you?"

"Yes, he's been notified that you're here," the resident said matter-of-factly.

Preston was temporarily stabilized with diuretics that did what his brain couldn't do. The famous neurosurgeon was still a no-show. After hours of calling his office with no response, Sam decided to park himself at his office, refusing to leave until we were given an answer. At last, we were informed that he would be gracing us with his presence.

The three of us were escorted into a small examination room. Preston was placed on an exam table. I stood next to him with his tiny hand draped softly around my finger. He looked content, wrapped snugly in a blanket as he slept. We waited another thirty minutes for our mystery doctor to appear.

His arrogance preceded him as he walked abruptly into the room. He seemed annoyed at the very sight of us. There was something in the way his body talked for him that put a great distance between himself—two desperate parents and an acutely sick infant. He said a scant hi to Sam and I, never looking at Preston. His arm made a sweeping gesture in front of his face as he checked the time on his expensive watch. He quickly placed Preston's CT scan in the lighted box. Still staring at the scan he muttered, "This looks horrible. There's nothing I can do for him. If he lives, you'll be lucky if he ever even smiles at you. Any questions?"

"Any questions? How about—why aren't you examining our son?" I pleaded.

"There's no point," he said dismissively. "Any other questions?"

Sam took a step toward the good doctor, stopping just shy of him, crossing his arms over his chest. His steely eyes shot the most disgusted look into Dr. Rolex's eyes. "How fast can we get our son out of here?" Moving hastily toward the door, he muttered, "I'll start the necessary paperwork. It shouldn't be long." At this point it was painfully clear he was moving quicker to get away from us than he did to get to us.

We stood in the room looking at our baby boy, feeling more helpless than ever. Sam gave me a reassuring hug, trying hard not to let his uncertainty show. "It will be alright, I promise." My finger still wrapped in Preston's velvet grip, I looked at our innocent baby boy and then at Sam, searching for answers in his eyes. While fighting back tears of frustration, I asked:

"How can a human being be so pointless you can't even look at him?"

Sam called our NICU hospital and relayed our newest nightmare to Preston's neurologist. "I'll send an ambulance to pick him up; we have to hurry," he stated in a frustrated tone. "Time is of the essence. I hope it's not too late."

rapid/rap-id/ ~

occurring within a short time; happening speedily

Origin ~

Latin rapidus seizing, sweeping

shock/shok/ ~

a sudden or violent disturbance of the mind, emotion, or sensibilities

Origin ~

Middle English; akin to Middle High German schoc heap

process/pros-es ~

a systematic series of actions directed to some end

Origin ~

Middle English process, from Latin processus, from procedere

rapid shock process ~

a protection mechanism, which makes itself available to all souls who experience repeat trauma

a coordinated system that allows a human being to remain calm when you would otherwise be hysterical

a mental process of receiving the unexpected as routine

a big soft rubber bumper on life's long and winding road

Chapter 16

On the Cusp of Heaven and Hell: Part Two

*I*T WAS THE FRIDAY BEFORE THE LONG LABOR DAY WEEK-
end. Preston had only been home for one brief ten-day visit since
his birth in July. Sam's parents had come for the weekend to help with the
renovations of our neglected but quaint farmhouse that I'd envisioned in
my head. It had great bones, was painted a faint blue with white trim, and
was perched on a hill overlooking a picturesque valley. A few rolling hills
led the eye to a pond below that appeared to have been spit squarely from
the mouths of the hills. A single row of knotty pine cabinets lined the front
kitchen wall. I envisioned a big old island with a butcher-block counter
top for entertaining and a long, white built-in bench and wall of windows
that ran the entire length of our large country kitchen wall overlooking the
pond. Directly outside the windows stood our graceful old weeping willow
tree. From it hung a swing that Sam had made for our future child. It stood
waiting for a little boy's squeals. I could almost hear, *push me again, higher.*
It all looked so certain.

Sam's dad, Emory, tall and lean, with a smile that made you feel good in
its presence, worked away on rebuilding the front porch. It was a beautiful
summer morning with just a hint of a breeze that reminded you not to get
hot. I watched Emory in his usual short-sleeved chambray work shirt and
jeans from the kitchen window while I prepared chicken salad for lunch,

thinking how happy Sam would be seeing the progress his dad had made when he arrived home.

The phone rang.

The ringing of our telephone was no longer an ordinary occurrence. A sound that once blended in with the humming of our dryer, now, rang shrill and alarming to our ears. It'd become a declaration of either wonderfully good or awfully bad news.

Such extremes—that was our new life.

Emory stood transfixed on the porch outside watching me through the kitchen window. My stomach twisted into knots with each ring, pleading for the voice on the other end to be the bearer of good news.

Answering the phone, now, required an unfamiliar courage.

Simple hellos took on a strange new meaning. My body froze, wanting both to run from impending bad news or run to news of a miracle. A constant battle as wanting and not wanting fought to be heard.

"Hello," I answered confidently as if securing good news. It was Preston's primary care nurse. "Hi Karen, this is Paulette." Her usual colorful personality was vacant in her tone. While always professional, she made us feel as if we were her one and only family. She provided the warmth and humor that allayed our fears, if only momentarily. That was the art of being a fine nurse, I suppose.

We'd bonded quickly the way I imagine you bond with anyone you share a trauma with. "Is Sam with you?" she asked. "No, he's not home yet. Why? Paulette you're scaring me." Her voice now sounded tender and precise. "I'm afraid I have bad news to tell you. Preston has taken a turn for the worse. You need to get here as fast as you can. Dr. Howl and Dr. Lily are with him. They don't think he'll make it through the night, Karen. I'm so sorry."

A turn for the worse. Isn't *worse* where we've been, for god's sake! Of course, I realized in my new Mothers Being there was one more *worse*. The worse we had been practicing for and fighting against.

I remember coming back from our first lesson on how to bring him home to die. It felt unreal in that we simultaneously spoke of death and miracles all in the same sentence like it was normal for new parents to do. We still held out hope for a Hail Mary of a miracle. Stepping onto the front porch, through the window, we could see all four parents busily milling about the kitchen with bowls and platters in hand. Seeing us, they smiled softly saying hello, because how in God's name do you ask your children how their first lesson went? And how the hell would we answer? Our emotions felt too wild to understand, so we talked about food and how hungry we were. Emory motioned toward the dining table saying, "Sit and relax." His eyes studied Sam. I settled next to him on the long window seat bench. Through the wall of windows, the warmth of the late afternoon sun drenched my back, making me feel like I could stretch out and sleep for days. Instead I rested my heavy head on Sam's shoulder.

The kitchen smelled alive with fried chicken, mashed potatoes and corn. Mom set the table placing blue and white striped napkins on each plate and Sam's mother, Lorraine, poured iced tea from a glass pitcher, while Dad and Emory attempted to make light-hearted conversation. Now both fathers were studying us, their faces took the same concerned shape, like they had just seconds ago strategized about our situation. Sam and I supposed this was what people did when someone was dying. Maybe they could see it too. Death's insistence was like a shadow that wouldn't fade.

My mother baked a three-layer lemon cake with light-as-air lemon custard filling. I remembered having it last summer and the summer before. It tasted like home. It was the first thing my stomach enjoyed since Preston's birth. Everything before carried with it the personality of a protein shake.

Over the last rapid-fire month and a half, our son's little body had become languid from the catastrophic damage to his brain. Now, even the dignity of bringing him home to die was being taken from us. My heart broke wide open inside of me. Wide as the sky over the universe. Maybe one day, when the pain sinks into a different place in me it will break into stars. And there I will find the light again.

I hung the phone up but didn't, my hand still clutched its beige receiver on the wall. Stepping away from it meant walking through the kitchen past the chicken salad with the grapes still waiting on the cutting board. Past a few minutes ago when I ingenuously thought our baby still had a chance against all odds.

It meant disconnecting from the mom who stood at the kitchen sink in her favorite lavender sundress washing grapes, while eagerly anticipating this afternoon's NICU visit. From the wife who assumed her husband would be happy when he arrived home. Everything had been tainted by the ringing phone's grim proclamation.

My psyche now recognized shock. It'd learned to process bad news rapidly for efficiency's sake. Not this time though. I rounded the corner into our kitchen, the shock dissolving into my open heart. I stopped and reached out to touch the wall for validation this was all real. I leaned my back into the wall hoping it would swallow me whole. My now exposed heart felt the burn of Paulette's news like some caustic cocktail had been poured fast into my heart. Stinging its way down until I couldn't contain it anymore. Angry, confused tears poured down my cheek at a rate I'd never before experienced. Breathing seemed secondary to this deluge.

My father raised his daughters to be strong, his definition of strong. *Don't cry. People will assume you're weak.* He meant well. He was right for the most part. *As a girl you'll have to work twice as hard as a man to get half the recognition,* he would say. Standing emotionless as my father yelled at me became second nature. I grew skilled at camouflaging my teenager emotions in public. Now—my adult persona.

Emory stood in the front parlor facing me. Our blue-striped Duncan Phyfe sofa behind him called out to me as though begging me to sit down. I could barely make it to Emory, let alone navigate past him. Yes. I had lost all navigational sense.

The pain in my eyes was mirrored in his. The words wouldn't come. They stayed lodged in my throat as if releasing them into the air gave them life. All the strength I'd reserved had vanished with Paulette's call. I collapsed into his arms, choking up the necessary words. "I'll have Sam paged," he said. "I'll call your parents. Don't worry. I'll take care of everything until Sam arrives," he assured me.

Lorraine stood on the perimeter with her detached look I was all too familiar with. Not even a hug to offer. A woman, who by her own admission, liked everything plain and simple. While I embraced simple, plain was everything I was not. I had grown tired of remarks about my nail polish, make-up and jewelry, tired of being judged by my outward appearance.

All these things were such a tiny part of me, but for some reason she clung to them. Our relationship had become perfunctory. The saddest part of all was her detachment from Sam for marrying me.

I wanted what all young girls wanted—for the mother of the man I loved to like me. Being young and naïve; I tried lessening my makeup, nail polish and jewelry around her. Then one day I looked in the mirror and realized I had lessened myself.

I recalled our first chat after Sam and I announced our engagement. Lorraine looked directly at Sam and told him I was a prima donna, and that his marriage to me would never last, as if I wasn't there. I nervously told her how deeply I loved her son. My proclamation would make everything better, I convinced myself. Her ambivalence filled the air almost smothering my spirit. "I'm sure you do love him, but I don't know how he could love the likes of you!" she responded curtly.

Sam's mouth flew open in disbelief; her words stunned him, making him feel like he didn't know his mother at all in that moment.

The likes of you . . . the Irish in me rose up to meet her.

The air cleared restoring my spirit. "You don't know me at all, and you couldn't describe the true likes of me if you had to," I shot back. I knew in that moment I would always be—her version of me in her mind—conceivably forever.

Emory, who was an equally good communicator and listener, was the heart and soul of my husband's family. Being a successful insurance agent afforded him the opportunity to retire soon. He and Sam had recently become close after Sam's tumultuous college years. They were kindred spirits and Sam had inherited his dad's gentle nature. I never needed it more than I did on this surreal day that felt freshly spun from a nightmare.

I excused myself, explaining that I needed to clear my head before Sam arrived. I sat on the knoll overlooking the rolling hills that tipped toward our neighbor's pond below. This heavenly view overwhelmed me. *Does heaven look like this?* I cried out to the universe. *Is Preston already hovering between two worlds? Hurry, Sam.*

Palpable fear consumed my Mothers Being. Was this it? Is this all we would know of our precious baby? Why? Sitting with my knees scrunched up to my chest, my head fell hard into my hands as the exhaustion of the past few months gushed out of me, leaving me afraid. Afraid of how extraordinarily much I already loved him and felt connected to him. Even more afraid of how I would exist in this world without him.

Suddenly, I sensed someone behind me. Lorraine stood five feet away. "Do you need anything?" she asked benignly. Her demeanor like that of a child coerced into apologizing but didn't want to. I could only assume Emory sent her thinking I needed a mother figure that could reach out to me woman to woman. If only he knew. Still looming awkwardly behind me, she never reached out to put her hand on my shoulder or stand in front of me to look into my brokenhearted eyes for one moment. That's all I wanted from her: understanding. Her distant stance behind me and refusal to look at me were metaphors for our relationship. I couldn't understand how a mature mother could watch a new mother in such pain and not offer anything more.

"Do I need anything? Just for Preston to live. That's all," I declared through sobs.

"He'll be okay," she said from behind me.

She was gone. I was alone. Still.

While I waited for Sam my head needed something to do, so I wrote a short letter to our baby boy. The one in route to a destination not ever supposed or understood.

Dear Preston,

The doctors are telling us it doesn't look good. That you're not going to make it. I can't stop crying. I'm so scared. I don't know how to do this. Don't know if my arms will be able to let you go. I know my heart can't. I'm still not experienced with this whole mommy thing, but I've learned that I really don't need to be. Something brand new deep inside of me is showing me the way. It's pretty instantaneous and all-encompassing this brand new mommy love. I love you. In every way, shape and manner there is for a mother to love her son. I claim them all . . . no matter what.

So if this is our life with you, contained in a small matter of months and experiences, of touches and feels, kisses and hugs; my mommy's heart will just have to do all the work. Don't worry, not one bit, 'cause you'll have Daddy's heart holding you too. And that heart of your Daddy's, well, it's pretty amazing. How I wish you could know it more. God, how I wish we could know you more. This isn't fair. We have so much love to give you and so much to tell you and teach you, like why the sky is blue and if Santa is real. However many minutes or hours we're given with you I promise they will be the most precious because we will make them so. Our hearts will grab each and every one for the miracle they are. We will hold you here forever little one. Forever and ever.

Love you always and forever,
Mommy

Sam wore a stunned, scared look as he hurriedly got out of the car. I wondered could anything still shock us, really? He too was practicing his version of strong for me. We fell into each other's arms. There was no comforting each other, just an exchange of pain. We held each other and sobbed as one.

We arrived at the NICU to grim but relieved faces. We made it before our son drew his last breath. The fluid around his brain gave him an alien-like appearance. His skin was transparent as paper. Tiny blue veins ran around his bulbous head like a chaotic road map. His lips had lost the rich pinkness of life. Paulette tearfully handed us a picture. "Here, this is for you to remember him by." It was part of the job description for a NICU nurse—snapping the last picture, just in case.

His big eyes and button nose looked beautiful. But his ashen skin, his lifeless lips, and his huge head told a different story.

We were escorted a few feet away to an area that had been sectioned off with privacy screens. Inside were two wooden rocking chairs and a small gray metal table that held a box of Kleenex. I sat in my designated chair while Sam watched carefully: waiting for the moment it all became real to me. His eyes scoped out our clinically necessary surroundings. Paulette placed Preston in my arms. This was it. The death countdown could commence. Our guttural sobs could be heard throughout the NICU as tears plummeted from our eyes. With every fleeting moment I held him I begged God to please let this be over. Looking into his piercing but vacant eyes, I grew more in love. Would my arms physically be able to release him when the time came? It was too impossible to comprehend.

This was all so peculiar, shrouded by a not so private screen. Taking turns rocking our baby as if it were a game of hot potato as ten sets of medical eyes kept watch. Whose arms would he die in? This place that smelled of soft baby scents mixed with the sharpness of alcohol and betadine.

This place. Where heartbroken parents go to rock their babies into heaven.

The next hour (or so) would define the rest of my life. It would forever be implanted in my memory place.

The rocking him in to heaven hour: when the angels would come to take his living soul from our arms and carry him off to heaven. It was a point from which I would slowly disintegrate or one from where I would step off and recreate myself. My humanness reordered.

I sat in the rocking chair staring into his dimmed blue eyes, trying my best to record this in my memory place for safekeeping. Sam and I held hands, wondering who and what he would have been, whose sense of humor he would have had. Who he would have looked like? I silently asked him how tall he would be in heaven.

Why does he have to be so utterly beautiful? It was as if all the beauty of life lay in his face. I suppose all angels look this way, especially the very young ones.

Though there were alarms going off and machines busy with life-sustaining humming noises, our world was quiet and gray. The darkest gray I've ever known. The purity and privilege of holding his body until his being slipped away, against the agony of surrendering his newly formed body we would never know past this, leave our trembling hands.

We teetered precariously on the cusp of heaven and hell.

Paulette appeared from behind the screen. "Karen, your parents have arrived," she said gently.

I laid Preston in his Dad's arms; wondering if this would be the last time I held our baby's warm body. Leaving the NICU, I could already feel myself falling apart. As much as I didn't want to admit it, I still needed my parents. I walked out the door hesitantly, glancing once more at Sam and Preston.

My father, Joe: an artistic, volatile, yet tender man, with a John Wayne-like presence. A man of few words when it came to idle chat, but when he spoke; the intelligent lilt of his words seemed to capture a room. His brilliance had earned him a career as a self-taught systems engineer. However, he had within him the heat of a fire-breathing dragon and the lure of a deep, placid lake.

My mother, Jane, a pretty, petite woman with short dark brown hair, wore her heart on her sleeve, but often criticized by my Dad for being too honest. A homemaker by choice, happily serving up whatever meals my Dad requested. Her hobbies were meticulously taking care of the house and their four children.

My parents stood at the other end of the hallway. My father tried to remain stoic, but the pained look in his eyes gave him away. He wasn't Superman after all. My father couldn't fix Preston and seeing the brokenness in his eyes wrecked me even more. Not known for displaying his emotions, I'd come to learn that a scant squeeze on my shoulder meant *I love you*; still, I longed to hear those words leave his lips. I ran down the hall as fast as my tears, disintegrating into his open arms and big chest. He hugged me tighter than he ever had before.

He softly cupped my head with his big hands the way fathers do. "Go ahead and cry babe, it's okay," he whispered. His words fell gently over us, enveloping me like a warm blanket. I cried as if my tears would never cease.

Permission to cry granted. This was a first. It was the most tender, awful thing to hear simultaneously. I was his little girl for an instant. This time I could cry.

My mother had been crying since the moment she appeared in the hallway. I'd grown used to seeing the emotions she wore on her sleeve. Her and my father's personalities were polar opposites and for the most part, I had inherited his.

Hours passed as both families waited nervously across the hall.

Our team of doctors huddled together in the corner of the NICU, just out of earshot. Something had changed. These last few hours had been the longest we'd ever held Preston but for the worst of reasons.

I continued to fall more in love; not giving two damns about the future devastation to my Mothers Being. Sam looked at me half-questioningly, "Did you see that?" Finally saying what both of us were afraid to say. "He's moving around."

"What does this mean?" I asked him, "Nothing at all or everything?"

The team of doctors walked over, asking to examine Preston. Dr. Lily, a neurologist, finished his exam and handed him to a nurse. "Would you and Sam please come with us?" he asked. At this point my mind was an unreliable blankness at best, it'd already received the worst news. There was no need for my Rapid Shock Process this time. Sam took my hand and we walked into a small room around the corner from the NICU.

Our team of doctors and nurses wore surprised, cautious looks on their faces. They were taking time choosing their words. I couldn't stand it. "How much longer does Preston have?" I asked softly. Is this why we're here, to get a countdown update? My Mothers Being was protecting me. I'd been living the nothing at all scenario. Did I dare allow myself to think that his movement meant everything? This change of thought terrified me. After months of turmoil, we'd become two rubber bands stretched beyond limits.

With compassion in his light blue eyes, Dr. Lily looked at us and uttered the most profound statement. One that would remain imbedded in my brain forever. I'd recall it when I needed reassurance. It served as a reminder of the strength of the human spirit, of Preston's spirit and the absolute mystery of the possibility in the impossible.

"Preston is as close to death as a human being can be without being dead."

His words reverberated in our ears as we tried hard to quiet their impact. Our brains automatically deciphered and dissected his sentence.

Which is it? Is he half alive or half dead? Which way do we look—towards nothing at all or everything?

We hadn't arrived at hopelessness recklessly. The hopelessness we felt initially startled me, it was as real and fleeting as a moment of deja vu. Our hearts were broken open, yet still held on to a scant bit of hope. But as we rocked Preston we came to hopelessness from a place of dignity and respect by embracing death. We had reached a place of peace more for our baby boy than for us. Now here we were again.

Hope can be the scariest thing in the room when the curtains have already been drawn with hopelessness. We had adjusted. We were devastated beyond all reason but had accepted the fact that he was going to die. This may sound crazy, but the thought of hoping again only to find out he was dying after all was terrifying. It seemed like an offering too good to be true. A mirage. Maybe our brains had come to accept bad news more readily. Still, the thought of putting our fragile hearts outside ourselves to possibly be shattered again felt daunting.

"I don't understand," Sam said.

Dr. Young, a neurosurgeon, spoke up, "I've never seen someone fight this hard. We have to do something to help him, even if we don't have a pediatric neurosurgeon on staff. I'm willing to operate if you'll trust me."

Watching their faces I wondered if this was one of those moments that doctors wait for all their lives. Were we about to get our miracle? Our everything? The neurosurgeon explained the brain surgery necessary to potentially save his life. A shunt would be inserted, then a tube would run from his brain into his abdominal cavity where excess fluid would drain. It all sounded so sci-fi in our crash medical course marathon. The expression on Dr. Young's face quickly fell as he warned us, "There is a fifty percent chance we could lose him on the table. He's still very weak."

In the few minutes we had to decide whether or not to give the doctors permission to operate during this window of opportunity nobody ever fathomed. Sam and I didn't leave the room to talk or ask for a minute alone. "Of course. Of course we will do whatever we can to help him fight." Sam said. Everyone scattered like ants at *of course*.

Nurses moved at breakneck speed prepping our baby boy for surgery. STAT was called out repeatedly as everyone raced to beat the clock.

We bent down and kissed Preston with magnificent smiles on our faces. If this was to be his last memory of us, we would be strong and good and happy for him.

After he disappeared from view, Sam and I sobbed together again—as one. Nothing at all. Or everything. Soon we would know. Everyone nervously watched the clock.

As the estimated surgery time passed, I noticed Paulette busying herself with anything she could find. She stopped looking at us. We grew more anxious with each pass of the minute hand, now our focal point.

Paulette raced to the ringing NICU phone. We prepared ourselves for nothing at all; it was easier that way. "Uh huh, uh huh," her head bobbed up and down. She hung up the phone. Our hearts beat out of our chest as we braced ourselves.

"He made it!" she yelled. "He's alive and doing well." She ran around the corner to give us the most wondrous details our ears had ever heard. The three of us held each other tightly; gratitude and joy consumed us, spilling into the NICU. Our parents hugged and then embraced us as echoes of Thank God filled the room. I even caught my Dad blinking away a tear he was trying hard to disguise.

From around the corner the team of doctors appeared with Preston. Their guarded smiles couldn't hide the delight peeking out from the corner of their mouths. Cue the Rocky music because they looked every bit like victorious super heroes to us. Dr. Young tried to remain composed. He shook Sam's hand and gave me a hug. "He did very well; he surprised us again," he told us. Our son had color in his beautiful baby face. His blue eyes were bright and curious, looking around as if seeing everything for the first time. "Hello little guy. Welcome to our world," I whispered.

In less than two months we had witnessed not one but two miracles. The birth of our son as he emerged from the womb, and the birth of our son as he emerged from the operating room. Two miracles. We felt weightless. This was our everything. The world around us suddenly appeared in

Technicolor. This wondrous September day existed within us. For the first time since his birth, we could touch and hold a miracle unencumbered by fear.

Whatever happened from this point on, however our future everything was defined, we'd remember the lightness we felt, and the gratitude we shared for the simplicity of the complex Miracle of Life. Einstein tells us, *'There are two ways to live your life. One is as though nothing is a miracle. The other is as though everything is a miracle.'* Another realization. This was to be one of many realizations peppered throughout the years, waiting and watching for the surprises life had in store for us.

Though it felt as if the odds were stacked against us, our eyes had been keenly opened to see everyday miracles. With each one we peeled back the layers, threw away another bit of fear and unpacked our hearts once again. That is how is realization was born. How we were born. We had become different and new from Preston's birth and almost death, but before we could fully welcome our new life, we had to unknow most of what our previous life told us.

Some realizations quickened into us the minute they happened. Others shouted, leaving us wide-eyed and open-mouthed. Though often they came softly the next day or week, at bedtime when Sam and I had each other to hold onto, in a hospital elevator, around an IEP table, when I felt inadequate as a mom, in the faces of Preston's peer buddies, and in his sister's smile. They were in uncomfortable stares and admiring glances. In moments that made us jump for joy or brought us to our knees. Our realizations, invited or otherwise, were life's lessons that formed themselves into teachable moments. Ones that helped us arrive at the place of us no matter where we were.

Chapter 2

Everyday Angels

*A*N ORANGE AND A SYRINGE WAITED ON THE ROLLING hospital tray. I would never see an orange the same way again. I stood eyeballing the innocent fruit as if it silently insulted me. My feet seemed to be adhered to a fixed spot on the mottled linoleum floor. I picked up the odd combination of orange and syringe, and with shaky hands practiced stabbing the poor thing with conviction. Tonight the orange would be replaced by my eight-month old baby's chubby little leg. I didn't know if I was up for this. Stabbing a needle with force into an orange was a far cry from Preston's leg. A nurse would hold his leg while I meticulously stabbed a needle into a muscle, hoping this drug would stop his infantile spasms, a rare form of epilepsy.

My Mothers Being needed time to prepare me, time it didn't have. Time to tell me that instead of being the mom who winces inside as she holds her little one's leg while a nurse administers a shot that would surely result in a blood-curdling cry, the kind of cry where there exists a missed breath before a sound is heard. Then whispers, *Sssh, all done.* My list of firsts was being haplessly rearranged, allowing no time to prepare. Maybe that's the point— there is no preparing. I'd forfeited the moment I'd imagined. Instead, I was now assigned the charge of being the giver of pain. My Mothers Being tried desperately to guide me to a place of courage in this strange position I now found myself in.

A gentle-faced, silver-haired man wearing a long white coat walked into our room. His eyes peered out over his wire-rimmed glasses as he approached Preston's bed. He was tall and walked with authority but spoke the way someone who already knows you would speak. "It looks like that orange is giving you a hard time," he said with a smile.

"Yes, I'm afraid the orange is winning," I told him, sharing the frustration I'd failed to hide on my anxious face.

"Do you mind if I help?"

"Please do," I sighed, releasing a deep long breath my stress held captive. He asked the nurse for some backup oranges and syringes. "Well, I must have undoubtedly impressed you," I said with a laugh. Smiling back at me, he assured me that it was simply for time's sake. He explained the process of IM (intra-muscular) injections to me. His warm demeanor felt like a friend. He played with Preston for a while, laughing with him; attempting to distract me for a few lighthearted moments.

He gave me a hug, then placed a hand on my shoulder. "I think you've mastered this. You'll do wonderfully. Don't worry," he assured me, and wished us well as he left the room.

"Well, you know people in high places, don't you?" our nurse said with a smile.

"What do you mean?"

"Do you know who that was?" she asked.

"A doctor," I answered flatly.

"Not just any doctor. That was the Chief of Pediatrics here," she added. *Here* happened to be Johns Hopkins Hospital in Baltimore, MD.

I felt honored that such a busy doctor took time for us. Not because he was the Chief of Pediatrics in a well-known hospital, but because he didn't have the need to tell me who or what he was. His Doctors Being saved my Mothers Being that morning. He did what good doctors do. He showed compassion in his wisdom and humanity in his Doctors Being.

Feeling pleased with my stellar nursing skills, I rewarded myself with a cappuccino and a few precious moments to myself. Sitting in the café sipping my coffee, I wondered how I would muster up enough strength to literally stab a needle into a muscle in my baby's leg. What if I missed the muscle or didn't administer it with enough quick force? The thought of hurting him crushed me.

I remembered how nervous I was giving my classmate an injection during my brief stint in Medical Secretarial School. It felt like time had allowed me to stay in school long enough to practice the art of injecting a needle into someone's arm before I got up the nerve to tell my father it wasn't for me. I had to wonder if that moment was in preparation for Preston and this moment. My Mothers Being nodded.

The café sat alongside one of the hospital's busy corridors, affording me a view of visitors, medical staff and patients going about their day. Or in this case, patients that appeared to be fighting for their life. I looked up from my steamy cup and saw a pale, bone-skinny woman with patches of hair hanging from her head, dressed in a gray sweat suit that hung from her. She struggled with every step as she clung to her IV pole. I was initially jolted by her stark, wan appearance. Everything about her looked unjustly fragile except for her fierce green eyes. They contained the spirit of a warrior. People stared or looked away as she made her loop around. When she passed by my table, I looked directly at her and said, "Hi, how are you?"

She looked at me, surprised that someone had acknowledged her humanness and said with a faint smile, "Doing better, thanks for asking."

I leaned back in my chair, ashamed for feeling overwhelmed by anything in my small world. My heart pounded a rhythm of awe at her courage and willpower. The physical pain of each step: obvious by the shuffled wince of her feet as they maneuvered down the corridor like they were dodging landmines. How far had she walked to arrive here to be stared at or ignored instead of applauded, I wondered.

I couldn't help but be mesmerized by her warrior soul. It was her eyes staring back at me that made me feel stronger. They held a thousand stories of vulnerability. I suppose people turned away because of their own vulnerability. Mine had been stripped bare like hers, but for different reasons. Yet in the moment when our eyes met, we knew each other. I realized deep down in my Mothers Being that she was meant to walk by me. To exchange courage: more from her than me. The universe had arranged a lesson for me in openness. My Mothers Being had been gently tapping on my guarded shoulder since Preston's birth. Trying to awaken the openness within me. Helping me to be open to the kindness of a doctor, to the willpower of a sick woman, and to finding my own untapped courage.

Having a child so developmentally imperfect caused me to step out of my thoroughly planned world of to dos and organizational lists and showed me how to be vulnerable. Preston grabbed my vulnerability and stuck it on a neon sign for the world to see, forcing me to walk through all the nonsense to my vulnerability. I'd somehow find a way to be open to whatever the universe had to offer—to not worry everything into tomorrow. I was realizing that within each individual moment there exists a more generous moment in which one can begin again.

At twenty-six, I began to understand that courage doesn't always look strong. Sometimes courage is pale and weak, walks with tentative steps, where somewhere inside a light is fighting hard to be seen. Courage is in the frantic pace of a dad as he juggles work and hospital stays, it's in shaky hands practicing with a needle, and it's in the smiles and coos of a baby boy after his mom correctly administers the first injection.

Courage is in the act of being human when life happens. Courage is vulnerability.

Preston caused me to visit the dark unreachable places within my soul until I had the courage to stay awhile. To sit within its walls until there were no walls. This would take some time.

Along with Preston, we were being birthed into a new consciousness. Another realization.

Walking down the hallway to Preston's room, still savoring my cappuccino and newfound courage, I overheard nurses talking about a virus on our floor. With his weakened immune system I worried he would catch it. Our little guy became seriously sick quickly. Before we knew it he had spiked an unheard fever of 108.9. Doctor after doctor came to check the reading, skeptical of its accuracy, confounded that Preston wasn't doing any of the things their medical books said he should be doing. We were told that a shift for the worse usually occurs at a temperature of 105. Not Preston. No coma, no seizures; his eyes still followed each doctor's light back and forth, back and forth. He was still alive: a very sick baby on a bed of ice.

When days were too illogical and too unreasonable to deal with, without realizing it we started a family tradition. If it didn't make sense, not even to doctors; then for god's sake let's stick a silly name on it so we could laugh, if just for one ridiculous second. Maybe a generous breath of laughter would be the very thing that helped him to get better. Our son's bizarre fever was the first to be written under the heading of things that don't make sense. This anomaly would be forever known as The Preston Percentile.

I had to wonder—*was* our child born to confuse and confound doctors? To pull them off their charts and into the faces of patients and parents who knew them best? Was he here to teach us all?

Like a playback from the past, our families had come to the hospital. The news was not good. His condition was guarded. He looked so helpless on the large bed of ice. His lips dry from the fever, his body still as death. Preston looked like he was slipping away on an iceberg of a bed as if cold packed to preserve him for a future date.

His developmental pediatrician, Dr. Nelson, wore black-rimmed glasses that sat on a prominent nose, his round, marble-like hazel eyes were big with curiosity, and a constant array of bowties overwhelmed his long skinny neck. His slight, almost anemic looking frame, topped off with a mop of black wavy hair, held an inquisitive mind and a gracious heart. We felt grateful that our son was in the charge of a compassionate man whose brain never stopped. He paced back and forth while his hands moved over his face organically—first stopping at his chin, then, rhythmically touching his temple with two fingers as if tapping the answers in Morse code. "I'm afraid this has the potential to cause more damage to his brain," Dr. Nelson told us as he shined his penlight into Preston's eyes, "but I must say I'm surprised that he's still responsive. We'll continue monitoring him closely. Hopefully the new regimen of drugs will address the fever." I looked up at the IV pole now enshrined by a bounteous amount of bags fat with new meds.

Emory insisted on taking everyone to dinner in Little Italy. We were exhausted from the blissful sleep that hospitals ensure. Worry consumed us. We protested, not wanting to leave our son. Sharon, his nurse, assured us she'd stay with Preston, promising to call if anything changed.

The restaurant was lovely, but we were too preoccupied with ominous temperature readings to care. I played with my spaghetti, pretending to enjoy it. We didn't eat in the conventional sense like everyone else at the table, oohing and aahing over the conglomerate of flavors. We merely processed the food into our mouths then vapidly down to our stomachs for fortification. Sam and I sat tightly in our chairs forcing smiles in response to encouraging words from family. We falsely participated in conversation that had the clarity of static to our already disquieted minds. Looking around our big table as heads bobbed in conversational agreement, hands flew in descriptive mannerism, and mouths remained in a state of constant motion, was overwhelming, like being in the middle of a speedway as cars whooshed around us at two hundred miles an hour. We were in the center of nothingness as it screamed loudly around us.

The night passed slowly as we waited for Preston's condition to change. Eventually, around four am, Sam and I passed out by his bedside, each in a fold-out bed chair. We awoke to a collection of doctors talking excitedly in our doorway. For a split second, my sleepy mind couldn't decipher the commotion. I quickly looked at Preston, fearful of what I would see. Sam jumped up. "Hey buddy, you gave us quite a scare!" He kissed his baby cheeks with tender excited pecks and Preston reciprocated with a grin from ear to ear. Our son's face was happy and bright. Sam and I glanced at each other with surprise. Was it possible that his eyes looked more aware? Yes. But why?

Dr. Nelson and his team entered the room. "Good morning," he said, beaming a curious smile at us. "This little guy is full of surprises, isn't he?" He appeared thrilled by Preston's condition but bewildered by his alert state.

"It's as if the fever somehow cleansed him," we joked to Dr. Nelson. He returned throughout the day to examine him; thinking that his fever should have damaged his already damaged brain further. He acknowledged, with a puzzled look, that he too thought Preston was more alert.

The treatments worked and we were released from the hospital several days later. Dr. Nelson handed us a card with his private number written on it. "Call me whenever you need me . . . anytime," he said. He shared his intrigue with Preston, urging us to let him care for our son. We agreed, realizing that we'd met a one of a kind doctor whose curiosity and humanity *was* his long white coat.

Sam and I had recently moved from rural Pennsylvania back to Maryland, closer to major hospitals and family. It came as no surprise when Sam lost his job. His employer's severance package was more than generous and the push we desperately needed. Although we'd made lifelong friends in Pennsylvania, we wanted to be home.

My mind wandered, traveling back in time; carefully scanning the events of the past few months since Preston's birth. There was no making sense of any of it. It just was. Maybe remembering them, or better yet, storing them in my memory place, would help me to right myself again. I tried hard to catalog them under something other than chaos or heartbreak. This wasn't supposed to happen to us. I'd taken such good care of my pregnant self. I did the why us, and why our baby questions to God. He answered quickly: why *not* us? If not us, then who? No one is ever suited for trauma. Until it finds you all happy and carefree.

A human heart either breaks open or closed.

Sam and I hadn't been given any choices so far that I could see; perhaps our move was a window of opportunity. For all I knew, the curious feeling inside of me I couldn't fully identify with was my heart breaking open. I could sense our old life falling away, leaving a vacancy to be filled with a fresh sense of duty. Another realization. Sorry, God.

Still an eager checker of to dos, I needed desperately to chart the past few months in order to make way for whatever lay ahead. I needed to file them away so I had room to face the unknown.

I would never forget seeing Preston for the first time after Dr. Baer broke the news to me.

I could tell Sam had been racing to get to us from the moment he'd hung up the phone. His eyes looked enormous with shock. His body wore the intent of an Olympic runner. His fast, hurried strides carried him to my bed as if he was tagging me on his way to Preston at the finish line. He sat on my bed holding me tightly, our bodies swayed back and forth together in disbelief. We were different now. Time and health were a new luxury. He held my face in his hands and said, "It will be alright, I promise. I'm going to go see our son and talk with Dr. Baer, I'll be back." Fifteen minutes later Sam returned to my room with a nurse. They moved quickly and purposefully toward me. He spoke fast as he told me, "The NICU team is on their way. Your nurse and I are going to help you into a wheelchair so you can see Preston before he is taken to the hospital."

I had no control over the lump that climbed into the entirety of my throat. In the isolation room I could see what looked like an eerily still doll from a scary movie. Preston was the worst color of white I'd ever seen. Purple shadows outlined his eyes. Needles and tubes engulfed him. It was hard to find our baby boy in the midst of the intimidating sterile box that contained and protected him. Not being able to hold him made it unbearable. It seemed like a nanosecond that I'd been given to spend with Preston, but I knew time was of the essence. Every minute away from the NICU was costly.

A team of doctors and nurses arrived and quickly prepared Preston for transport. They moved with precision, calling out instructions to team members, a verbal lifesaving checklist.

Sam followed behind the ambulance's siren. I watched them run down the hallway with Preston in tow realizing I might never see him again, and whatever hadn't felt real before now took on a scary, three-dimensional form. Overnight, our life had lost its order. All of the joyous feelings I anticipated had been washed away in a flood of shock and worry I'd never before known. A strange new loneliness slithered inside of me like it meant business. My body was free of the life it had nurtured. It longed for the touch of Preston's cottony-soft skin. Sitting alone in my hospital bed, emptiness filled my new Mothers Being. I was more than confident though, that Sam would do anything and everything necessary for our newborn son. The only certainty I knew for now was that Sam was born to be a father.

Sam, the man I married, my best friend and lover. I could tell by our first kiss, a single, gentle kiss on my lips as snow swirled around us, that he was as uncommon as that kiss. His mischievous eyes were irresistible to mine. Boyishly handsome with wavy brown hair and warm hazel eyes that smiled in unison with his mouth invited you to smile back. Until Sam, I didn't know it was possible to like a man as much as I loved him. Kind and gentle with a quiet strength, he was a banker by profession, and yet had practical hands-on know-how to work on cars, build furniture and wire houses. Because he could fix just about anything. I saw a glimmer of my Dad in him. However, I knew I'd fallen in love with this man because he was, for the most part, not like my Dad.

We'd been good friends since middle school, years before we became romantically involved during college. Our bond as friends fostered a deeper union that sustained us when life seemed impossible. It helped us forgive each other when we were too tired to love each other carefully. Sam and I had taken turns falling apart. It was as if, by osmosis, our hearts and souls had secretly met and created a survival plan just for us.

Our agreement was quickly put to the test after Preston's birth. Leaving the hospital empty handed, devoid of balloons and flowers and stripped of all the fanfare that having a newborn brings, opposed everything I'd imagined. With my wheelchair click clacking down the quiet hallway, I felt like there was a spotlight on my vacant lap. Yes, I'm the mom going home without a baby. If my still swollen belly wasn't enough of a clue, our scared, swollen eyes gave us away.

Stepping outside it felt as if the sun was directing all of its rays on us alone. The heaviness of the hot, humid July afternoon seemed to mirror our emotions. It was hard to breathe it in.

Coming home from the hospital empty-handed was tortuous. I sat in the front seat like it was natural to be sitting there, knowing full well our hearts were in dire trouble. Driving down the hill from the hospital, I could see the bank clock blinking 85 degrees. *Every Breath You Take* played on the car radio. Sam quickly reached over to turn it off. Funny how a second can change the force at which a song arrives on your heart. Sam and I were years older, it seemed, than when we heard it just the other day.

The radio was supposed to fill a void; instead it triggered one. The span of emptiness we sped past—winding country roads, farm fields and apple orchards—filled the entire car. We had imagined this trip before. Sam would carefully place Preston in his car seat then cautiously maneuver through familiar roads as if we were on some treacherous safari. I would sit in the back, glued to our baby's car seat watching his every breath, feeling blessed beyond measure while repeatedly reminding Sam to drive carefully. That was *supposed* to be the scariest thing, the first ride home, the first night. Instead, the uninhabited car seat radiated pain at a frequency that was almost unbearable.

Before now we were only acting the grown-up role, playing fix-up the farmhouse, pasting magazine cut-outs on our dream boards. Walking through the doorway of our family home, symbol of hope and growth, empty hands intertwined, we felt small and insignificant against our problems. For the past nine months, Preston's presence had been right there with us when we unpacked the first box. We feared that our careful nursery preparations, our planning, and the fresh paint were now done in vain. Our family home that had been singing with enthusiasm awaiting the arrival of our son now took on a strange energy like the flat line on a NICU monitor we feared.

I looked pleadingly into Sam's eyes as if silently asking permission to fall apart. "Are you ready to shower, so we can leave for the hospital?" he asked me. Sam had slept at the hospital since Preston's birth. We slowly walked up the short flight of stairs, stopping on the landing. "I can't do this," I cried.

Sam looked at me bewildered, "You can't do what?"

I stood on the landing pointing up to the end of the stairway. "That. That is what I can't do." One more flight of stairs and there it was. The empty nursery. Suddenly everything seemed unfamiliar, like I was looking at a stage that was set up for a play that never ran.

Everything up to this point had been frantically held in by shock. Shock is like a frenemy, smiling to your face as it wraps its ambiguous arms around you. Tricking you into thinking that what you're not feeling will remain that way. And it did until that moment when every inanimate object in the nursery took on life-like form. His empty crib seemed to be screaming at me. The nursery was supposed to smell like him by now. The clothes hamper should be filled to the brim. The scent of baby lotion, powder and *him* was supposed to meet us at the door. The oak rocking chair Sam refinished saddened me the most. It represented lullabies and snuggles and dreams coming true that for now lived in some mysterious fairy tale I couldn't reach.

In just two and a half days my senses had been overwhelmed by so many errant emotions I couldn't grab hold of any one. My adrenaline had been pumping as fast as humanly possible for Preston and Preston alone. But now, seeing the nursery brought the last several days crashing hard into this minute. I could feel insistent, heavy tears rising inside of me the way that dreaded sense of nausea hits you unwittingly, and try as you may, you can't squelch it. Then suddenly you lose all control—you vomit. I ran to our bedroom lying on the bed, vomiting tear after tear until the nausea of fear left me. I was beginning to understand fear and how the only way it had a hold on me was when I kept it hidden. Sam was my rock, he held me, allowing me to disintegrate before his eyes. I showered, freeing more tears as the hot water cascaded down my face, melting them away. I quickly changed into fresh clothes and we left for the hospital. Because of Sam's strong arms, because I let myself sink deeper than I ever had before, I was now ready to face whatever lie ahead.

My first visit to the NICU collected all my senses and tossed them in the corner like an old rag doll. Paulette had curly reddish-brown hair that skimmed her shoulders, brown eyes and olive skin. I already liked her. She reminded me of an Italian family I knew in Philadelphia. She walked toward me with eyes that were bright from laughing a lot. Her personality was like a warm smile wrapped in a careful hug. She reached out her arms to greet me. I could tell that Sam and her had already bonded. "I know it's a lot to take in all at once, but it's not as scary as it looks," she reassured me, her hand still on my shoulder. Sam escorted me to the sink so we could scrub with betadine and put our hospital gowns on.

She was right. There was so much to look at, but all I could see was Preston lying in his incubator. Paulette had dressed him in a light blue and white gingham outfit. That's what I looked at first. In my peripheral I could see the IV in my sweet baby's head. My heart bounced off every wall of the NICU until it toughened enough to withstand such images. It would get used to this I promised myself. Strange juxtapositions jumped out in each direction: needles pierced baby's heads and feet dotted with Polaroid pictures of mommy and daddy. Angel pictures of an everlasting glance offered to reluctant hands. Constant beeps and humming noises that sustained life. Baby coos and cries. Parents painted with silent tears, their faces sporadically bursting into laughter at the slightest movement of their clear-plastic-cube-bound child. Handmade pastel blankets and tiny newborn hats pleased my eyes and spoke to my heart of a place far away. A place called home. Where we all longed to be; outside of the huge plastic NICU cube that took care of us all. That for now—strangely felt like home.

At the farmhouse that night, I sensed I was losing Sam. His body language was tight and his eyes were distant. I chattered away about our day in the NICU but his answers came in deflated tones. We climbed into bed, mentally and physically exhausted. Outside our bedroom window the weeping willow swooshed in the breeze. I leaned over to kiss him goodnight and my lips tasted the saltiness of his tears. "Go ahead," I whispered, "let it out." I'd never heard my husband cry like he did that night. Proud, controlled, silent cries began until his heart cried scared, angry tears. Then frustration and worry crept in summoning a perfect storm.

His cries came from the depths of his father's being, from a place of hurt for not being able to make it better for his son. For not being able to transfer the pain from his son's weak little body to his strong fatherly body. From deeply and unconditionally loving another human being in a way his heart had never known. That's what our falling apart moments were—our parental bodies oozing out the hurt and fear so they could scab over, protecting us for next time. Now I was his rock. I wiped away his tears, telling him, "It will be all right. I promise. We'll face this together, no matter what."

The support we experienced was at times, astounding. We were overcome by the kindness of new friends and strangers in our small Pennsylvania community. Early one morning I was in the kitchen making sandwiches before leaving for the hospital when I heard a lawnmower. I ran to the window wall at the side of our house to see our neighbor mowing our lawn. In the yard I waved her down and explained that we would mow the grass over the weekend. Jean got off the mower, reaching for my hand, putting it in hers saying, "Your only chore is to bring that baby home. This is the very least we can do."

After one exhausting day in the NICU, we arrived home to find baskets of meals on our front porch. We received everything from canned goods, homemade cakes to three course dinners. The common thread of generosity that ran through our porch gifts was in the fact that no one left a card. Our meals were prepared out of the goodness of very kind hearts that didn't require a thank you.

Our hearts were healed by the generosity of spirit, and the outpouring of humanity displayed to us. Our souls had been fed by a remarkable bounty of love and friendship, by extraordinary human beings who after a long day of work and taking care of their own family, bothered to care just a little bit more than the average person.

We would miss our new friends, but I knew we'd formed an extraordinary bond that would last forever.

Preston's first birthday arrived. Sam and I were elated and exhausted. A peaceful night's slumber was something we hadn't experienced since his birth. Our son was one year old. A milestone most families expect without the angst and anticipation of what might not be. How we'd changed in just a year's time. Our Buffet of Life fluctuated with each passing day. Medical jargon became as common as asking someone to pass the butter. We had happily conformed to our new reality. We didn't resemble our former selves. The essence of our love had grown stronger than I thought possible. Born of necessity. Yet deeply rooted in a great friendship for one another.

My Mothers Being had changed. Life demanded it. While still soft and pliable on the inside, a hard shell had formed to protect it from crumbling. I stopped fully immersing myself in the grace of a good day. I thought too much.

I found myself spinning scenarios in my head and strategically prepping for them. Never telling a soul. Why did a good day with Preston make me more anxious than a bad day? I wondered.

My Mothers Being already knew; it waited patiently until I was ready to listen.

The normalcy of our lives was now filled with specialists for special children, early intervention teachers, physical and occupational therapists, developmental pediatricians, surgeons, leg braces, surgery schedules, and whispers of Cerebral Palsy and a future wheelchair. We'd been drop kicked into a new existence—an exceptionally wonderful and scary world full of special needs.

Everyone gathered at my parent's house for Preston's birthday celebration. We were living with them temporarily while our house was being built across the road. My father had bought twenty-seven acres on top of South Mountain fourteen years ago. We'd initially thought he was crazy for buying land so remote. Our only neighbors were deer. This place was growing on me, though. I'd come to love its quiet beauty.

Preston was the picture of health complete with chubby legs that stuck out from under his navy blue shorts. Today there was no talk of illness or hospitals. Everyone flowed in and out of the house refilling their plates with an abundance of picnic food. Poplar, Red Oak and pine trees filled the perimeter where we'd all gathered on the patio outside the dining room.

Stories and laughter echoed through the woods around us. Everyone basked in the glory of a beautiful summer day, celebrating our little family.

Sam and I were busy with hosting duties and more than happy to pass Preston around to eager arms. Emory was particularly zeroed in on him though. With each passing glance I caught Emory stealing him right and left. Nobody said a word. We'd all slipped into another dimension. The universe consorted with our subconscious minds while the angels conspired to help Emory out. He stared into Preston's eyes as if their souls were having a private conversation. I wondered what Preston heard.

The next morning, Sam had to leave for a meeting in DC. He poured his coffee, wearing a smile left over from yesterday. "You look handsome in your new gray suit and tie," I told him.

"Why thank you my dear," he said. He stole a quick kiss, grabbed his coffee mug and was out the door. Mom and I sat at the kitchen table reminiscing about the party over a cup of coffee while Preston napped.

"Did I tell you what I overheard Emory saying to Preston?" Mom asked.

"No, what did he say?"

"He said 'You're a wonder.'"

Just as we finished our second cup, the phone rang. Emory had suffered a massive heart attack and was in the ICU. How ironic, I thought, a man with one of the biggest hearts I know. Now, this big heart of his was failing him.

I quickly showered and waited for Sam to arrive. The color of our world had been stripped away, leaving all that remained dismal in our eyes.

This time someone else was slipping into heaven as I sat rocking Preston, feeding him his bottle. "You and your future siblings and cousins might never know his immense love," I worried.

Emory fought to hang on as best as he could given the damage to his heart. The family kept a bedside vigil as they came to grips with the reality of Emory's dire prognosis. It was hard to look at him hooked up to a ventilator and various machines that seemed to devour him. His anxious eyes darting from one family member to the next said *I have so much left to tell you.* Now, the only thing he could do was try to prepare them for life without him. Emory had been best friend and advisor to each of his four children. That was his gift. After several tortuous weeks, our world went black. Sam's father, his best friend and advisor, was gone. The foundation on which his family stood was reduced to improbable pieces. The aftermath of Sam's visits to his dad's bedside was profound as again he had to watch someone he loved slip away.

In a year's time he'd prepared to kiss his son goodbye twice. Now, the sudden death of his beloved father at fifty-five had disrupted his core beyond comprehension. Sam was lost.

Lying in bed, our limbs entwined, he asked, "Is this going to be our journey? One good thing followed by an equally bad thing?" He released all his pent-up tears that shock hadn't allowed. Our unspoken rhythm of one falling and one catching had already been established.

Our heartbeats knew this dance. I kissed him realizing he was not capable of words anymore. My arms were all he needed as he buried his head and broken heart into my chest. Life had felt confusing and fragile since Preston's birth. Was our life to be a succession of bright beautiful colors followed immediately by flat lifeless ones?

Was this to be our journey? To view the world through black and white lenses while everyone else saw it in living color? I loved black and white photographs, though. They had character that allowed a glimpse of the soul, with shadows and gray areas that drew me in. Perhaps black and white would afford a new mindset, a new way of looking at everything and everyone. Preston's way.

Perhaps there was a strange new beauty in the undefined.

mother /muhth-er/ ~

a female parent

Origin ~

Middle English moder, from Old English modor

being /bee-ing/ ~

that which has actuality either materially or in idea

absolute existence in a complete or perfect state, lacking no essential characteristic; essence

Origin ~

Middle English from gerund of been

Mothers Being ~

a soft veil—transparent enough for me to see through: yet vaporous to shield me from harm

my Zen Warrior

my knowing soul, my higher intuition,

my other heart.

Chapter 3

Reflections

OUTSIDE, MELTED SNOW RAN OFF TREE BRANCHES IN defeat. Watching the symphony of water droplets made it hard to imagine the two feet of snow that looked like something out of a winter wonderland just eight days ago. High winds had sculpted the snow into alabaster drifts. Frosty peaks reached upward almost touching glassy icicles dangling from overwrought branches. And the white horse barn all but disappeared from view except for hoof prints leading to the meadow behind it.

Today was an unusually mild January day, calm and still as if winter were playing hide and seek. The cold wind took Preston's breath away, so I decided to take advantage of the calm. I bundled him up and walked down my parent's wooded lane, across the gravel road to the construction site of our new home. Its foundation had been mortared together by Sam and my father's capable hands. It looked strong and ready to hold whatever life brought our way. The earth would soon cover it in, forever protecting us the way roots push from the darkness all things that grow by seeking the light. As I started up our hilly driveway, across the road I noticed two deer watching us from the pond in the lower meadow. This was what I loved about the mountain. The serenity I disliked as a child now enchanted me.

Preston smiled, kicking his legs excitedly the minute he saw his beloved Pop. Dad wore his usual uniform of a brown and rust plaid shirt, brown pants and a straw hat with a brown band wrapping its rim.

His pipe dangled out of the right side of his mouth. Steam rose from his coffee mug on a nearby wooden workbench. He was in the middle of laying brickwork. It was almost therapeutic to sit on the floor with Preston on my lap and watch my father finesse the brick around the fireplace as if he'd been a mason all his life. His big hands manipulated the bricks and mortar effortlessly. "Dad, how can you simply read a book on masonry and be this skilled?" I asked him.

"I don't know babe, you pay attention to the little details; they're not as little as you would think, and after that it's just a matter of practice and patience." I thought it ironic that such a mercurial man had the ability to be astoundingly practiced and patient when mastering a craft. I guess it was why I loved watching the calm in a sometimes stormy Irishman. He stopped long enough to play with Preston who was now laughing at his pop's silly noises. I left wearing a big smile, knowing the love that went into his fastidious craftsmanship would be a part of our new home.

Our Dutch Colonial sat in the middle of a three-acre corner lot bordered by two gravel roads with 200 acres of wooded land behind it. It's grayish green siding and burgundy front door were our nod to Williamsburg, Virginia. We'd designed it ourselves with open, airy rooms that had ample space for a future wheelchair, therapy mat and other things beyond what we were capable of knowing right now. A central stairway divided the long spacious family room from the open kitchen and dining area. I envisioned myself preparing meals in the kitchen while watching the kids in the family room beside me.

From the kitchen sink I could see the pond where the deer liked to linger. I imagined soon they would be our new guests. This house would be our respite from the world.

My Mothers Being had found its center again. It was ready for some serious nesting. Our recent to do lists often felt all consuming in their nature, with items like—call insurance company, schedule physical therapy, order syringes, refill meds, call neurologist regarding Preston's last seizure, schedule fitting for leg braces. I'd forgotten what it was like to have a to do list full of things like—pick paint color for bedroom and buy picture for fireplace mantel. Interior design was my first love . . . the one that got away.

My father, the intellectual, considered my dream of becoming an interior designer to be frivolous.

On my birthday Sam arrived at my parent's house wearing childlike excitement on his face. "Hurry up, we can't be late," he said. He opened the car door for me and off we went. A mere two minutes later, we pulled into the driveway of our almost finished house. "Close your eyes," he told me, as he escorted me out of the car. "No peeking, just let me lead the way." He walked me into the dining area. "Okay, now open your eyes!"

The first thing I saw was a beautiful crystal vase full of pale pink roses. The vase rested on a makeshift plywood table that Sam had draped with a white tablecloth and next to it was a full array of Chinese takeout. A single white candle's glow was reflected in the crystal vase. Two blue toile pillows were arranged on either side of our plywood table. It was the most stunning table setting I'd ever seen. It was made with love and hope, fashioned from unlikely materials.

Sam got up to uncork a bottle of white wine. "Happy Birthday my dear. I think we have the best table in the house," he said, grinning from ear to ear, proud for having pulled off my birthday surprise.

"Thank you, my sweetheart, this is exactly what I needed." For a few glorious hours we were a young couple sitting in our new house dreaming of a future without complication.

Sam reached for the bottle of wine, moving his pillow next to mine. His comfortable smile was replaced by an intense look. "Something on your mind?" I asked.

"Do you think it's a coincidence that Preston has been better since my dad's death?" he asked. "It's almost as if Dad's dying made him stronger."

My sister, Julie, and I had spent hours discussing intuition—how we all have it but don't know how to tap into it. If intuition was really valuable, why weren't we taught to use it? Was every human being born with it? Was a mother's intuition different from that of a father?

My Mothers Being had taken many forms since Preston's birth. Was it a typical Mothers Being or was it developing differently to meet the needs of a disabled child? I wondered if my intuition had grown into something more. I thought back to the birthday party. The image of Emory staring intently into Preston's eyes wouldn't leave me. It was the first thing I recalled after Emory died. Somewhere, somehow, I was being given a message. Was I developing a keener intuitive process, or was Preston on a higher intuitive plane than all of us? Or both?

It was true that Preston had been better since Emory's death. My Mothers Being felt blessed; it had been shown a sacred gift. It'd witnessed a kind soul breathing life into a new soul in preparation to leave this world in an exchange of energy or transference of willpower.

It was interesting that he had used plywood. It wasn't a high grade of wood that was admired by anyone; its purpose wasn't for making a dining table. All of its defects were quite obvious just as our son's were. The world would give him labels to wear. He would be known by his defects first.

Sam and I were made of love, hope and defects like the table. Now, we too, had an unlikely product in Preston. I didn't know what Preston would be or even if he would be. But I knew for certain that he didn't fight so hard to live for a boilerplate, predetermined existence. His worth wouldn't be mandated by society. Not if we had anything to do with it. His spirit pointed boldly to the possibility in the impossible. He had cheated death. Hell, he even managed to smile.

My Mothers Being felt reenergized from the calm of the last several months, though our new calm was not as calm as we would have liked. It had a newfound determination; ready to take on whatever path we were meant to walk. Sam and I would explore all the possibilities for our son, no matter what anyone said, while still realistically recognizing his defects.

Everything in our life seemed to be laid out in black and white terms. Just black and white was unsatisfactory, begging us to think from an entirely different set of brainwaves.

Like the black and white photos that gained depths in gray. I found that my Mothers Being gained depth in these grays. Not dismal, forlorn gray but the introspective grays of a rainy day.

It seemed as if most of my adult life was in preparation for experiencing the inside of Preston's soul from the outside of my existence. A shifting of inside to outside: then back to inside—to the soul.

A quiet melody on paper was, at last, given a voice.

He had chosen us, and we, him.

We would be the crystal vase reflecting the candles glow.

Sam leaned into me, kissing my neck long and tenderly. "I love you my dear."

"I love you more," I whispered. This home of ours would be a place that celebrated diversity. A place of immense love.

We christened our new home.

Loving a child with special needs is like having a hummingbird land on your heart.

Leaving it awestruck and fluttering. Forever.

Chapter 4

Cha Cha Changes

"We must always change, renew, rejuvenate ourselves; otherwise we harden."
Von Goethe

*P*RESTON WAS HOSPITALIZED FOR A POSSIBLE SHUNT REVI-
sion. The shunt, originally placed in one of the ventricles in his brain
to treat the abnormal drainage of cerebrospinal fluid due to hydrocephalus,
needed to be adjusted. I realized that in the world of neurosurgery this was
a simple procedure, but for my Mothers Being, brain surgery was an assault
on her two-and-a-half-year old's body.

Preston's nurse walked into his room to announce that a parent support
group was being held on our floor in fifteen minutes. "No thanks," I said,
rolling my eyes.

"Why?" she asked.

"I don't want to air my private thoughts to a group of strangers, nor do
I want to listen to parents whine like children," I said, with a sarcastic smile
on my face.

She tilted her head at me in a disapproving but friendly manner, "There's
coffee and donuts, and it will give you a break. Go. I'll stay with this redheaded cutie!" As if on cue, Preston smiled his ornery smile at her, kicking
his legs with such excitement it convinced me to go.

Five other parents gathered around the coffeepot in the lounge area.
I politely said hello, still wondering why I allowed myself to be talked into

this. I heard a husband and wife commiserating over their little girl's appendectomy, causing me to regret my decision even more.

Linda, the social worker wore black pants and a light pink shirt that looked even brighter against her long platinum hair. She had a pleasant face with considerate brown eyes. She gathered everyone onto two red sofas that faced each other, asking us to introduce ourselves and tell why we were here. Sharing private details with strangers was not something the guarded side of my family easily did. Ugh.

Clark, an average looking man in his late twenties, sat fidgeting with his coffee cup, intermittently touching his dark wavy hair to make sure it was in place. He was fashionably decked out in khaki pants, a navy blue and white checked shirt and proper manners that said this was the biggest problem he ever expected to have in his life. His entire being appeared purposefully distant, as though the very idea of how this unfortunate matter happened to his son hadn't caught up to him yet. His eyes seemed arrogant with self-pity and gave me the impression that the only reason he came was to talk, not to listen. "I'll go first," he said. *Of course you will,* I thought. "My son had his tonsils removed. It's been very stressful and I'm glad he pulled through, but his throat is still sore, and he keeps asking when he can have French fries."

His problem didn't seem like much of a problem to me. Brain surgery sounded like a problem. Clark's eyes darted ambiguously around the room as he spoke, making it harder still to listen. At the exact moment I heard him explain his particular brand of ordeal, I regretted having come.

And directly inside that place in my head I heard, *see, I told you,* from the fierce little Irish redhead who bounced around my brain when things got tough. At times, it was hard to contain her (I pictured her with heels and a kick-ass green dress to match her feisty spirit). Just knowing she was there—doing her Irish thing all up in my head made me smile on the inside when I wanted to scream on the outside. For now I would let the little person in my brain rant while I sat with my knees crossed, arms resting calmly on my lap politely listening. Guarding my truth.

It was just as I thought. The first sofa was filled with stories of parental woe, each one sounding similar to the next. There was no demarcation of anything unusual or particularly scary until Ally.

Her brunette hair was bluntly cut in a way that said it was as much for maintenance as it was for style. She wore a white linen shirt, loose jeans and Bjorn clogs. I guessed that she was in her mid-thirties by the experience in her voice. It was clear by the ease at which she moved through the area and found her place on the sofa she had done this before "Hello everyone, I'll miss coming to these coffee klatches that Linda so thoughtfully puts together. We're not going to be in the hospital much longer." I thought to myself—hmm, maybe another appendectomy? She carefully paused, drawing in a deep breath as she adjusted herself on the sofa. "My daughter has end stage leukemia," she said calmly. My Mothers Being sat staring into the eyes of another Mothers Being it knew all too well, but different. My heart started beating fast. She appeared strong and calm on the outside. What made her want to share one precious moment with a group of strangers? I wondered.

I already knew the answer—she wanted a few sacred moments of *normal* with a cup of coffee and friendly chatter, maybe even laughter, before her Mothers Being morphed into something she didn't recognize. Her Mothers Being had helped her escape the pain. She was busy breathing in life before death came. There was a wise peacefulness to this woman that humbled me. I wanted to absorb it into my Mothers Being. It's hard shell would need to soften first. I wondered, how many years she had gone through this with her daughter? What did she learn? How many hospital stays? She didn't look wrecked though—that would come later.

News of her eight-year-old daughter's death trickled down the hallway. I thought about my state of mind at the coffee klatch yesterday morning. Had I become the emotionless robot on the outside my father groomed me to be, while also resembling the cheerleader from hell? I'd just received the wake up call of my life. I was learning quickly as I witnessed numerous life stories passing by me in hallways. Our bubble of a world, known as a hospital, was filled with all walks of life. Full of sad and happy stories. Mediocre stories. Even miracles. The magnitudinous force of nervous tension, sadness and profound gratitude bouncing off hospital walls was generally overwhelming. How many extraordinary life stories did I walk by on a given day? Being in a hospital was exhausting. Not solely due to our circumstance. But because all the intense emotions encased within the microcosm of its walls sometimes collided as they passed in the hallways—or at a parent's coffee klatch.

My Mothers Being grew a lot that day. It would continue to feel whatever Preston felt. It would know, sometimes before others knew. It would sense things before my heart was prepared to feel them. It was tuned in to the unknown. Tuned in to the unimaginable. It was learning to adapt to all the new realities circling around us, sometimes like vultures.

Its hard shell was formed with the best of intentions, to help me to breathe, to think, to grow, and to love. And to adjust so I wouldn't crumble from the pressure. Now, I was ready for a deeper realization. My Mothers Being had lived a thousand lives. It knew more than it could say. It was a wise old soul, connected to Preston's soul.

Today, its hard shell became porous allowing a new reality to filter through. The realization that to the dad whose son had a tonsillectomy— that was brain surgery to him. I was so caught up in our perfect storm that I'd mistakenly shut out the rest of the world. My Mothers Being had been adjusting. Our brains were on a crash course, cramming for anything and everything, whose major changed at the blink of an eye. We'd lost our direction. I allowed our challenges to consume me.

I remembered the lightness we vowed never to forget.

It was time to live our life again, time to establish the place of us no matter where we were. Knowing it sure as hell wouldn't be typical.

Children inevitably change us. Having Preston changed me suddenly in an explosion of color and force. His persistent challenges made him a continual catalyst of change.

I would need both the little Irish redhead and my Mothers Being. Perhaps together they'd keep me spirited and grounded enough to someday let down my guard and show my humanness, all of it. I don't know what's ahead; I just know today I've been changed. And that gives me strength for tomorrow. Another realization.

There was fragility in having a severely disabled child the world would judge, or worse yet—dismiss. We worried with every seizure as we held Preston in our arms waiting for it to stop. The fear of what lie ahead would never leave us; but we'd no longer allow it to define us. It didn't matter where we were, in a hospital or at home, we were together and we would make the most of whatever time we had.

My Mothers Being kept that a closely guarded secret for now.

possibility/pa-se-bi-le-te/ ~

a chance that something might exist, happen, or be true

Origin ~

Late Middle English; from Old French possibilite, from late Latin possibilitas, possibilis 'able to be done'

I dwell in possibility. Emily Dickinson

possibility ~

an imagination of expectations from the heart of your soul.

Chapter 5

In the Slow Blink of an Eye

SAM AND I CLIMBED THE STAIRS. IT WAS ELEVEN P.M. HE cast his pensive look at me. The one I had come to know, his eyes telepathically saying, *here comes another long and sleepless night.* Both of us knew we had a few scant hours before Preston woke up screaming uncontrollably. This had become our silent march up the stairs to our bedroom as our minds came to grips with what was to come. What we were afraid to say out loud for fear the universe would think us ungrateful. We didn't dare make the slightest noise. Preston's hypersensitive hearing could pick up the sound of a cricket in the basement it seemed.

Our nights had become an inescapable nightmare. The eerie anticipation of night as it turned abruptly into morning was our harsh reality. We'd all been robbed of the gift of laying down to sleep in peace; robbed of the best meditation. We attempted taking turns with him throughout the night, but it was impossible to elude our son's loud cries. His crying was nearly a scream, loud and high-pitched. We went from pediatrician to pediatrician to get to the bottom if it, only to be told he was gassy due to his cerebral palsy, or that he was possibly colicky. We were prescribed every colic and acid reflux medication on the market. It was perplexing to us that each failed attempt was never followed by a doctor's question just an absurd knowingness that there was nothing wrong past that.

We continued walking the hallways in the not so quiet hours from one to six almost every night. There's something magical about being able to lie down, shut out the world, shut off your mind, and fall into a restful slumber, awaking refreshed. I realized that sleeping through the night, something we took for granted before Preston's birth, now seemed like a small miracle as the abruptness of morning forced the weight of our eyes open.

Morning came loud and fast like a trumpet blast, our senses dulled by only a momentary slumber. A haze of time and space had grown over my memory of sleeping through the night the way fog slips a curtain between here and there. So far, parenthood was an enigma most unlike what we envisioned.

From the moment cerebral palsy was practically whispered in our ears; everything regarding our strange new world had become a mystery. We were now detectives, doctors, nurses and psychics attempting to navigate through the vagueness of our universe.

My Mothers Being felt conflicted. Anger and frustration poured in, clogging its shell's porous surface; endangering its pliability. It was going to have to help me with the new reality of feeling helpless for not being able to quell our son's distress. This ongoing feeling of helplessness is not what a parent expects to feel so early on. It's supposed to come later during the frustrating teenage years, but here we were, frustrated and tired beyond what was conceivable to most. My Mothers Being was a chameleon, though. It camouflaged itself to protect me from the unknown. That's what you do when you don't know what else to do—you protect yourself.

Morning kept coming too soon. We'd been functioning on a few hours of sleep for three years, now. With the light of day came Preston's smiling face as if last night was but a dream.

Sam and I sucked down our morning coffee summoning life back into our bone-weary bodies. "I'm calling Dr. Nelson," I said sluggishly. I leaned into the table, my head propped against my hand as if I was whispering to it, "We can't keep doing this night after night. Where do we reach a saturation point in all this? You and I are already at the point where the nights scare us awake before we even lay our heads on a pillow. We are that tired, Sam."

In a frustrated voice he answered, "I know. I'm fed up with pediatricians telling us it's because of his cerebral palsy like that's an acceptable blanket answer."

Seeing the worried look on his face, I stood beside Sam who was staring at the purple and white phlox through the French doors of the family room like they held the key to unlocking our mystery of sleepless nights. The phlox gracefully spilled over a twenty-foot long limestone rock wall that bordered a brick patio in our backyard. They poured over the rocks in the most delicate, charming way. It all but suggested they had been painted on. Sam's far-off gaze reminded me of all the times I'd spent digging in the earth looking for answers in our flowers. Our perennial flower garden sat to the right of the rock wall just off the patio. A purple butterfly bush greeted pass-ersby at the end of the first path; around it were four more beds full of laven-der, campanula, Shasta daisies, yellow and orange lilies, coreopsis and herbs.

In a thinking-out-loud tone, still looking at the phlox, he continued, "I'm worried that Preston is already being put in generic categories instead of being looked at as an individual. What's it going to take to get people to see him? Just him."

Dr. Nelson had a serious but pleasant look on his face as he shared the test results with us. I didn't feel panicked this time. Speculation swirled around my Mothers Being. Had all this become ordinary or was I so exhausted that any answer was met with ease? At last we had a diagnosis, and hopefully, relief for Preston: Gastroesophageal Reflux Disease (GERD).

A surgical procedure would be necessary to correct his condition, a Nis-sen fundoplication, they called it. The upper part of his stomach would be wrapped around the lower end of his esophagus, tightening the sphincter valve and hopefully preventing reflux. We'd become comfortable in hospi-tals—our second home. Preston greeted the familiar faces of his favorite nurses with a big smile and his joke of the day on his Tech Talk—a four-square communication device that enabled us to record messages such as *Hi, I'm Preston*. This and another one with eight squares was his verbal link to the rest of the world.

Most doctors saw that even though he couldn't speak, he could listen and understand. We came to realize that their opinions on what he under-stood varied. We knew, as well, that they didn't have time beyond the scope of their specialty, to conceptualize his life's map.

They knew that our opinion about treating our son with respect didn't vary. Any doctor who didn't treat Preston as a person first was politely shown the door.

Sending your child through the doors of an operating room is obviously never easy for any parent. Thoughts of what could go wrong taunted us as soon as the double doors swung shut. At age three this was Preston's third surgery and seventh hospitalization. Knowing there were probably many more of both ahead it was essential that we remained as calm as possible. We never wanted to appear worried in front of him—our routine was to reassure him he would be all right and remind him that we would see him very soon. We needed our calm energy to permeate his psyche. Just like we had done for his first surgery, we kissed him with magnificent smiles on our faces. And when they had taken him, we prayed.

Surgery was a success. We were granted a brief reprieve but no pardon from our sleepless nights. The seizures and muscle spasms that woke him through the night remained. Our bodies adapted, or so we thought, as well as our routine. We'd started taking shifts as much as possible. We had even purchased a waterbed in hopes it would soothe his tight, spastic muscle tone and lull him to sleep.

Sam and I were like two ships passing in the night. Hell, who am I kidding? I only wish it were that calm. It was more like two cars frantically racing down the highway, pursued by a chase car with a very loud siren.

Sam had taken the one-thirty wakeup call. Now it was my turn. Three a.m., as I lay in Preston's bed beside him, afraid to move, I watched as he effortlessly breathed in and out. No memory of an earlier time when the faint rise and fall of his chest was like a metronome counting his last minutes of life lingered. It was precious to watch our little guy sleeping, temporarily unimpeded by cerebral palsy. I wanted nothing more than to be in this place of thankfulness regardless of the hour. The nightlight cast a soft glow on his dark eyebrows and long lashes that outlined his face. I lay within the shadow of his profile, exhausted but content. Across the room, the rocking horse lamp stood tall on a maple dresser. I looked around Preston's room, wide-eyed awake, smiling inwardly at being surrounded by such beautiful things all made from love.

Preston had a small seizure at three-thirty, it was now four-fifteen and he was finally back to sleep. He stirred at the slightest movement, and was often startled awake, which in turn caused another seizure. We had thus adopted a ridiculous, stealthy, Ninja-like, rolling off the bed exit strategy so as not to disturb the best cure in the world.

All we really needed was to see his handsome face each morning. It was the lightness that would carry us for now. We would sleep . . . eventually, we reassured each other. For now, we celebrated the lightness, and the fact that he was alive and doing remarkably well, considering.

Before Preston, I thought that a miraculous moment was one so theatrical you couldn't deny its occurrence.

For instance, those dramatic movie scenes with emotive, swelling music. We did have swelling music miracles, like our Labor Day weekend, when the earth shook something within us and it seemed the ground really did move beneath our feet, making it obvious to all that, yes, this is a miracle. Tears and smiles were simultaneously draped across the faces of those blessed to be involved.

But, we were learning that miracles no longer needed background music. That sometimes the quiet, demure ones were the most impressive of all. Our grateful hearts now looked for the smallest nuance in each day.

It wasn't that long ago I thought all of our moments with our first child were gone before they'd begun. It's said you can't know true happiness unless you've experienced pain. Perhaps it's true. I thought we were perfectly happy before, but now I know a different kind of happiness, like I left and came back with a resplendent realization I could have never known in my old life. I imagine though, that in order to feel this kind of happiness we had to lose some of the supposed things the way you lose something you never expected to lose; making the lost thing seem invaluable. Then you either spend an exhausting amount of time trying to find it or you look around at what's left and you adapt. Another realization.

You begin again. And what you lost is lost again in your memory.

We were sitting on our screen porch, propped against a wicker sofa, a soft green braided rug beneath us. What looked like an ordinary moment: a mom sipping coffee, yawning herself back to life while her child wrapped between her legs, playing with a toy was really an OT/PT session, teaching our son cause and effect that was crucial to helping him develop communication skills. I slyly stretched his tight body in between belly laughs, cataloguing it in my memory place for a time less forgiving.

This gentle late summer day whispered of fall. Preston reaching out to touch the fuzzy yellow tennis ball with a smiley face on the joystick toy his Pop made and belly laughing when it buzzed. This is what miracles look like.

I realized acutely in this moment of awareness, that if it hadn't been for the other moment, I would certainly not have the awareness, let alone the appreciation for this extraordinarily ordinary day in the life of a mom and her differently-abled little boy.

I too had become differently-abled. My Mothers Being made sure of it.

We vowed never to forget rocking him into heaven. We had learned in that moment we were capable of doing what we once perceived as impossible. It was the most profoundly vulnerable and courageous moment of our lives. Holding our dying baby allowed us a tiny bitter taste of how life would feel without him. It was as if we had been allowed to taste a crumb on a plate full of food.

Before the day Sam and I had acknowledged and felt a miracle, we began each extraordinary day the same way most people do. We moved freely, unencumbered by prior thought or effort. We rose from our bed, feet touching the floor—full of the sensation of a soft rug under our toes. Our feet automatically balanced and supported the weight of our bodies. We mouthed sleepy good mornings to each other without thinking of how we would get the words out. We walked, talked and moved about our world freely, never thinking fully what utterly divine miracles we were experiencing.

Watching Preston fight for a breath of life, we began to understand how assuming we had been. From that moment on we made a conscious decision to be more grateful for what we did have rather than wishing for what we didn't have. The word conscious is not quite correct. It was an organic process that opened us up when we needed it most. Things we used to complain about seemed embarrassingly insignificant these days, like who would mow the grass and when. It quiets me still, to think we ever gave such importance to a single blade of grass. Now a simple arm movement required Herculean effort. Preston would never feel the freedom of each new day the way we so effortlessly and unknowingly did. His feet would never touch the floor as he got out of bed. He was completely dependent on us to start his day in motion, to help him feel the sensation of ordinary miracles . . . forever.

Little by little, we soaked in another layer of Preston's silent lessons.

Our perspective changed in the slow blink of an eye—everywhere we looked, miracles now existed. Every little thing had changed, including us, yet they were all the same. Another realization.

Preston turned our eyes to keenly pay attention. To regard what we used to take for granted. A smile: moving your body freely: sleeping through the night: the spoken word: a day free of seizures. Humanity. Did I mention a smile? His beautiful, full-faced, crooked, eyes-twinkling, melt your heart smile.

The good doctor who predicted he probably wouldn't live, as well as never even smile, was sent a Polaroid photograph from the NICU hospital. It was a picture of Preston laughing and smiling from ear to ear. On it was written four words:

A picture will suffice.

Indeed. A picture will more than suffice.

I'd hoped Dr. Rolex had paused for a profound, insightful moment and would maybe actually look at the next sick human being, no matter what their test results showed. That he wouldn't give up or assume or make them feel like an inconvenience. That maybe, just maybe, he realized he wasn't the all-knowing person he perceived himself to be.

No, he was not God but a mere mortal of a neurosurgeon. I wish we could have been there secretly watching, as he first laid eyes on Preston's picture.

The little Irish redhead in my brain likes to imagine that every time our son smiled, somehow through the universe Dr. Rolex felt an unexplainable twinge.

We could only hope that beyond anything else he would remember— when in doubt, *look* at the patient! They tell a story that often precludes a medical book. With each and every person comes an energy force and a will that sometimes defy logic.

And medicine.

Preston's silent lessons had begun.

Chapter 6

The Truest Part

TWO STALWART BRICK BUILDINGS STOOD FACING EACH other through their respective parking lots as if it were a harbinger of things to come.

One: a typical elementary school and the other, a not so typical school for children with disabilities—a segregated center.

At the mention of starting pre-school Preston's eyes eagerly popped wide open the same way his smile overwhelmed his cute little face. His smaller than average body wiggled from side to side in his wheelchair, while his skinny legs kicked with excitement. A dolphin-like squeal of joy echoed throughout our house whenever he heard something funny or exciting. And to his ears, this was as good as Christmas morning.

Preston was beginning pre-school, a milestone for most parents. But for me, it was a quandary of sorts. Where he was going and the absence of choice was a concept I struggled with. I asked myself. Was this my ego or was Preston's soul reaching out to my Mothers Being? Was there more?

Our parental hearts and minds had digested so much in the past three years. This was an odd day for us, to say the least. It marked the realization of a segregated education. Separateness. And as much as I tried to embrace this concept, it felt uncomfortable.

Yet, we were wonderfully happy for Preston and for the opportunity to learn. Still, I felt as if all my beliefs had been sifted through a colander, coming out jumbled together with no identity.

Tomorrow the short yellow bus, the one referred to in jokes, would take Preston to a school far away from his neighborhood school. The present me had no problem with his bus, but the future me wondered how the Irish redhead would handle people making what they considered to be funny remarks about *being on the short bus*. Another layer of reality stood bigger than life in front of us. He would never ride the big bus. Nevertheless, our reality for our red headed boy wouldn't be diminished by the size of a silly bus.

Miss Steph—a name that would become synonymous with family.

I remember meeting Preston's teacher for the first time. Wheeling him down the hallway to his classroom we passed a nurse walking with an IV pole, which felt both comforting and unnerving. It was wonderful to know they were there in the school and chill-worthy to know we might one day need that IV pole. The gym, at first glance, looked like any other elementary school gym. Two basketball hoops anchored its court. Though around it was adapted swings, walkers, prone-standers, canes and other strange looking things I couldn't yet identify.

Red and bright blue therapy mats and wedges punctuated the spaces in between the equipment, their colors calling out our new normal. I knew that someday, probably soon; all the disability apparatus and medically necessary equipment would look as ordinary as the basketball lying on the floor at center court. Another realization.

We rolled Preston into the classroom in his awesomely cool first wheelchair. He telescoped his head around the room like a human computer, his eyes digitalizing the classroom in his memory bank—his way of soaking in a new environment.

We were so proud of him. He was our little warrior who looked no worse for the wear. We'd become accustomed to people's surprised look upon seeing such a happy, healthy looking child, given the already thick stack of medical records.

Miss Steph's face wore the same surprised look as she warmly greeted us at the door of her classroom. She was a handsome woman, horsey perhaps, I thought. She had sky blue eyes that spoke of summer. Her chiseled, make-up free cheekbones and very short blonde hair told me she valued her time in nature rather than primping in front of a mirror. Her tanned body and muscular hands told a story of long days spent outside gardening.

She didn't mince words—I liked that. An immense love for her students was obvious the way her face softened as she spoke of how she ran her classroom.

To her they were children first; their disabilities came second. We were off to a good start—we already shared a common thread of philosophy.

She had a Buddha-like essence that drew me in. As uncomfortable as I was with coming to grips about the segregated school; I was excited at the prospect of having Miss Steph as his teacher.

She felt like an old friend from the start. Yet, I was intrigued. There was something mysterious about her I couldn't quite put my finger on.

Preston and she locked eyes and their souls became bound together forever like they had met before. The handsome woman and the handsome angel (as she called him) fell in love. Miss Steph's dynamic calm and humor along with Preston's soulful energy and humor matched the way two halves make a whole and, together they spoke to each other's uncommon story. He loved her immediately and she in turn, loved him unconditionally.

Together, we shared a belief in the person he would grow into—a person with potential in spite of his many limitations. Our potential looked different. It was encouraging, hopeful and accepting of whatever. A potential that lay in exploring the possibility in the impossible.

Miss Steph had already spoiled us for future teachers. There were no limited expectations in her classroom: only the belief that each and every unique child had the potential to learn and to enlighten her.

We had entrusted her with our most precious being, and she in turn, entrusted us with her most precious secret—her true identity.

"This is it Pumpkin, today is your first day of school!" His eyes opened wide with a child's delight, and when we told him he would soon see Miss Steph, his entire body rose up from the seat of his wheelchair as much as his CP allowed. He extended his legs in unison with his arms that were stretched out over the wooden tray atop his wheelchair as if to say, "Let's go!" His face took on an almost mischievous expression as if he knew something we didn't. His eyes regarded us with their usual impishness and his crooked, ornery smile flaunted his sense of humor.

We dressed him in khaki shorts and a green and blue striped polo shirt, over which was draped a bright new, green bandana. His new green backpack with his name embroidered on it hung across the backside of his wheelchair. Inside was a change of clothes, a sweater, diapers, lunch, leg braces, medication, and extra bandanas. His backpack would never come home overloaded with books and homework assignments looking like it could tip him over backwards. It did, however, contain the essence of who he was and as long as we honored that, we knew everything would be all right.

Having a non-verbal child mutes the back and forth verbal dialogue a typical family relies on. It's hard enough being a parent without having to play guess your best. Questions such as: "How was your day? What did you learn today? What was the best/worst part of your day?" are crucial. A typical dialogue filled with questions in order to glean valuable tidbits about how well your child is adapting to their emerging world.

It was hard sending our non-verbal, totally dependent child off into the arms of virtual strangers. Initially we worried that his unique signals wouldn't be read correctly. The first day of school, Miss Steph started a daily communication book that went back and forth. Our dialogue on paper had begun. A story was about to be told. A history of likes and dislikes, successes and failures, how well he ate, illnesses, how many times he correctly identified a picture or object, how he made her laugh, what he laughed at, whether or not he had a seizure—its type and duration, whether he seemed mysteriously uncomfortable, if he had muscle spasms, how he did in PT, OT, Vision or Speech Therapy, whether he said uh huh aloud or remained silent, along with snippets of personal notes as we began to share each other's human story.

A chronology of good days and bad days and what made them so, was our lifeline between home and school. We had broken ground on our new village.

Our school village was comprised of special education teachers, classroom aides, special education administrators, principals, physical, occupational and speech therapists, vision and hearing specialists, psychologists, social workers and nurses.

Miss Steph began to work with him and told us, "There's a little boy in there dammit; I can see wisdom in his eyes. I can feel his unique energy. Boy, he's been through a lot. He's one tough little bird. You would never know he's been so sick by looking at him today. I can't properly put it into words, but there's a kind of curiousness in his blue eyes. The kind that makes you want to peek around the corner because what you can see is so intriguing. Does that make sense?"

"It sure does," we answered, nodding our heads as we smiled at each other.

"We understand exactly what you mean. I guess we'll have to peel back the layers together, won't we," Sam said. I could tell by the approving look in his eyes that he too was a little smitten to have Miss Steph as Preston's teacher.

With the onset of school came a rush of PTA and other parent support group meetings.

At one such meeting a specialist spoke of her special view on how special parents should feel about their special needs children. It made us feel, at times, as if we were being lumped into a generic category, as well. She told us that we were grieving or would soon be grieving for the child we lost. In other words—the normal, full of potential child we didn't get.

Sitting on facing sofas in the school lobby, other parents nodded their heads in agreement as she spoke. Some pulled out tissues dabbing the corner of their eyes. It was clear by the salty heaviness in the air most parents were already there.

I've never fully understood why we didn't grieve the way other parents did. I felt like an emotional outcast at times. Was there a subliminal message written in the parental sky that we were missing?

I was beginning to believe our DNA actually had been changed while rocking him into heaven in the NICU. When we let go of how we thought our life was supposed to be, it was as if a different knowingness entered. Everything familiar had been swept from inside us, like an accidental deletion of pages on a computer screen. A blank page to be rewritten with a different remembrance. It didn't mean we weren't stressed or worried or tired, it only meant we celebrated what we did have. Perhaps it was another miracle of sorts. Darkness and lightness had come so close together they practically sat on one another. It was that moment when time isn't measured but differently felt, when the darkness conceded to the lightness of the supernal in between. Another realization.

We've never grieved for what could have been. It seemed disrespectful to the little human being we did have—senseless, like throwing away a gift that had never been open, yet wishing for a different one. Preston was our gift. At times, I felt as if some didn't understand why we were celebrating the child we had. Experience trumps assumption, that's what I believed and felt deep in my Mothers Being. How dare the world assume we should grieve, based on what? Our only reality was that we fell fully in love with our little guy. I saw no point in grieving for something we didn't have. Preston was who we were meant to have and for whatever reason, he was what he was meant to be.

Our life with him, in all its gritty reality, all its joy, and all its gray areas, was here and now. What if seemed pointless.

How can you bask in the warmth of the sun if you've never danced in the glow of a moonlit evening? That's what being a parent to Preston felt like. While it's true, having a child who needs you to bathe, dress and feed him twenty-four seven, is exhausting—somewhat unbearable at times. And not having a neighborhood full of parents who live it on a regular basis made it isolating, at times. Yet in the darkness of all the mundane and tiring necessities of his care came an illumination so beautiful and unknown to most.

While it appeared reduced to some, the aperture of our life experience was filled with light.

The night before Halloween we gave Preston four costume choices, and he used his Tech Talk to indicate he wanted to be a scarecrow. Sam and I stayed up half the night creating a costume that would incorporate his wheelchair. We wanted him to be proud of his wheelchair. We attached ridiculous amounts of straw to the back of it so he appeared to be popping out of straw. Red bandanas hung on the back of the chair along with the straw bundles. Sam made a black felt hat and I glued straw at the top. He made a felt and muslin top to go over Preston's shirt. We stuffed fake felt booties that went over his shoes with straw. The next morning, he sat on my lap looking in the makeup mirror as I painted a red triangle on his nose and darkened his eyebrows.

Pink blushed cheeks finished his face. "You're the cutest scarecrow I've ever seen," I told him. He smiled at me, arching his back against my chest in excitement and let out one of his happy squeals. One last look in the mirror and off he went on the bus for his unveiling. An hour later the phone rang. "Are you happy? You just made a grown-ass woman cry," Steph told me. "Seriously, the way you dressed every bit of him, including his wheel-chair moved me to tears. That and the fact that I've never seen anything so stinking cute in my life."

Preston was adapting to his new routine. He loved every aspect of going to school.

And I too was relishing a bit of a break. Projects around the house that had to be left undone were now getting looked at and some, miraculously, were getting finished. One of the projects that weighed heavily on my mind was having another child. It was time to think of the future—time to talk to Sam about adding to our family. We didn't want our children to be too far apart in age. Yet, we knew that physically it would be like having twins. Preston's developmental stages weren't going to change drastically in terms of his physical care. There would never be a perfect time, but now with only a minor eye surgery scheduled it was as close to perfect as we were going to get. A getaway weekend was in order.

The minute we walked into Steph's house to pick Preston up after our respite weekend it became clear that something was on her mind. Seeing us, Preston kicked his legs and let out his usual happy squeal.

He was sitting in a recliner chair watching Raffi and Miss Steph was sitting beside him on the floor massaging warmth back into his cold feet. Sam and I joined her. "So did you two have a fun weekend?" Sam asked.

"He was an angel as usual, weren't you mister? Let's see, we went for ice cream yesterday and tonight he ate a big plate of spaghetti for dinner. And should we tell mom and dad?" They both smiled at each other as Preston babbled away. He was trying to tell us. Miss Steph laughed at him, saying, "Okay I'll tell them . . . he slept all night long."

"What! Well of course you slept all night mister, you're always good for Miss Steph! You just like to play games with mom and dad," Sam said as he tickled him.

"I think the boy plays games with his eyes too. I know his curious eyes, his 'tuning you out' eyes, and there's the way his eyes light up when he sees someone he loves or when he smiles or gets a joke; but there's another one. He has a super intense look when his body goes really still. You know which one I mean?" Steph asked.

"Ah, yes. That's what we call his listening eyes—when cerebral palsy doesn't have such a tight grip on him and all systems are able to focus as a whole. Sam and I always say figuring Preston out is like looking at one of those random dot pictures. I think they're called stereograms or something like that. You know the ones that, at first glance, appear to be a confusion of colors that don't make sense. But when you focus your eyes on the center, really focus, a beautiful 3-D picture emerges like magic. And you happily startle at what was there all along, perplexed by what you couldn't see at first. Then with a quick shift of your eyes, it disappears.

"And in that moment you realize that today and for the rest of your life you have to repeatedly focus on the center if you want to learn and be surprised. His listening eyes—they're his center. His soul. They are the key to unlocking the mystery of Preston. Some days it seems like we focus for hours and can't interpret anything, no matter how hard we try. And the others, they're the wonderful days that fill our soul for the days we lose focus. The days that Preston's image is locked tightly in cerebral palsy's grip. His body is limited, as you know. Extremely limited. But his eyes, they tell a story. They are the sheer physicality of his being. In unknowing the knowing, we realized his center never leaves—just our gaze." Another realization.

Steph's eyes moistened, "Wow, that's beautiful and so true. I completely agree. Well this little bean-head has certainly gotten to my center and he knows it. Don't you?" Preston grinned his crooked, mischievous grin at Miss Steph. "From the first time I met you guys I've been moved by how you looked at this guy with such pride while still remaining realistic about all his challenges. And speaking of telling a story, there's something I need to tell you. I've been putting it off, afraid of how you'll react. Afraid of what I might lose."

I leaned in putting my hand on her shoulder, "Steph, what is it? Are you alright?"

"Hey, whatever it is just tell us," Sam added.

"I have an older sister who is gay. Growing up I hated her being gay and all the embarrassment it caused. I wanted nothing to do with her or it. So I dated guys in high school, I tried and I tried to be normal cause I didn't want to be seen the same as her. I didn't want to have my car egged like hers. I didn't want to be called horrible names that had nothing to do with who I was as a person. I ran from her and her gayness as fast as I could, but I knew deep down all the running couldn't change who I really was.

"When I first met your family, I felt such an instant connection. And this little redhead—he went straight to my heart without stopping. I've learned a great deal from watching the way you two present your boy to the world. I've seen him clearly through you, realistically, and now I want the world to see me clearly. Your openness and acceptance of Preston has given me the courage to accept myself for who I truly am. It's something more though. I don't see you just accepting him; I see you celebrating every part of him. I stopped celebrating who I am a long time ago. When I saw the Halloween costume—the way you embraced the chair made me cry. You and Sam embraced what some people see as sad. Through the way you present Preston you've given me the strength to come out of the closet. I'm a lesbian. There, I said it."

"Is that all?" Sam asked with an ornery smile. "Did you seriously think you could get rid of us that easily?"

"Oh, Steph, the wheelchair, the bandana, the CP—they're all part of Preston's truest being, and in each and every one we see beauty not shame nor sadness. Don't you see, your being gay is the truest part of you. It's what makes you, you. Being a lesbian is what makes you beautiful and it's to be celebrated, not hidden, my friend. Hiding it is the ugly part," I reassured her.

Steph drew in a long breath and exhaled with such a thorough, expansive smile. Far different from the one we had seen before. "Whew, I'm so glad this didn't change anything," she sighed. "Did you hear that mister? You're stuck with me!" Preston babbled back to her and they both laughed as she patted his leg.

"Well of course nothing has changed for us, Steph. Wait. I take that back. Something has changed. It's so nice to finally meet the woman you were meant to be. The other one held something back. I could never quite put my finger on it, but now as I look at you I see what had gone missing in your eyes before."

"My God, you must be exhausted. You held back your soul, Steph. For all these years, you held back your soul."

"I'm so sorry for what you've had to endure and for all you'll continue to go through thanks to what society deems right or wrong. Looking at you now though, I can finally see your center. And I love what I see." I leaned over to give her a big hug.

"It all makes perfect sense. No wonder you're so good with these guys," Sam marveled. "You know what it feels like to be judged and discriminated against. More than anyone else, you get it. Your students not only receive your amazing teaching skills, but they get an extra dose of compassion every single day."

"Thanks, you have no idea what a relief this is," she added. "I still haven't told everyone yet, so I need you to keep my secret for a while.

"But I had to tell you guys in case you didn't want me to watch Preston anymore. I'm so happy you're good with who I am 'cause that would have broken my heart more than any of this. I love this little redhead and you guys, too."

"We love you too. You know what, Steph? Whether love comes from a nonverbal boy who happens to be in a wheelchair, or from a wonderful human being who happens to be gay, it only matters that love comes from the truest part of you—wholly and infinitely. People make it so damn complicated, don't they? This entity called love that they make so specific or rigid, isn't. No one can convince me otherwise. At its core, embracing the truest part of ourselves so we can then embrace the truest part of another human being is all that really matters."

"Isn't that what love should be for everyone?"

"Did you know that most of the earth's gold is buried deep in its core? It's so practical and divine I could cry, because deep in the center it's all the same. In your center. And in my center.

"At the shiniest part, where all the gold is stashed. Love is love. Period."

begin/bi-gin/ ~

to do the first part of an action: to start doing something

Origin ~

Old English onginnan "to be at a starting point"

again/e-gen/ ~

once more; another time

Origin ~

Middle English, opposite, again, from Old English ongean opposite, back. For a sense of "lined up facing, opposite," and "in the opposite direction, returning."

begin again ~

an opening of one's heart and spirit

a fortification of the soul to start anew with a fresh mindset and a strong will

Chapter 7

Message and Mirth

OUTSIDE OUR BEDROOM WINDOW A GENTLE BLUE SKY hinted of dawn. The horizon looked like it had been faintly outlined with an orange magic marker. As pretty as the twilight colors were, there was something else that had breathed me awake at this unusual hour. And for some bizarre reason I wasn't hysterically upset when the warmth of my blood woke me just before sunrise. Perhaps my Rapid Shock Process had automatically kicked in from past experience, or I had already resigned myself to the fact that I was losing the baby, or my Mothers Being was keeping me calm for another reason I couldn't yet tap into. Which was it? I was stuck in that weird place of knowing and not knowing, and then trying to unknow what I thought I knew. I wish I wasn't the woman who philosophizes and spins scenarios until it makes me dizzy. The one whose brain attracts word groups like metal attracts magnets. But I am. I am absolutely that woman.

I watched Sam sleeping peacefully, knowing in mere seconds I was going to disrupt his calm the same way my call had disrupted him three years ago. His face wore the same look he tried hard to camouflage before, as apparent to me as neon orange in a forest of green. I already supposed we had and would put in enough *bad things that happen to good parents* to last us a lifetime. That was the look I dreaded seeing: his face fell as his jaw tightened around his open mouth, and his eyes—oh his eyes—lit with fear and disbelief like a confused light bulb.

Running to call my obstetrician, his face morphed into a familiar look of brave and comforting, like his facial muscles were pre-set for crisis mode. Within minutes we were on our way to his office. On the way we pretended that the bad thing wasn't there, but it took up all the space in our car like noxious emanations from the past.

Leaning back in his big, brown leather chair, Dr. George slowly and deliberately rubbed his handlebar mustache as if it was an essential part of his thought process, curiously reminding me of Dr. Nelson's process. Watching him made me think that all good doctors must go through this outwardly human process of letting their struggle show. I wondered how many times he had done the exact same thing with other patients. The haunting familiarity of a problem with our baby, sat as uncomfortably in the room as an uninvited person.

He looked warily up at the ceiling, the way you do when trying to figure out what to say first—carefully pausing before he told us his findings, like he was trying to fit it into one neat sentence. Medicine has neat sentences that always end with a period. Life does not. Life has commas and pauses and question marks and exclamation points—the ones that say: *shit, it's happening to us again! Why?* Its hard edges fall sharply on soft human hearts not prepared to hear the ambiguous news they're about to hear, the kind of news that turns your world upside-down and inside out, making you go still because you had supposed that you were exempt from such sentences.

What I'd already supposed we would hear was that I lost the baby. I had said it over and over in my head on the way to the doctor's office. Preparing myself for the worst so I wouldn't be shocked when it was said out loud.

After the brief pause that felt more like a stuck yellow caution light he began, "The problem is you're carrying twins, and you're either losing one or both, or we'll have to carefully monitor this pregnancy." There it was, captured in one neat sentence . . . two babies, one baby or no baby. He continued, "We'll have to wait until we can do the sonogram later this afternoon. Until then, try not to worry; go home, drink eight glasses of water, put your feet up and I'll see you at four o'clock."

My body seemed to be locked tight as my mind floated chaotically outside of itself. I sat motionless, shocked by the unlikelihood of the news. Twins? I stared at his brass nameplate in front of me with my mouth agape. Hundreds of medical books ran the length of the wall behind Dr. Francis

George's desk. I sat in a stupor thinking of the vast amount of knowledge sitting on those bookshelves, yet here we were, again. All at once, I heard Sam, sitting to my right, nervously laughing as if trying to tender the uncertainty of it all. He sat firmly against the back of his chair, both hands gripping its wooden arms, attempting with all his might to push away the worst-case scenario. Sam removed his left hand from the chair and covered my right hand with his, saying once again, "It will be alright, I promise."

Walking in the back door, the lingering smell of last night's herbed chicken dinner greeted us as if to reassure us that some things were still the same. Sam ordered me to the sofa the moment we stepped foot into the house. The phone rang; Mom was on the other end listening to Sam in disbelief. "Don't worry about dinner, I'm fixing meatloaf and we'll bring plates over for everyone," she said.

Sam's next call was to Preston's school to ask that he be dropped off at his grandparents' house across the street. We were lucky for sure—my parents had helped with taking care of Preston whenever they could. Whether it was sitting with him so I could shower or make dinner or rest, which I didn't easily do. There were dinner invitations when they knew we'd had a long day, groceries that appeared without asking, and the loops they made around the staircase with their grandson when he wasn't feeling well—knowing Sam and I were exhausted. Their generous acts of love always seemed to appear out of nowhere when we needed them most.

My view from this still point where I lay on the camelback sofa, my legs propped on multiple pillows strategically stacked by Sam, was oddly comforting. The French doors to my left were open and I could smell the last of our white roses whose petals were beginning to surrender to the potential of autumn.

Sam appeared from the kitchen carrying a white wicker tray containing a tuna sandwich and dill pickle, a pitcher of water with one glass already filled, and a napkin printed with a blue hydrangea he knew would make me smile.

"Here's your lunch so you don't have to get up. I've got to run into the office for a while. Your dad will be checking on you later; did you know that twins run in his side of the family? I'll be home at 3:15. Until then, you need to stay put. And don't worry."

"I know . . . it will be alright," I added with a smile.

I could almost hear the gust blow in the minute Sam opened the door to leave—the mind storm in my head had begun. Pregnant with twins. Why us? Taking care of Preston and another baby already seemed as laborious as having twins, but now triplets? How did we get here again; potentially stuck on a rickety bridge between hello and goodbye little ones(s)? Around me the quiet stillness of an empty house caused me to turn on the TV then quickly click it off. I couldn't not worry. Were we about to lose this child? Both children? Did I dare hope once more? I couldn't begin to understand why we would be given twins. Why not a woman who could only have one pregnancy? It seemed to make sense that blessings should be spread in a more equitable manner. I found myself questioning everything, so I tried to stop thinking and just exist. I looked outside at the wilted edges of the roses once more. I couldn't help but fear that I too was being asked to surrender what I had been nurturing inside of me.

Why wasn't I crying? Perhaps my Mothers Being knew it was either meant to be: that Preston's care would be enough for us, or it knew everything would be all right. This strange calmness was surely telling me something. Maybe the little being(s) were speaking to me, telling me not to worry.

A connectivity of heart and mind had already begun—it must be why mothers who miscarry or deliver a stillborn grieve the same as mothers who successfully deliver. They've already spoken to each other's soul. Something I never really thought about until now. I needed to pay attention to my Mothers Being and just exist on this mysterious fall-like day as either one or two beautiful souls were preparing to leave this world or fighting like hell to stay.

There are days, I was beginning to learn, where one can do nothing more than exist, and this was one of them. I would simply exist in this hush of quiet space, free of guilt, encapsulated within my seven-hour wait time as the sunlight danced across objects inviting me to play. It was almost merry in its insistence as it highlighted the folk art painting of a child sitting on a rocking horse above the fireplace as if to say, *Did you notice what beautiful colors exist in this picture over your mantel? Do you know what clever power I have to change their intensity? Have you ever stopped to look?* Watching as this torch of light moved about the family room, carefully selecting what it gave life to, then swiftly taking it away as it moved from the picture to the pewter vase filled with purple dahlias.

I prayed that God had carefully selected what was growing inside of me, that he had chosen to give life to this baby. I called upon my Mothers Being, my Zen warrior, as I waited out the seven hours, drinking my eight glasses of water. It was her that would help me breathe in life and sustain calm while my extra heart dealt with worry and fear.

By late afternoon the room had darkened as if the sun was pushing my mind away from objects it had captured and my attention back into my conscious thoughts. Soon we would know.

Jeff, the sonogram technician, prepped my belly. Everyone stared at the screen. Dr. George announced quickly, "See this flash, that's your baby's heartbeat and everything appears to be fine. However this empty sac is where the other baby was and I'm afraid it's gone."

"Thank God," organically fell from my mouth as if it was hiding there on the tip of my tongue without my knowledge. But I did know. I thought back to earlier in the afternoon when I prayed that God would give life to this baby, not babies. Jeff looked confused, not knowing where my thank God belonged. Dr. George added, "We'll do another sonogram in a few weeks just to be sure, but everything looks fine. There's no need to worry. Understand?"

On the car ride home I asked Sam, "Was it wrong that I felt relieved that there was only one baby?"

"No, because we already knew that our baby was fine. Let's just think about that, okay? Haven't we done enough worrying for one day?" Sam asked. "I know, I know. Did you see how Jeff looked at me? He must think I'm nuts! I can't help it though; you know that saying *when one door closes another opens?*"

"Yeah?"

"Well I want to think that somehow through the goodness of the universe, the baby we lost was given to someone else who really needed just one baby to love."

"Then that is what we'll think, my dear. Now turn your brain to the off position, please. Let's go home and enjoy your mom's meat loaf dinner, I sure hope she made mashed potatoes. I'm starving."

"When Dad came over this afternoon he told me Mom was thinking about making the chocolate cake. I sure hope she did, after today I need some deep, dark, chocolate cake love!"

"Every particle of creation sings its own song of what is and what is not. Hearing what is can make you wise; hearing what is not can drive you mad."

Galib

I believe to a higher degree than what is perceptible that Preston came from another world, that all children with disabilities do. And we can either enter it or stand on the outside wishing our old world back. I began to understand that Preston had come to redefine my humaneness. From the second his being attempted to breathe in life, his presence was born from unending questions.

His birth opened the privacy gate that had been guarding my truest self. Slowly, carefully and sometimes sharply, I stepped through it all at once.

It was a joy to observe Miss Steph's class as she creatively pulled the most out of every student. Preston had begun saying, "uh huh" consistently and appropriately (as they say in the special ed world). However, he refused to say it in front of Miss Steph. While Sam and I were observing we decided some trickery was in order. Sam pretended to be going to the front office with Steph and while they hid around the corner in the hall, I asked him a few questions.

"Hey pumpkin, this sure was nice watching you in class; you did a great job. Are you happy that Mom and Dad came to visit?"

"Uh huh," he answered smiling.

"Would you like to get ice cream after class is over?"

"Uh HUH," he said loudly, kicking his legs from side to side.

Miss Steph walked in saying, "All right mister the gig is up! I now know you can say 'uh huh' and you, sir, are going to have to say it in my class if you want something. Understand?"

Preston looked down at his tray and muttered the glummest, "Uh huh," we had ever heard. The three of us quickly turned away from him so he couldn't see us laughing to ourselves.

Becky, who had Down syndrome, stopped to quickly brush her hand across the top of Preston's head as we wheeled him down the hallway. "Bye,

Preston; see you tomorrow." His thicket of red hair with a cowlick on top seemed to be a talisman of good luck for everyone at school.

He smiled back at Becky, saying, "Oh," for bye.

Sam and I had a long talk after observing the class. I asked him, "Do you think I was wrong for thinking this wasn't enough?"

He put his arm around me saying, "As long as he is happy and learning, let's leave things alone for now. If anyone can help him it's Miss Steph." Sam said. I agreed. Preston was making great progress.

Being the parents of a child with severe disabilities meant that the developmental seasons of life remain still. Our baby would surpass Preston in gross and fine motor skills within the first year. We had no choice in that. Our intention for his life was that it would be beautiful and love-filled in every way. Our big intention wasn't going to be influenced by his condition.

Realistically, however, it was bound within the parameters of his disabling condition, bound within his wheelchair, nonverbal language and health concerns. Our job as parents was to empower Preston to succeed within the many restrictions his severely disabling condition had imposed, yet also leave room at the table for the unexpected to come into our reality. It's scarier than you would think to leave room for the unknown. It says, "I welcome all, no matter in what form they appear." Preston saying 'uh huh' at the age of three and a half would seem ridiculous to most parents, never written down as a goal or milestone. But for a child who was never supposed to live, let alone utter a sound or form his mouth into a smile, 'uh huh' was an affirmation of hope and lightness. The lightness we vowed never to forget. It was time to forget what was lost in the shadows of his disabilities and establish some new kick-ass goals based on his current achievements.

Individualized Education Program (IEP) meetings are strange creatures for parents to adapt to. No matter the issues, big or small, they had an across the table feeling to them depending on who was at the table. The sheer number alone was daunting even if the meeting was amicable. Seated at the head of the table at Preston's segregated school was the principal followed by the special educator, physical, occupational and speech therapists, guidance counselor, psychologist, vision specialist, school nurse and mom and dad.

Sam and I sat at the table listening to mostly good reports from all the experts, particularly from Miss Steph and Debbie, his speech therapist. The four of us had agreed beforehand that we would ask for fifteen minutes more of speech therapy.

Fifteen minutes. Due to Preston's tight tone, Debbie felt that she needed more time to get him adjusted and ready to work. Aware of the principal, Ethel's, firm hand we went into the meeting knowing this wasn't going to be easy to achieve.

After everyone spoke, I said, "Based on the reports, we strongly feel the need for fifteen minutes more of speech therapy, too."

Ethel leaned across the table the way you lean towards a child who doesn't understand what you're saying. "Mrs. Draper, fifteen minutes more of speech therapy isn't going to do anything *magic* for Preston."

Her emphasis on magic along with the condescending look on her face gave her intentions away. Everyone around the table sat still as inanimate objects, like they'd been carved into their chairs. Under the table my shoe touched Sam's as if tapping my anger into his. The two of us were an efficient machine and since she directed her comment at me, I took the lead. I could feel my spine stiffen at her improbable words. I sat tall in my chair calmly saying, "You must have misunderstood me, I didn't ask for magic. I asked for more education. Isn't that what you're supposed to provide here? Education?" Letting the last word be a question unto itself.

This was the fateful second everything we thought we knew to be true began to shift in a rather seismic way. The insulted look on her face told me this was personal. Ethel turned to her guidance counselor quickly demanding that he start the voting process with such arrogance it blew me away. I wanted so badly to ask her, "What is it you're fighting so vehemently for or against and why?"

He voted yes, for an additional fifteen minutes of education.

As soon as he cast his vote her head snapped in his direction and she curtly stated, "We'll talk later," reprimanding the counselor and warning the others. Miss Steph, Yes. Debbie, Yes. PT, Yes. OT, Yes. Everyone but the school nurse voted yes. It never made sense to us why the school nurse was given a say regarding educational matters anyway. Ethel left the meeting without saying good-bye to us. It was clear that she thought we had turned everyone against her. In our minds, education won. Preston won.

Each had drawn battle lines for different reasons. From our viewpoint this had absolutely nothing to do with her. I respected Ethel for everything she had done for children with disabilities when she first opened a school in the fifties. She gave children a place to go at a time when society believed they should either stay home or be institutionalized. And I would think she, better than anyone else, would understand my advocacy. What I faulted her for was not being open to other ways of thinking and learning. Along with Sam, I was advocating for our son. We were the voice for a voiceless little boy and nothing, and no one, would silence us.

I wished I had leaned across the table at the end of the meeting and said, "Don't you see, the magic is in the trying," but I didn't. I knew for a certainty that each of our magic was formed from two separate principles. And whether it was across an IEP table, in the hallway or outside these walls, it was highly unlikely our divergent principles would ever meet.

I knew certain people thought I didn't like *her,* specifically. It was never about her. It was always about Preston.

It was about the right to pursue any and all forms of education that could potentially benefit our son. All I knew of her so far was her practice of sprinkling her beliefs, like crumbs in a trail for all to follow, and those who didn't follow were cast out. I had officially been cast out. It was clear that I had been branded a troublemaker by the way people turned their heads away from me as we passed in the hallway. I would gladly write troublemaker on my nametag, in all caps any day of the week. If paying attention to our son's signals and advocating on his behalf meant being a troublemaker, then so be it. Whether he succeeded or failed or fell somewhere in between, at least we fought for the opportunity to learn beyond what was expected for his condition.

If advocate is spelled with a capital T, then a T it shall be.

We would continue to be the vase reflecting the candles glow as long as there was but one glimmer of light.

The icy tone of our IEP meeting served as the cornerstone for a newfound curiosity of the human, social and educational kind. I was an advocate housed in the body of a mama bear, so basically nothing and no one was going to stop me.

Sam's cousin, Cathy, by serendipitous fate, lay on the other side of the swinging labor room doors, and delivered her son just minutes before our daughter was born.

Dr. George almost called security when seconds after I gave birth, my legs still in stirrups, her husband appeared in the doorway of our labor room asking, "What did you have?" The next morning Cathy came by to say hello. She had already nursed Jacob. I hadn't yet seen Samantha. Panic set in. I tried not to, but I couldn't help myself; sometimes yesterday's worries scattered like ants into today. I called Sam but he had already left. While waiting anxiously for our new little girl I couldn't deny how eerily similar this felt to the morning after Preston's birth four years ago. Then Dr. Mathis walked in. Seeing the worried look in my eyes he flashed an instant smile and said, "She's perfectly fine; her nurse has had a busy morning with some other babies. Sorry for the delay."

He pulled a chair beside my bed and took my hand, "Please don't worry about her. There is nothing wrong and there won't be anything wrong tomorrow either. You need to get used to normal. You and Sam will have plenty to worry about when she's older, like skinned knees, homework, boys, curfew, and what to wear to the school dance. But this is one time in her life when you get to be carefree. Look, I know after all you and Sam have been through your brains are pre-wired for emergencies. All you have to do with this one, though, is feed her and bathe her. You already love her. Just take her home and enjoy your beautiful new miracle. That's all there is," he tenderly instructed.

I sat rocking Samantha in the oak rocker; her silky newborn head snuggled in the crook of my neck like its sole purpose was for just that. I held her for the longest time, crying soft, carefree tears of joy I hadn't cried for Preston—not in this way. Newborn skin against lived in skin—scars and all. A brand new heart against a seasoned heart—broken pieces and all. Our way of thinking had become so complex. Could it truly be this simple like Dr. Mathis said? Nursing, bathing, snuggling and sleep. No wonder there are so many lullabies.

I didn't need to don a hospital gown or watch where my hand touched her head for fear I would disturb an IV. Betadine and metallic smells had been replaced with baby lotion, powder and her—honeysuckle and springtime. Samantha's smell was curiously comforting, like I already knew it. And I did. I was still unsure of so much: like how we would manage when Preston had a bad seizure or illness, or worse yet, how I would ever be able to leave her when he was hospitalized, but what I did know was the calm I experienced from the still point on the sofa was Samantha. It was her all along. We already knew each other. This was the other moment my heart had been made for, why I didn't cry as I sat at home waiting for my sonogram.

Deep down where my Mothers Being lived, I already knew I was getting Samantha. For her heart was imprinted in mine. She was familiar the way the ocean is familiar no matter where you see it. Holding this beautiful angel of a daughter turned on the music in my head.

The one that made my spirit dance and my soul come alive. Looking at her rosy cheeks and happy blue eyes, her fair skin against her light brown hair made me wonder how we got so lucky.

I guess sometimes, just sometimes, life works out the way it's supposed to. In this moment my hard, secure edges melted away like a popsicle on a hot summer day. When I stilled my heart long enough, I could feel it transforming. And while I didn't think it possible to alter it any more, I felt my heart soften the exact moment I first laid eyes on her.

How brilliantly amazing this feeling was. The softer my heart muscle became the more it could hold. Another realization.

Samantha was the other half of my Mothers Being that made me whole.

It was okay to be carefree. We deserved a little carefree. Four years is a long time to not be carefree, to constantly have our brains in problem-solving mode like mice on a wheel. I looked around her bedroom: medical equipment had been replaced by pink and blue bows I'd stenciled on the walls, Dr. Seuss books and a Beatrix Potter tea set sat on a wooden shelf her Pop built, a framed quilted heart hung on the wall above her crib and now we had to allow all the supposed, dreamed of things to seep into our souls like water dripping onto a sponge, until we believed them.

Seeing the tenderness in Sam's eyes as he held almost all of her being in his big, daddy hands was the stuff that movie soundtracks must be made from, I thought. The kind that stirs up the sediment at the bottom of your soul—where the joy we forgot to use had settled. Watching Sam with his brand new little girl, a feeling of sheer contentment came over me filling my chest until a warm quiver released it. It felt lighthearted and gracious.

His look said, you got me. All you ever need to do is look at me with those smiling blue eyes of yours. Without even trying, you are Daddy's little girl—now and forever.

What a contrast these two babies we made were, one soft and pliable, the other tight and rigid, a duality of typical and not so typical.

Preston's official diagnosis was Spastic Quadriplegia Cerebral Palsy. This meant he could not walk and that his speech was profoundly affected. It also meant that his limbs were extremely stiff requiring an outrageous amount of physical therapy just to maintain them, and possibly several corrective surgeries. We were instructed how to hold him to prevent potential deformities and to maximize the stretching of his limbs whenever possible.

With his body being as tight and tense as a brand new drumhead, both of his hips had popped out of alignment, which set the stage for a double hip osteotomy. He wasn't in pain now but if we didn't take care of it soon it could lead to deformity of his hip joints which would cause a lot of pain.

Preston was now four and Samantha was just three months old. Our worry of having to leave her was coming true sooner than we'd imagined. Sam and I were on emotional and physical overload, like crazed spinning tops with no barriers to stop us.

Samantha slept all night until her six am feeding, however Preston was still waking up several times between one and six. When Samantha fell asleep she was out—what a blessing; I don't know what we would've done if Preston woke her with his screaming. Nevertheless, we were exhausted.

In preparation for his fifth surgery we went through all the usual parental woes: praying our son made it through a major surgery, upset at the very thought of leaving our baby girl, and worrying how in the hell we were going to handle it all once we returned from the hospital with Preston in a double hip Spica cast. This cast began just under his ribcage and ran the entire length of his body, covering both feet. A two feet wide bar separated his legs creating the letter 'A' with his lower extremities. Suffice it to say, changing a diaper required channeling Houdini.

A hospital bed sat in the back corner of our family room by the French doors because carrying him upstairs was out of the question. He was in a lot of discomfort so Dr. Nelson prescribed Valium to address the muscle spasms and pain. Sleep in our house had become optional.

If this all wasn't enough, and surely it was, Sam's oldest sister, Sue's marriage was coming to a tumultuous end. She and her two children needed to stay with us for a few days. To say that this wasn't a good time was laughable—but family is family and the only thing to do was to open the back door wide.

Undoubtedly our house resembled a three-ring circus by now and we both felt like one-armed jugglers. Preston's unhappy volume and pitch grew by the hour. Sam phoned Dr. Nelson hoping for a remedy. He increased his painkiller thinking it wasn't doing the trick. Samantha was happily teetering around in her walker with a teddy bear on its tray giving intermittent hugs as needed. Sue attempted to talk to Sam at the dining room table but with its openness to the kitchen, it was clear they needed to go elsewhere away from her children's ears. Sue was devastated by what she'd discovered and it was clear that her children had seen and heard things they never thought they would. Their happy family as they knew it had disintegrated into a heap of mistakes. At eight years old, Andy was remarkably bright and complex, and sometimes had trouble expressing his feelings. Anna, six, was wonderfully calm and obliging, never any trouble, but I could tell she held something back on account of her brother.

Sam's youngest sister Sarah had arrived for back up. Sue called her kids into the kitchen, kneeling down she told them, "Mommy and Uncle Sam have to go out for awhile and you're going to stay here with Aunt Karen and Aunt Sarah. You can keep Preston and Samantha company while we're gone. Be good, okay? We'll be back as soon as we can. I love you." Standing against the back door, Andy pulled at Sue's arm. Sam had to dislodge him from his mother, telling him it would be all right. Sue opened the back door and Andy sprung at her angrier than before, this time grabbing her legs. Anna sat on the floor by Samantha between the kitchen and dining area helplessly watching the tug of war. When Samantha dropped her teddy bear Anna began dancing it across the tray, trying as always to blithely distract herself from the chaos.

Preston had dozed off for a while but now he was awake sounding more in pain than ever. I motioned for Sam and his sister to leave the way you motion for someone to abandon ship. With the kaleidoscope of confusion that had fallen over us, if they didn't run I was going to. I had to lock the back door to prevent Andy from going after them. Sarah and I made an effort to comfort Andy, but he cowered in the corner yelling at us to get away. He wanted to be left alone—we would have to honor that for now.

This was a wretched day; an abundance of the worst kind, fraught with worry and tension. Sue's children were upset, sad and confused and I didn't blame them one bit. I couldn't heal them today, that was time's assignment. All I could do was love them and try to give them a few moments of fun and laughter and help them forget the hurt in their young hearts if just for today. Preston's screaming grew louder. His eyes looked mean and angry, with a strange kind of awake about them. He was trying to tell me something. I'd have to focus harder.

I phoned Dr. Nelson's private number. An answer came in the form of the Preston Percentile. He was experiencing an adverse reaction to the Valium. Everything it was supposed to do for him did the exact opposite. Samantha was down for her afternoon nap; she seemed to be happy and content despite the circus around her. I remained in awe at what a good baby she was.

Still, I felt inept, like no matter what I did something or someone was going to be overlooked. Sarah and I wheeled Preston's hospital bed in front of the TV so Raffi could entertain him and hopefully take his mind off the cast that imprisoned his body until my Dad arrived with the new prescription. In the kitchen we began making chocolate chip cookies with Anna. Eventually Andy left the security of his corner to join us.

Sam and Sue walked in the back door with pizzas just as I pulled out the last batch of cookies. Dad arrived shortly after with the new medication. Samantha had woken up and Sarah sat at the dining room table, giving her a bottle.

All of this was crazy for sure. We had lost control briefly, each one of us, overwhelmed by all the disproportionate odds and ends we were being asked to juggle. But we were all still here. We strange and wonderful creatures gathered around the table together. Inwardly we still held the woes of this day, but outwardly we laughed. And we loved, probably a little more than yesterday.

We would let this bad day fall away from us the way a bad sunburn peels away leaving fresh tender skin with a faint memory of sunburn's pain. And tomorrow, begin again.

Chapter 8

Labels and Tigers and Bears, Oh My!

*B*EING DISABLED IS HARD. BEING DISABLED IN AN OUT-wardly non-disabled world is harder still. Being the parents who, with our human hearts, witnessed the indifference towards Preston left us bewildered at times.

Preston was small for his age, so for a while, rather than disassembling his wheelchair in order to load it into the trunk of our old Volvo, we transported him in a foldable McLaren stroller. Then when Samantha was born it was easier for us to put them in a double stroller with foam wedges propping him up. People stopped to talk to them both, commenting on the forever topic of Preston's red hair and Samantha's rosy cheeks and blue eyes, saying what beautiful children we had—the usual stuff. The kids giggled and smiled back, earning their praise. While it was obvious that there was something different about Preston, nobody said a thing. They spoke to him the same way they spoke to his sister.

Now our car looked like we were going away for the weekend. We had a stroller and a wheelchair to load into the car, two children, a diaper and wheelchair bag filled with Preston's many necessities, just in case. Sometimes the mere thought of going anywhere made me want to curl up with a blankie and a glass of wine.

I remember, vividly, our first outing in his wheelchair. Imagine us—excited to show it off (such naïveté)—assuming this typical trip to the mall that always culminated with ice cream sundaes at Friendly's would be no different than others.

But now the same redheaded, handsome, little boy who people stopped to chat with was being looked at peculiarly. Even our favorite department store sales clerk who always took the time to say hi acted strangely. As we turned into the children's clothing section amongst little pink dresses she stared through us as if we weren't there. My eyes scrunched together at Sam, making my eyebrows dip towards my nose, "Did you see that?" I mouthed.

Eventually, with such indifference in her voice it made the hair on my arms stand on end, she said, "If you need any help let me know." We had become strangers. Her indifference felt like a cruel insult had been shouted at us over top the cotton sleepers and stuffed animals.

People sometimes did a double take, stared, or purposely looked away. They reminded me of the warrior woman in the hospital, never imagining we would know how she felt. Every so often a child could be heard saying, "Mommy what's wrong with him?" or "Why is he wearing that thing around his neck?" Worse was hearing his mom say, "Never mind, come one." All of this felt especially unkind knowing we were out and about in our own community. But no one knew him. They hadn't seen Preston at their neighborhood school. They hadn't learned about his disability or heard him laugh. To them he was a wheelchair that happened to contain a boy wearing a confusing label at best.

The wheelchair seemed to make some people incredibly uneasy, even rude. The randomness of it almost felt like bullying, though we knew it never was anyone's intention. It was pure ignorance. The wheelchair represented what they didn't understand and had never seen.

Ignorance, it seemed, lead to general assumption. With assumption there was no curiosity, and without curiosity, there could be no wisdom. So how would we break this cycle?

Maybe these moments we wanted to push away were meant to make us uncomfortable. Uncomfortable was the place we would grow from or retreat from. It was our choice. We didn't have a clue what to do. As far as I knew there wasn't a guidebook for parents on how to deal with prejudice of this kind. But what I did know was how thoughtfully we treated this moment determined so many future things. We were hell-bent on making some kind of personal connection with the ones who stared. We couldn't help the ones who turned away. For whatever reason they couldn't look. Perhaps they would never see a human being with a feeling heart.

This moment needed to represent something more than hurt and indifference. There had to be a teaching moment in here somewhere instead of the inhumane pointing and staring. If we looked away too, then what had we become? What were we teaching our children to be? So for every awkward stare, we bent over Preston's wheelchair and with the most pleasant voice we could muster, said, "Preston, say hi to the nice person."

And not always, but often enough his eyes warmed his face; he smiled his crooked smile and he looked up and said, "Ooh," in his enthusiastic manner. Sometimes people startled away, but mostly they said hi back; some even came over to chat. A cold, ugly moment had been turned back into a warm human one. Another realization.

Obviously we couldn't control the way everyone felt but by controlling the way we reacted to these moments, hopefully, we reopened some hearts and minds and sent a message regarding labels.

Some things are difficult to wear, like new braces and tight-fitting jeans. There's no graceful way to describe their effects, because certain things are infinitely undeserving of grace. Labels suck when put on a human being. Labels are ugly. Disgusting. They wear you like a second skin; falsely imprisoning you within a solitary identification, shrinking you down to a place no one can see. Labels tell us what is in the food we eat, not what's in another human being. Our son would always be a label to some and no matter how much that sucked we needed to be free from the illusionary mask of the self-contaminated opinion of others.

Sometimes I felt like I would explode if I didn't verbalize the particulars of being a differently-abled parent to another mom. At times, when I overheard other women sitting in a café discussing the woes of teething I couldn't help feel a little jealous.

There was no other mom I could talk to who would understand except for Sue. Certain friends and family members always listened with great love and intention but they couldn't know. They weren't living it. Sue and I talked the same language without even opening our mouths. She used to say that we must have existed together in another lifetime. I agreed. With Sue there was no explanation needed, no concern over being seen as not handling things well, or feeling sorry for ourselves, or dwelling on it. Despite the fact that our outward appearance was completely different we were kindred souls. Sue's idea of a good outfit was a pair of jeans and a tee shirt imprinted with the last festival she'd attended. In fact when she first saw me she thought I was some color coordinated stuck-up fashionista with a matching mindset. Then I opened my mouth. She was fascinated by the redheaded mother and child but assumed we couldn't possibly have anything more in common beyond two boys with special needs.

I met Sue and Nick in a physical therapy room the size of a classroom. Blue and green bouncy therapy balls of all sizes dotted the room. Nick and his physical therapist sat on one of the light blue mats that lined two adjacent mirrored walls while his mom looked on. Nick and Preston were classmates.

Preston's body was being finagled by his physical therapist, Barb. She was trying unsuccessfully to get him to bend toward her left shoulder, which for Preston meant coming directly under her armpit. We had known Barb for years now; together we shared a mutual love for Preston and sarcasm. After several more attempts he started to protest, his body growing increasingly tighter.

She looked down at him kissing his cheeks and said, "What's a girl gotta do to get some cooperation around here?"

"Well maybe if you wore deodorant once in a while he could lean into your armpit," I joked.

She playfully shook him and in her usual gregarious way said, "Preston did you hear what your MAMA said about me? I'm gonna get her!" He belly laughed. His entire body loosened and Barb was able to bend him the way she needed to.

Sue was surprised by what I said, claiming it as the exact moment she knew she liked me. I could feel her watching us, so afterwards I introduced myself saying we should get together. Now we were the women having coffee together but instead talked about special education rights and diversity.

Sue felt like an old friend from the start. I think in some remote corner of our minds, we both knew that our old souls had been linked together in another lifetime. Somehow we had met and played and laughed and cried together for the sole purpose of this moment that might have otherwise been lost. Little did we know the work of our lives was before us.

Sue had been talking to me about inclusion for a while now. She'd met some people affiliated with a group called Maryland Coalition for Inclusive Education (MCIE). Inclusion had always made sense to me, but I was skeptical, thinking it was too improbable for kids like Preston and Nick given the current situation in our school system.

Now the boys had a new teacher and as they began to experience segregation—lunch alone outside the school cafeteria, for instance—inclusion made more and more sense.

It was my regular day to volunteer in Preston's classroom. Mildred greeted me at the classroom door in her pink fuzzy slippers. Even though it made my skin crawl I had grown accustomed to seeing several of the teachers wear bedroom slippers in class. Another issue Sue and I were advocating to have changed. Jimmy was using the computer and Preston was next. Mildred was already irritated with me (and Sue) for pushing Edith to make the class eat in the cafeteria. It seemed ridiculous that we'd ever have to fight against segregation within the walls of the segregated center. But we did. "Ok Preston it's your turn," she said.

I wheeled him in front of the computer. "Hello Jimmy," it said.

"Oh, Mildred, it's still saying Jimmy's name, just tell me how to change it."

"You don't need to change it. It doesn't matter," she declared.

The entire program had each student's name inserted in different parts to help encourage them, so I thought I must have misunderstood her. "No, can you please help me change it to say Preston?" I asked.

"It doesn't matter, just use it the way it is, two more students are still waiting for a turn."

I excused myself from Preston who was growing irritated; he loved working on the computer. I walked toward her icy stare. Her mouth tightened around her words. She repeated, "It doesn't matter, just let him have his turn." *It doesn't matter* darted around the room like some misguided missile. Its intended target, me: its victim—our son.

"Mildred could you step out in the hallway for a minute? I'm shocked by what just happened." I waited for her to offer an apology during a long, awkward pause as our eyes silently duked it out.

Finally, in a flat voice she said, "You're making way too much of this, I was just trying to save time."

"Oh, so saving time is more important than calling my son by his given name? Do you see those unique human beings in that room? Their names are not interchangeable for the sake of time or anything else. They are not interchangeable for your convenience. And what exactly do you mean by it doesn't matter?"

"Oh come on Karen, he still would have enjoyed using the computer program. It doesn't matter whose name it's saying. That's what I mean."

"Well you know, Mildred, just because he can't say, 'Hey, my name isn't Jimmy, don't call me that.' Just because he can't walk away and go pout in the corner doesn't mean it doesn't matter. Your assumption isn't knowledge. Do you call your cat by the same name? Uh huh. Well let me make this perfectly clear. His name matters because he matters. So stop it. Stop saying it doesn't matter."

There's a cause and effect for everything. And sometimes it's the little things that matter most of all. It's as if they exist in the universe as a hint of what's to come. Little whispers that lead us in the direction we're meant to go. It's the space in between. And that space in between all that matters, matters even more. That's where we breathe and think and grow and love. And that space of time in the classroom just now didn't help Preston to do any of those things.

"Don't you get it? Everything matters. So stop saying that our son, the one who smiles when he's happy, pouts when he's sad, the boy who loves to tell jokes, the one in there with an unexplainable energy that attracts people like magnets, the boy whose face lights up when he sees someone he loves—yeah, that one. Don't ever, ever again, say it doesn't matter. His name happens to be attached to his humanness. Or did you forget?"

Her dark brown eyes looked bored, they had dismissed me long ago. She asked if we were done. "Yes, we're done for now. I'm going to say good-bye to Preston. But just so you know, this is the short list. I'm far from being done. If there's any doubt—what just happened matters greatly to me. Good-bye, Maude. Oh you don't mind if I change your name too, since saving time is so important; it's quicker to say than your real name."

The pure, organic anger of a woman when her child is humiliated should be filed under the category of hurricane force winds and other such things of unstoppable nature. The mama tiger in me had been unleashed and completely set free by one careless act. Apathy. She would now move mountains for the pure joy of watching something move that someone said not to move. She would quietly ascend the mountain, gathering all the tools along the way, learning the secret language of the forest I now found myself in. She would recognize the poisonous plants and walk around them until I was armed with the proper gloves. The goal wasn't solely to move mountains, but rather to view the entire lay of the land from the mountain's peak so I could see all of the paths and in which direction they lead to figure out the best route for our son with a clear perspective, unimpeded by the trees.

Driving up South Mountain, both hands looked as if they were glued to the steering wheel. Eight white knuckles appeared like flagpoles, gripping it the way you hold tight to something being pulled from you. I couldn't help wonder if this had happened before on another busy day. I knew that I was meant to be in his room today. This was one of those moments my heart broke at Preston being non-verbal.

How many words that were lost to CP did he want to tell me? How many times did he come home feeling sad and couldn't say?

I couldn't contain my tears anymore; they spattered from my eyes like hot oil off a frying pan. "Dammit! He didn't fight so hard to live for this bullshit," I yelled. I was the crazy woman talking to myself in the car. The world outside looked cold and unforgiving. The further I went up the mountain the bleaker it got. A few scant leaves clung to branches. I hurt so badly for Preston. This feeling of insult and injury felt too close to my heart. My human heart broke from the first day of Preston's life, as I feared for his life, and it would continue to break through the years for reasons like this. Sometimes life gets so close to your skin and bones it hurts. You need a mechanism to help you cope. That's what my Mothers Being was for. She was my separation of heart and mind so I could breathe and think and grow and love. Her heart was wise and learned.

And it was most often in the bleakness, through her, on the other side of the looking glass where I could see my way to beautiful once again. Had my Mothers Being not crafted an extra heart to take the lead for my human heart when it was broken, I would have broken. My extra heart would take over from here. My human heart needed time to heal. To believe in the human race again. I wondered where we would go from here and how and when. My Mothers Being whispered, *don't worry; you'll know where to start. The rest will follow*. Okay then. We would start with humanity.

I called Sue. She was surprised but not shocked. "Another one to add to the list." We arranged to meet for coffee and strategize further about inclusion. Perhaps this was the moment that all the other moments since Preston's birth had been waiting for. They had been circling the universe gathering energy; waiting for me to meet Sue. Maybe it was all prearranged or preordained in preparation for this solitary, heartrending moment. As outrage met coincidence, when humanity was forgotten and our son's dignity forsaken. With Sue I could cry without crying, because I didn't really want to cry at being Preston's mom; I wanted to cry because the world misunderstood him. I wanted to cry for the million things that had to be explained or fought for as if he didn't have the same humaneness as others. Sue and I could talk seizures and shopping, inclusion, adaptation and marriage adaptation the way the women in the café talked about teething.

We had a general and most specific understanding of each other's lives. Together we weren't alone in our words.

I paced back and forth between the kitchen and dining area, wringing the anger through my hands.

Mildred's words banged around my brain like an obnoxiously loud children's toy. I'd been taken to that place where you don't care anymore, where stunned outrage towers mountainous over any other emotion. Preston's bus ride was long. I needed something to do and drinking wine wasn't an option right now. I reached for my family's famous chocolate cake recipe. This dark, dense cake could fix anything from a brush-burned elbow to a broken heart. It would cheer me up. Just seeing the chunks of dark chocolate waiting on the counter, ready to jump into the mixer made me smile. The strong coffee was brewing, one cup for the cake and two for me. While the cake baked I made the thick fudge-like icing that was as dark as the cake. I smiled thinking of all the times growing up, my family had made this cureall cake. And now our kids would remember it too. I could see a grown up Samantha one day making this cake.

After dinner Sam got Preston ready for bed and I took care of Samantha. Looking at her sweet, innocent face I knew I wanted more for her; more understanding of her brother, more humanity for them both. There had to be more out there. I thought if we searched and found more there would be fewer questions, fewer stares, less prejudice. She shouldn't have to be expected to explain her brother to the world. I kissed her goodnight and silently promised we would do whatever we needed to do for both of them to be happy in this world. I kissed Preston goodnight. A few teardrops slid quietly from my eyes. I wanted to chant his name a million times to make up for the one time when his teacher said it didn't matter. I wanted to sing it and shout it aloud until I laughed the hurt out. "I promise, things are going to change. Always remember how much you matter. Good night, pumpkin," I whispered.

Sam and I sat on the sofa eating our cake. I filled him in on the incident in Mildred's class. "How can a person specially trained to educate our son at a school solely for children with disabilities be so disrespectful? I don't get it."

"Well, this isn't the first problem you know. There are teachers wearing bedroom slippers as if they're at home, a principal who doesn't welcome change. Look what you and Sue had to go through for their class to eat in the cafeteria with everyone else," he reminded me.

I leaned my head on his shoulder and said, "You know the irony of it really gets me. This place where I thought he was free from pre-conceived ideas about what he could or couldn't do, like when he was with Miss Steph, now, seems to be the very place that breeds them."

There's a saying: "If the map doesn't agree with the ground, the map is wrong." The special ed map that told us how and where to educate our son didn't agree with our ground of full inclusiveness in our community. The map wasn't wrong for everyone. It was right and helpful for many parents of children with disabilities. It provided the support and direction they needed on new and unfamiliar ground. And while we respected their right to follow their personal map, it no longer worked for us.

We crawled into bed exhausted from the harshness of a day that screamed at us. I lay beside Sam who was worn out from working a long day after being up with Preston last night, wired with worry and caffeine.

Outside, the moon was full and bright in the midnight sky. I got up to look out the window staring numbly at the goodnight moon, searching for wisdom in its face. "Where do we go from here, and how?" I muttered to the moon. It just smiled back. I crawled into bed and then glanced at our wedding picture on the nightstand. A silver shred of moonlight entered through the window, finding life on the brass frame. It danced around as if reminding me how our love had gotten us this far; and somehow, someway, it would take us wherever we needed to go. I thought of the lightness we vowed never to forget. I didn't have the answers tonight; only a clue of where we were heading and that was okay. I was learning more and more to listen to the quiet. Thank you moon. Thank you chocolate cake. Thank you sweet husband of mine.

We needed to pick up a few things at the grocery store on our way back from an eye exam in Baltimore. Sam ran to get eggs and I took Preston with me to find pasta for tonight's dinner. The little boy walking toward us smiled with curiosity. Preston smiled back, tucking his chin into his chest; his head began the process of helping his eyes zero in on his *Hi, I'm Preston* square on his communication device. I could tell by the way his eyes lit up, he was excited to say hi. I had to practice patience and not intervene, wanting this to be Preston's moment with a new friend. His arm moved quicker than normal across his tray toward his Tech Talk. Just as his hand hovered an inch away from hitting the green square that would introduce him to the little boy, just before the little boy would then say his name, his mother came from around the end aisle with a bewildered look on her face.

Grabbing her son's shirtsleeve, she yanked him away as if he was about to run onto a busy street. Her panic-stricken voice warned, "Get away from him," like actual harm would come to her son if he stepped any closer. She shot one more disturbed glance in the direction of Preston's bandana, never looking at his face or me.

Stunned, I stood behind Preston's wheelchair staring at a box of penne pasta. Just then a voice from inside my head said *Clean up in aisle three!* It was the little Irish redhead in my brain and she was boiling mad, madder that I've ever seen her with her heels kicked off, hands on hips, legs in warrior stance. Those piercing blue Irish eyes of hers were ready to inflict serious damage. I'll stand by and let her do her Irish thing in my head and hope it saves me from verbally taking down that woman myself. I was seriously conflicted. Part of me wanted Preston to see his mom defend his humanness and the other part, my Mothers Being, whispered grace and said leave it alone. In my brain she stomped over to the little boy's mother and demanded to know what her problem was *He drools a little—get over it! He also laughs and smiles and loves a lot, way more than he drools. Imagine for one non-judgmental moment how you would want people to treat your son if he was sitting in that wheelchair. And speaking of your son, you should probably pay more attention to his cues. He's very wise you know.* Then I reached for the pasta and kissed Preston on his forehead, thinking how the mom should consider herself lucky for having been saved by the little Irish redhead. In her prejudice she couldn't have known this was his bandana of love and courage. It appeared that to her, it represented shame. Her ignorance blinded her.

Funny though, all her little boy saw was another little boy smiling at him. If only she could have seen that part. The human part.

In December of 1775 Martha Washington commissioned a bandana bearing the likeness of her husband, George. It became popular for promoting political campaigns and in celebrating victories and heroes. It was born out of the struggle for independence. How fitting, I thought. Through the years, anything noteworthy from popular movies to sports heroes was displayed on what was originally called a little banner.

The bandana. Used for over two hundred years for a thousand things—headband, neck scarf, sun shield, tourniquet. Now the cotton cloth of endless color combinations was as integral to our life as an arm or leg—a necessary appendage that seemed as if it had been here all along. Folded in half into a triangle it served as a napkin of sorts for Preston, a fashionable necessity. Due to his CP, he drooled like a toddler. This triangular cloth of many colors was hugely symbolic of loving and celebrating the entirety of him. The Japanese believe that when something has suffered damage and has a history it becomes more beautiful, so they aggrandize the damage by filling the cracks with gold. Accordingly, we would aggrandize what seemed to be the ugly part to some by buying the brightest, coolest bandanas we could find in every color of the rainbow. That bandana didn't wear him; he wore it. Preston wore his bandana as proudly as he wore his shirt, as naturally and brightly as he wore his smile, enlivening everyone around him like fireflies in the night.

Everyone wears bandanas of some sort. Invisible for the days that overcome us, the ones that shrink us down to worry no one will see what's on our bandana. Bright for the days we overcome, the ones that cause us to stand tall with shoulders back so everyone can see what's emblazoned across the span of it. I had to wonder what was on the mother's bandana. She could have never imagined that two of the most profound emotions necessary for a human being to thrive in this world: love and courage, were woven through every thread of Preston's bandana. I cringed at what humanity was being squashed in that dear little boy. I shuddered to think what indifference would be taught to him on the car ride home. I imagined her telling him to stop asking questions, quickly changing the subject to something more manageable.

My heart broke thinking of what was happening inside of Preston's heart. What did he want to ask or say? How could I best address this situation? I bent down, whispering in his ear; appealing to his sense of humor, "Wow, she must be having a really bad day; she's as grouchy as an old bear. Grrrrrrr." He laughed his two-syllable laugh. "She wasn't being a very nice mom. I know that little boy wanted to meet you—sorry pumpkin." He smiled and said uh huh with the 'huh' in a deeper voice for emphasis. His eyes were half smiling like his mouth. He looked happy so I left it at that.

Not wanting to make too much of it I said, "Let's go find Dad, I bet he's in the ice cream aisle!" Preston extended his legs and arms in his usual manner, like his outstretched limbs actually started the wheelchair in motion, and when we were in charge they did, so off we went.

While I smiled outwardly there was no denying that this wretched experience fell heavy on my heart, yet another reason why inclusion made more and more sense. While it still may have happened, I don't think it would have felt as big as it did at the moment—like the them and us moment living in my brain.

I decided not to tell Sam about the little boy and his mother. I didn't necessarily like not telling him; we told each other everything. Even so, giving this anymore oxygen than what it already consumed felt worse. All of these startling lateral moments in our new world helped to shape us into what we were becoming. I'm sure that's how most defining moments occur. If we knew ahead of time, what would be the point?

I understood that no matter what anyone else said we needed to keep walking towards pursuing inclusion for Preston and Nick. It made sense that in order to celebrate diversity we must continue to think in different directions; rotating our thoughts so we could see all sides, otherwise we risked becoming emotionally and intellectually one-dimensional. Another realization.

mana/mah-nah/ ~

the power of the elemental forces of nature embodied in an object or person

a term used in Melanesian and Polynesian cultures to describe an extraordinary power or energy force residing in a person or object

Origin ~

of Polynesian origin; akin to Hawaiian and Maori mana mana

mana ~

a spiritual quality

the unconscious influence of one being on another

an unexplainable energy field

the power from within

Chapter 9

Proof of Life

PRESTON'S BODY WASN'T AVAILABLE TO HIM. NOT AT ANY consistent level. CP had segmented it into uncooperative parts. But his mana was whole. Ready and waiting for those curious enough to seek it. For the past seven years people had been talking about his unique energy, saying things like, *without using words he can spread joy. There's something about him. Incredible depth. He possesses an energy that speaks for him.*

The unalterable shape of his wheelchair, the curve of his crooked smile and the constant rigidity of his body where mere forms by which to carry the illimitable energy of his soul. His mana. A well-fed soul isn't an empty vessel. It has a dialogue and carries with it all the energy from the heart's universe.

Preston bonded with almost every person he came in contact with. Not the way you bond with an acquaintance but the way you bond with a for-ever friend. There was such an emotional energy traded back and forth you could almost reach out and touch it, like a black and white photo that sees only the soul. Maybe that was yet another reason inclusion consumed me. How could we allow his soul energy to be contained in a bubble?

I couldn't let go of what happened at the computer. More importantly, I couldn't let go of why it happened. Some thoughts are unputdownable.

Humanity needed to be redefined for children with disabilities. Old thought patterns needed to be edited. Even words needed to be rear-ranged—words like it doesn't matter. And ree-tard, needed to be stricken from the English language. If I had it my way it would be seen as the other 'n' word. Words can either be powerful weapons of destruction or they can inspire us to do more than we thought possible. Sue and Sam and I were realizing quickly, the way a spark becomes a flame that limited expectations further disabled our already disabled children. Our children with disabilities weren't born into a specific world; they were born into this diverse and vast universe of ours. Weren't they?

Our son saw the world through complicated blue eyes that needed so many things to work together that rarely did. When they did it was beautiful, miraculous, for it had taken such an outrageous amount of parts in his tight body and damaged brain to work together it was like asking the moon to bend a rock.

Because there were few verbal cues and physical validation coming from Preston, we had to learn to telescope our eyes to see any subtle nuance in the way he tilted his head or how tightly his fist was held. Small things indicated how comfortable he was in his body. Seeing the concentration in his eyes as he struggled to move his hand across the tray toward a communication device was life affirming.

And equally, watching the anger and frustration in his eyes as CP restricted his hands like tight rubber bands, snapping them back to start over again, was heartbreaking.

When he spoke or babbled conversationally, we leaned our ears in the way you lean forward to hear a complex sound, always listening for a new word or familiar cadence or tone. This required our utmost patience used in a careful way. We lived in the minute changes from one second to the next. But in Preston's world we needed to wait in silence with our senses queued up as well as being still for ten to twenty seconds so his intensive motor planning process could enable him to respond. If we spoke during his process we had to repeat the question all over again, and he had to repeat the arduous process of getting what his brain understood out through the convoluted confines of his body or mouth. Keats said, "Nothing ever becomes real until it is experienced." Ask someone a question. Wait fifteen seconds. Repeat this for a day, a week, a month. This was our extreme that became commonplace as we moved about our one-second world.

Patience. Just saying it teaches us to exhale. Yet this would become the hardest, core concept to get people to understand and to practice. What became a learned behavior for us, felt awkward as a baby's first steps for some. We thought the more people he was around and the more people were around him the less awkward this would become for everyone. Maybe they could hurry him up and maybe, just maybe, he could slow them down a bit.

There are a lot of myths regarding how much of our brain we use, but I wonder how much of our heart do we truly use? I had a feeling deep in my Mothers Being that Preston would be a catalyst in helping others to use more of their heart. More than they knew was there.

I think patience is the calm overriding a human being who wants to hurry along the inconvenience of the world. If we went about including him in his neighborhood school the right way maybe we could slow everyone down to his singular pace.

The truth of disabilities is raw and messy in its unedited way of life. A contradiction of emotions: beautiful, yet scary and frustrating. Having a child with special needs is often crisis driven, whether it's educational or medical, there always seems to be an issue waiting sharply around every corner.

However, to care for another human being so exhaustively, so exquisitely, is one of the greatest spiritual journeys we've ever taken.

Where there exists the most tender strength I've ever known.

It was the daily bending and stretching of my soul I thought so far beyond my grasp. When I reached it I had to stop and slowly breathe to feel its impact, which had begun to leave remnants imprinted on my being.

Everyday patience had finagled its way into my soul the way water reshapes a stone. You can't see it happening, the stone still looks the same as water flows around it. But in the looking back, over time the stone took on a new form.

It had crevices and chips, dents and scrapes—proof of life.

Preston wasn't a concise developmental age, nor would he ever be. At best he was a mixed bag of severely delayed fine and gross motor skills. And because of that his IQ couldn't be accurately tested. We were given depressing psychological test results the school system was required to administer. But due to his severe physical impairment they were never conclusive. We'd been told by physical therapists that he was trapped in a body that, for the most part, didn't work.

Imagine being trapped inside your own body. Hearing and watching the world: understanding most of it, but not always being able to show it. Imagine. People speaking to you fast; not giving you a chance to respond because linking your brain with your muscles took too long so they answered for you, but not necessarily how you would have answered. Imagine. Waiting for someone to feed you when you wanted to eat an hour ago. Imagine. Sitting in a wheelchair; always having to look up at everyone. Imagine. Watching people move around you and wanting to move yourself but you can't, you must wait for someone to move you. Imagine.

Imagine going out in the world with all your messiness and realness front and center for the entire world to see and judge. All the imperfect parts and insecurities flashing like a beacon. I suppose that's what it was like to be Preston—messy and real all at once. Messy and real: day in and day out. I didn't know if the world was ready for so much realness because of how naturally separate it was. It seemed the world was full of separate places for separate groups of people all wanting togetherness of some kind. People, who thought alike, believed alike, lived alike—so much likeness. We stay curled up in our separate principles and ideology; condemning those who don't think and look like us. Refusing to celebrate diversity. Yet not really understanding diversity because we're looking so hard for likeness. I don't know, maybe some people stay separate because they can't be messy and real themselves.

So how would we unfurl everyone's tightly knit beliefs to entertain real and messy and diverse? We would have to enter through their heart; to help them see a child first and foremost. A lot of educators still believed Preston should be taught separately from his community. They believed separate was better for him because his needs were too different, too special.

But maybe, they, like us, could come to a place of unknowing what our prior life had assumed. In that spot of grace that was currently out beyond the perception of most.

So where were we heading? What was this entity called inclusion? How does it live and breathe and work and grow in a neighborhood school? And why were some states doing it well while others rejected it completely?

One of our fundamental principles for including Preston was that he shouldn't solely have to adapt to the world, the world needed to do some adapting too. If he were a part of his neighborhood school from the start this would be a natural process, not a learned behavior. Secondly—he was a person first, not a label.

The more conferences on inclusion Sue and I attended, the more MCIE educated us on its merits, the more I shared with Sam, the more we were convinced that not only was it possible, but crucial. Though we knew accomplishing this wouldn't be an easy feat. It went beyond talking to Ethel, beyond what anyone could perceive at the moment. Now it was about opening minds and mouths and forming them into one cohesive voice. We were prepared for people thinking we were crazy for even entertaining such a thought. Prepared to hear the word impossible over and over. That was fine, we'd heard it before.

With the guidance of MCIE, Sue and I co-founded C.H.A.M.P.I.O.N.S. (Children Having A Major Part In Our Neighborhood Schools) in 1990. Our mission statement was: To ensure that the home school is a welcoming and accepting environment for all students, and to maintain a high level of community awareness about the importance of building inclusive schools.

Together, Sam, Sue, myself, and a host of amazing parents would navigate our new map. We would begin again in our own backyards.

A life pattern had been established for Sam and I. Whether we were in a hospital, or home, or wondering what else was out there for our son it repeated itself until we saw what the universe required of us.

Curiosity caused us to not just look but see. Seeing caused us to be grateful. And gratitude helped us to begin again. Curiosity, gratitude and beginning again had followed us throughout our life like the change of seasons.

One lingering just long enough to help us appreciate the newness of another. Another realization.

Chapter 10

How Do You Spell Possible?

*I*T DIDN'T HAPPEN OVERNIGHT. MOST TRANSCENDENT acts usually don't. It fell over everyone lightly and entirely, the way dust settles on furniture.

Sue and I bypassed Ethel and went straight to the Supervisor of Special Education and his boss the Assistant Superintendent of Schools. They agreed that it was our right to have our children in the least restrictive environment and their support helped make our dream a reality. At the time however, it was unheard of for a child with significant disabilities to be educated outside of a segregated school.

As soon as word got out that we were including Preston and Nick in their neighborhood schools it was made clear that our segregated school was not behind us.

Another battle that shouldn't be a battle, I thought.

It was sad to me that sides were perceived as right or wrong. Sad that some were angry because we had looked beyond the mandate we were initially given as if there wasn't a federal law in place that spoke specifically to our right as parents to make sure that the child has the maximum opportunity appropriate to learn with children who do not have disabilities—in academic, nonacademic, and extracurricular activities. (IDEA). There was no right or wrong. Only the right to pursue options that best worked for our children.

Though it wouldn't impact our decision there was another person I needed to tell. There weren't many subjects you could out talk my brainy father on, in fact none that I could think of but one—special education. As much as he tried, he didn't grasp its many layers, which is why I dreaded telling him about Myersville.

Mom invited us for dinner. She already knew. Samantha brought her play-doh along. Her and Gram sat at the kitchen peninsula molding flowers while Sam caught up on returning customer calls. Preston lay on a mat by the TV stretching the long bus ride out of his muscles and listened to Raffi on his boom box, intermittingly watching Samantha and Gram, smiling and verbalizing back and forth.

"Dad, Sam and I have come to a decision about including Preston." Before I could say another word, Samantha yelled excitedly over the stove-top, "Poppy, guess what? Preston and me are going to the same school next year! And I might even get to see him at recess—right buddy?" Preston beamed a smile back at his sister.

I could see the disappointment that made my father's eyes wearisome as if I had just committed some careless act unbefitting a mother. He poured two cups of coffee, handed mine to me and motioned toward their café size kitchen table, "Here, sit down."

He took in a long breath. I could still smell the cherry tobacco from his pipe he was smoking on the front porch when we arrived. "Are you sure you two have thought this through? What if he gets made fun of? He can't defend himself. You don't have to worry about that at Rock Creek." I knew my father was fiercely protective of both grandchildren. With Preston though it tortured him to see his grandson suffer.

After a surgery that left him in a cast, he would say, "They did it to you again didn't they bud?" Then he'd sit with him until he made him laugh and both their faces lit up and Poppy felt like he had taken a little of his grandson's pain away. "You don't understand, that's precisely why we're doing this. Hopefully he'll have friends who will speak for him and with him because they've hung out in class together, played together, ate lunch together, laughed together, or learned together.

"They'll look into each other's eyes the way children do and without us adults knowing, speak a language all their own to each other. Because that's what kids do."

"Yes, I can accept that might happen, but he's a lot different than those other kids, Karen."

"Well Dad, tell me why Samantha knows how to play with him or understand his signals—after all he's a lot different from his sister. I don't care how disabled he is; he's a child first and he deserves to be around other typical children. And you know what, they deserve to be around him just as much. He shouldn't be left out because he's disabled.

"I've got to believe his classmates will be his defenders because they will be his friends. You know sometimes an ignorant stare can be louder than words and we've already experienced those more times than I care to remember. Can you appreciate how amazing it would be to run into one of his classmates at the mall or grocery store—for both of those kids in there? How many lessons do you think other people would learn from watching their interactions? You've always told me to follow my gut, and I am. Every part of me is telling me it's the best thing we can possibly do for Preston.

"Your grandson is part of a whole, not a part floating out there separate from everything else. Preston has already taught us to see the world through a unique vantage point. Now we need to experience being in the world, the whole world in a new and different manner. I know you don't see how this will work, but trust me, okay; I know what I'm doing."

A wheel cannot move simply because it is round, it needs a surface and energy force by which to be propelled. Likewise, inclusion can't work simply because a child with disabilities is physically in their neighborhood school. Even though Preston and Nick were the first children with severe disabilities to be included we weren't about to sacrifice them to an ideology. We asked for proper training of the staff and students and we received just that. There was so much preparation to be done. Sue and I were like Santa's elves checking off a long list before Christmas.

MCIE helped educate us on various aspects of special education law, current inclusive education practices and community organizing. Sue and I began speaking in front of anyone who would listen. CHAMPIONS parents spoke at local BOE meetings regarding funding for educational assistants, the need for consistent training, as well as sharing our personal journeys on why inclusion made sense. Sue was a natural at presentations. Her eyes were the lightest blue that constantly smiled at you.

Tall with blonde hair and rosy cheeks and her no fuss, natural look, she appeared approachable and always sounded completely relaxed. I, on the other hand, did not.

I felt afraid and courageous at once if that's possible. And it is.

Through our advocacy I was beginning to know myself in ways I'd never imagined. Born with a cleft palate, I'd had three operations to repair the roof of my mouth, leaving me with a nasally sounding voice as a child. Growing up, I remember my mother over told the story of me saying, "Eet Yody eet," to my brother, Jody, her voice sounding like a clothespin was clamping her nose shut. Everyone at the table would laugh. I smiled outwardly not wanting them to know how much it hurt to be made fun of. While inwardly I sat with my fake smile remembering how hard I worked in speech therapy during my elementary school years to overcome my tiny nasal voice so no one would ever laugh at me again. I wondered how many times Preston had smiled outwardly when secretly, where it really mattered, he hurt too.

Even though I didn't know on a grand scale what it felt like to be Preston, I understood what it was like to be made fun of. For a second, fear kept me from entertaining the idea of getting on stage. Afraid made me human: hands sweating, heart racing, uneasy in front of an audience, but still standing. Fear tried to shout my nasally childhood voice at me, telling me no one would listen. It tried to fill my mouth with cotton so I couldn't speak.

And though my voice still bore remnants of my cleft palate, even though people's eyes squinted in curiosity when they first heard me or asked me to speak up when I already was: I spoke. Fear threatened to suppress the thinking, feeling me. Fear doesn't know or care to know. That's what fear wanted, to impale me with its frozen spear, minimizing me, permanently freezing me so I would never know what I was capable of.

But fear wasn't about to silence me the way CP had silenced our son. Fear had forgotten one thing. I held within me a superpower—the strength and depth of a mother's love for her children. That was my army and I was about to raise it up. My voice had been altered, quickly, before the knowing me could intervene, an evolution had begun. My altered voice now spoke from a place of love. And it was a strong voice. Asserting our beliefs on diversity, acceptance and inclusion had chased fear away. Every time I stepped up to the podium, still nervous and afraid, I dismissed fear. Not knowingly, but organically. Step by incremental step I came to see fear in human form—imagining it as the mean girl or schoolyard bully. A coward in altered form trying to convince me of its might, fear hadn't counted on the might of my Mothers Being. Fear had given rise to the truest part of me and it was stronger, and faster, and smarter than fear could ever hope to be. I could almost see it running from me fast with high-pitched screams, and arms flailing in the air like the sissy it was.

Next came the critical education and training on inclusive practices that both schools receiving teams needed to learn in order to understand how it could work at their school. They were sent to the Colorado Peak Center conference on inclusive education. Returning from the conference, Preston's teachers and principal shared how much talking with teachers who had successfully included children with disabilities for years had helped them. Hearing their real-life stories was a crucial part in shifting everyone's awareness from assumption to fact-based knowledge.

After that came observations of both boys from the receiving special ed. teachers. Then disability awareness lessons that simulated what it might feel like to have a disability were taught to the students. I made a collage of Preston swimming, horseback riding, sitting in a beanbag chair watching a movie with Samantha and sledding along with photos of him in his wheelchair so the kids could see he existed outside of his wheelchair too. I did disability awareness training with Samantha's kindergarten class because she was as much a part of this as her brother. Sam and I fielded questions over the phone relayed by the supervisor of special education from staff members regarding seizures and shunt failure and what if this and thats. They were good questions from good people who were scared. We realized not all people wanted to experience the 'Wonderful World of Disabilities Tour' and that was fine; we just asked that the people directly involved with him be open-minded and kind.

We also had to remind ourselves how intertwined our two worlds had become. The duality of talking about a play date for Samantha and a surgery date for Preston all in one breath was natural for us.

I thought back to a CHAMPIONS meeting Sam and I hosted at our house. It was a beautiful summer evening where everything felt right, like someone had purposely cued up 'play perfect summer evening.' The mosquitos appeared to have taken a holiday elsewhere. The temperature was short sleeve perfect. Lavender, coreopsis and Japanese anemones next to the brick patio were in full bloom. The lights Sam strung over the French doors gave the patio a magical glow. An ironstone vase full of cuttings from the garden, bright with pink, yellow and purple sat on the picnic table beside the double doors. It wasn't much; we were too tired and stressed most of the time for much, but there was just enough brightness and lightness to make it feel special.

Sue and I stood at the kitchen island prepping trays of spanakopita and roasted shrimp appetizers while Sam made strawberry daiquiris. We overheard conversations that reminded us we weren't in Kansas anymore. It looked like cocktail party conversation; it sounded anything but. I felt like I was watching a strange movie called Duality as everyone arrived and caught up with each other. Larry told Steve about his son's severe seizure that put him in the hospital last week. Then they talked about Larry's new business venture. Eventually laughter was heard. Helen was telling Patti about her son's heart surgery next month. Then they talked about an upcoming sale at their favorite clothing store. Eventually laughter was heard.

Terry told Diane about the serious implications of her son's rare syndrome. Then they talked about how much they wanted to start doing yoga. Eventually laughter was heard. Darkness and lightness, darkness and lightness; they repeated themselves and still laughter was heard through the rhyme of their souls.

We were all here for the same cause. Here for all of our children— our typical kids and our kids with disabilities. Collectively, we had been touched by darkness and lightness to a ridiculous degree. And still we laughed. Because of them.

Several summer in-service training sessions were planned for staff members. We brought Preston to the school after hours so he could take time soaking in his new environment. Myersville Elementary was a one-story brick building with a picturesque view of the Middletown Valley behind it. Tess, the special education teacher, met us in the front lobby that wasn't really a lobby, but more like a doublewide hallway. She was tiny and fair-skinned like me. I couldn't tell if her curly, shoulder length black hair was natural or permed. Her brown eyes were sincere and intelligent. She greeted Preston immediately; he struggled to say hi, he was too busy taking in his new environment but eventually quietly said oh.

We were ushered into the front office to our left. Nancy came out of her office behind the school secretary's desk with her eyes full of a million questions.

Our new principal was one of those women who immediately commanded respect. Not because she tried though. She was tall and direct when she looked at you. Anyone could see that she was a-pull-no-punches kind of woman in the best way possible. I got the sense that she was as good a listener as she was a talker. I wondered if all her years training and showing horses had given her a broader use of her senses around other human beings. Her big voice startled Preston at first and he almost pouted until Sam quickly asked him to tell his joke. He told his joke of the day and everyone laughed. Sam and I glanced at each other happily realizing how on he was. They saw the wisdom in his humor and that he understood the sequence of joke telling.

Tess lead us back out into the lobby where a banner with primary colored lettering reading more alike than different hung over a bulletin board. I hoped that the students at Myersville would somehow see a part of themselves in Preston. He relaxed upon re-entering the lobby. His legs and arms automatically stretched out in excitement. I secretly hoped this was an omen of good things to come. His eyes computerlike, digitally scanning the rooms, storing information for future use. We brought him back once more to briefly meet his future classmates. Everything was in place. All we needed was an instructional aide.

"No way!" Carol told Nancy after watching a video of Preston. "I'll help out until you find another aide, but that's all."

It had been a month since Preston was fully included in his neighborhood school. Being an open concept school made it easy to sneak in through the loose partitions in the back corner of the classroom.

Sam and I felt it was important to stay away for the first month so everyone could settle in and, equally, for everyone to establish a mutual trust.

Daily communication notes were sent back and forth along with a few phone calls to ensure us all was well. Still, I was anxious to sit on the floor and secretly observe him in a regular classroom for the first time.

Tess found a stool the same height as Preston's wheelchair so his classmates would be at eye level with him. Angie, his peer buddy for the day, sat on the stool beside him as Miss Daiger tried valiantly to get his attention. Preston's head was floppy due to neck muscle control issues, so he had to be prompted to pick his head up. We had already seen considerable improvement, and lately, he was much more interested in his environment. "Preston, Mrs. Daiger needs to see your handsome face." His head remained down. "Preston, Mrs. Daiger would like to see your beautiful blue eyes." I was more than familiar with Preston pretending not to hear or understand if he didn't feel like working. "Preston, Mrs. Daiger is waiting until you look at me to continue." I could see his eyes slyly shifting right and left as he gained more control over his environment. Wondering in how many ways he was going to keep his teacher's attention.

Finally, Angie had had it. She looked at him and in a tone that said, nice try, but you're not fooling me, demanded, "Preston, pick your head up or I'm not playing with you at recess!" His head sprang up like an overloaded jack-in-the-box. The astonished look on Mrs. Daiger's face mirrored mine. We had just witnessed two good friends; one disgusted with the other and calling him on it, the other friend knowing it.

And a teacher, who in that moment, became a student. Seeing the unfiltered brilliance of children had enlightened us all. I wanted to do cartwheels down the whole length of the hallway. Words swam in my head and dove way down into my heart. Words like humanity, friendship, love, acceptance—and pick your head up.

Preston knew he might be able to fool Mrs. Daiger, but he knew he couldn't fool Angie; they spoke the same secret language. His classmates didn't think of him as a severely disabled child. To them he was a friend who happened to be in a wheelchair, wore a bandana, and talked in an unconventional manner. His speech was garbled at best spoken in broken utterances that, most times, couldn't be understood. But he used it anyway. It was his voice. A human voice. And his friends at Myersville Elementary understood it perfectly.

They didn't overanalyze what to do or what not to say. They just did and said. There was no overthinking. If something didn't work, they moved on. No special education trial stats. (Student was able to complete task six times out of ten). Imagine being tested like that. For them no proof was necessary. Adaptations that at times seemed so complex to adults flew out of their mouths. When the morning pledge was said they worried that Preston couldn't see the flag clearly, so they made a stand to hold a flag on his prone stander tray and a classmate always stood beside him to say the pledge. As weeks went on Preston began verbalizing the pledge out loud as well.

Preston's hands were often fisted due to tight muscle tone, so his friends taught him to do high fives. Without knowing it, they were addressing PT goals as well as IEP goals such as making eye contact and following directions, while also helping him to be an active participant in his environment rather than a passive observer.

It was time for an adapted math activity and clearly Preston didn't 'do math.' I couldn't wait to see what Tess and Carol had come up with. Preston was seated in an adapted floor chair so he could sit on the floor with his classmates. It was a flash card activity, and Preston was the wild card. When Mrs. Daiger held up a flash card, students couldn't call out the answer until Preston hit his switch. She told the class that when they answered correctly they could return to their seats for free time. As each student yelled out the correct answer something amazing happened; instead of returning to their seat they sat by Preston.

As a mom who had never seen our son as a natural part of a group of kids it was mind-boggling to watch his friends cheer him on to hit the switch. He was no longer a separate entity. Then to see him get excited when one of his classmates shouted out the correct answer because he knew they would come sit by him. Even his hypersensitive hearing didn't mind the sudden outbursts of excited second graders.

Laura B. and Angie flanked him, sitting as close as they could, encouraging his every move. He was just one of the gang who happened to have a disability, but now you had to look close to find it. His disabilities were still obvious, they just weren't as obvious as his humanness.

In these friendship and learning moments, Preston's wheelchair fell away; his voice emerged and there was a sense of sameness, as completely differently-abled children existed as equals. Not because they were the same or learned at the same level, but because they didn't care they weren't the same. They got him. That is, after all, what we're all here for—to understand each other. From that was born a sense of belonging in each and every student.

That is what being part of a community feels like.

That is inclusion. Belonging.

Before I left, his instructional aide, Carol, stopped to talk with me in the hallway. "I'm having such a good time with your sweet boy. And he's funny too! This isn't as difficult as I thought it would be. The way the other kids are reacting to him is nothing short of amazing, Karen. I realize, now, that he's just a kid who happens to be in a wheelchair, that's all. But boy was I scared at first!" We both laughed. "You know this was my first experience being around a disabled kid. I'll tell you what though, this month with your redheaded boy has completely changed my perspective. Now I see a person first. And an ornery one at that!"

"Well thanks for sharing that with me, Carol. You have no idea how much it means to us. But more than anything thanks for being so open.

"There's a Picasso quote I absolutely love that relates to what you've experienced, 'There is only one way to look at things until someone shows us how to look at them with different eyes.' Isn't that beautiful?"

"It is," Carol replied, "and if someone would have told me two months ago I'd be doing this and loving it I would have told them they were nuts!"

"Well, I'm so happy you feel that way. We've already seen so much growth. Last weekend we were at a family picnic and several relatives commented on how much looser his arms were—probably from all those high fives I guess, huh. They also thought he sat up taller and was more observant. So thank you for all of your love and hard work. Your role is crucial in making this work. We honestly couldn't do it without you. And the fact that when you're not with Preston you can help Mrs. Daiger or one of the other students is an added bonus. This year is off to a great start. I only wish the naysayers were here to see what I saw today."

"You know what you said about how the kids are reacting to him? I think that children with disabilities somehow fill that space in between two people; serving as a mirror reflecting another's strengths and a barrier to their weaknesses. Don't get me wrong—I don't think Preston is some magical unicorn; I think all kids are magical unicorns. It's one of the many reasons inclusion makes sense. Everyone helps each other no matter what level they're at. Everyone wins. Oh my goodness! Speaking of kids, that reminds me—the note that came home the other day from Brandon, 'I like Preston a whole lot, do you know how much? I like him like a brother.' Ripped my heart out."

Then Carol added, "Oh I know. Well I have a feeling there will be many more notes just like that."

Who says Preston is too severely disabled to be a part of his whole environment?

Who says inclusion isn't possible for children with severe disabilities?

Who says it can't be done?

Not Laura B or Laura L. Not Angie or Sara. Not Lindsey or Brandon. Not Ian. The ones who couldn't spell possible didn't know about the unfiltered brilliance of children. All children.

Every time the universe shakes me a little more, I learn that anything is possible if you believe deep in that place that makes you afraid and courageous at once. Another realization.

After last week's class observation, Sam and I didn't think things could get any better. Tess called to say, "You're not going to believe this, but Lindsey's mom wrote a letter to the editor about how much it's meant to her and her daughter to have Preston in her class!" It's going to appear in *The Frederick News Post*, *The Citizen* and *The Mirror*. I'll send a copy of it home with Preston. Just be warned, it's going to make you cry." Tess was right. I cried tears of joy, and so did Sam.

After all the stares, after all the indifference, Preston was thanked for being his messy and real self. Lindsey's mother called it his gift.

A privilege in Myersville

To the Editor:

My daughter, Lindsey Silliman, a second grader at Myersville Elementary School, has the privilege of being part of a very special learning experience this year. A student in her class is physically handicapped.

For my daughter, this is very natural having this student in her class; there are no fears, only excitement and enthusiasm for this little boy. Each day a student is his buddy for the day, helping him with his wheelchair. Not a day has gone by since school began that we don't hear about Preston in the evening.

For Lindsey, this has been one of life's invaluable lessons that I couldn't have begun to teach her. She has learned what most people, if ever, don't learn until they're adults — that a handicapped person isn't "different" or "strange" or "someone to be stared at."

To quote Lindsey, "Preston is just like you and I, Mommy, except he was born with muscles that aren't as strong as ours. So, he can't talk like us, or use his arms and legs like we use ours. But otherwise, he's just like us. He eats and sleeps; smiles when he's happy, has a look when he's sad or angry; laughs and cries; loves us and we love him." This has been a tremendous learning experience for her, as well as I'm sure for Preston, and I know she will grow up with a different understanding and attitude towards handicapped persons than most of us did.

I hope to see this program, called CHAMPIONS (Children Having A Major Part In Our Local Schools), expand to other schools for the benefit of all children involved. It has already proven to have had a tremendous positive impact on Mrs. Daiger's second grade students.

I would like to thank Frederick County Public Schools, Myersville Elementary School and especially Mrs. Carolyn Daiger for her special gift of teaching her students the values of life and that everyone is special and important. And a very BIG thank you to Preston, for your very, very special and precious gift that you have shared with all your "buddies". It's one my daughter will cherish forever.

—Donna Silliman, Middletown

Letter

A privilege in Myersville

To the Editor:

My daughter, Lindsey Silliman, a second grader at Myersville Elementary School, has the privilege of being part of a very special learning experience this year. A student in her class is physically handicapped.

For my daughter, this is very natural having this student in her class; there are no fears, only excitement and enthusiasm for this little boy. Each day a student is his buddy for the day, helping him with his wheelchair. Not a day has gone by since school began that we don't hear about Preston in the evening.

For Lindsey, this has been one of life's invaluable lessons that I couldn't have begun to teach her. She has learned what most people, if ever, don't learn until they're adults—that a handicapped person isn't "different" or "strange" or "someone to be stared at."

To quote Lindsey, "Preston is just like you and I, Mommy, except he was born with muscles that aren't as strong as ours. So, he can't talk like us, or use his arms and legs like we use ours. But otherwise, he's just like us. He eats and sleeps; smiles when he's happy, has a look when he's sad or angry; laughs and cries; loves us and we love him." This has been a tremendous learning experience for her, as well as I'm sure for Preston, and I know she will grow up with a different understanding and attitude towards handicapped persons than most of us did.

I hope to see this program called CHAMPIONS (Children Having A Major Part In Our Neighborhood Schools), expand to other schools for the benefit of all children involved. It has already proven to have had a tremendous positive impact on Mrs. Daiger's second grade students.

I would like to thank Frederick County Public Schools, Myersville Elementary School and especially Mrs. Carol Daiger for her special gift of teaching her students the values of life and that everyone is special and important. And a very BIG thank you to Preston, for your very, very special and precious gift that you have shared with all your "buddies." It's one my daughter will cherish forever.

—Donna Silliman, Middletown

Two days after Christmas, halfway through feeding Preston dinner, he fell asleep—unusual for him. Then minutes later he let out a horrible scream, his eyes rolled back in his head and his left torso jerked violently. Sam ran to the phone to call the ambulance while Preston continued to seize for another twenty minutes in my arms. At almost five years old Samantha was used to moments like this that began normally and ended with an ambulance run. She got up from her chair and stood beside of me; patting Preston's leg saying, "It's okay Preston; I'm here."

In the emergency room, still shaken from the atypical seizure, Preston saw and heard too many things going on around him. He was pouting with his bottom lip turned as far down as it would go as tears streamed down his face faster than I could wipe them away. We hadn't seen him this scared in a long while. Nothing and no one could calm him except one very special nurse. I wish I remembered her name so I could acknowledge her properly. She respected him as a human being first and he knew it. She looked directly in his eyes and asked as she touched his wrist, "Do you want your ID bracelet on your wrist, Preston?"

He yelled at her. She then touched his foot and asked, "Do you want your ID bracelet on your foot?"

He then smiled at her and said, "Uh huh."

I wanted to clone this nurse. She could have rushed in amidst the screaming and crying and stuck the bracelet anywhere. In reality what she did, didn't take any longer than it would have taken to catch a flailing arm or leg. The way she spoke to him was so very simple.

It didn't require a tremendous amount of energy or thought process—just respect. Sometimes the simplest things are the most beautiful. She expected him to give her a sign as to what he wanted. In doing so she set his disabled body aside and spoke to his soul. And his soul answered hers.

Respect. It's a famous Aretha Franklin song and so much more. It is a one-word declaration for all people with emotional, mental or physical disabilities.

One word. Respect.

Preston taught us daily, we're all beautifully and perfectly made souls. Whether we're in an outwardly perfectly made body or an outwardly imperfectly made body.

Our souls have the same basic need.

To be seen.

Heard.

Loved.

And Respected.

realization/re(e)-le-za-SH-(e)n/ ~

an act of becoming fully aware of something as fact

Origin ~

French re'alisition, Middle French, equivalent to realis (er) to realize

realization ~

an enlightenment of the spirit and soul

a conscious or unconscious awakening of the mind

an epiphany in a life lesson

a moment in which you suddenly see something in a new way

an aha moment

Chapter 11

Oh the Places You Can Go!

OUTSIDE IT WAS WINTER DARK AND DREARY, A TYPICAL January evening in the northeast. A few inches of snow still lingered in perfect mounds where the sun's shallow rays had to work hard to find them through the oak and poplar trees surrounding our yard. The thermometer on the screen porch read twenty-seven degrees. Every once in awhile a gust of wind howled through the fireplace flue as though warning us not to go outside. The fireplace mantel was painted Bassett Hall Green, an official muted green from the Colonial Williamsburg paint line—my color bible for our entire house. Green was one of my favorite colors. I read that it symbolized growth and hope, which sat well with my Irish soul. Orange and yellow flames danced in the fireplace until a log burnt ashen enough to shift, crackling and popping them into a new spot on the grate. Preston lay on his mat wrapped tightly in a light blue fleece blanket beside the fireplace with our one-hundred-and-twenty-pound black lab, Buck, right beside his mat.

A note in his communication book said he had been uncomfortable at school. His body wore the weather like an ill-fitting suit. Extreme heat or cold lingered in the damaged places often causing great discomfort to him. Samantha sat on her dad's lap in her pink Beauty and the Beast pajamas snuggled in a blanket on the sofa reading *The Poky Little Puppy* as Preston listened from the comfort of his mat. I stayed in the kitchen overseeing our homemade pizza baking in the oven while I made brownies for our Friday night movie treat.

The phone rang.

Once in a while when I heard the ringing of the phone I couldn't help but breathe a huge sigh of gratitude at how nonchalantly we walked toward its ring, remembering the days it scared us so.

The voice on the other end of the phone was Sarah's mom—the mother of one of Preston's classmates. She was calling to invite him to her daughters's birthday party. "I'm sorry to bother you on a Friday night, and I apologize for calling so far in advance, but Sarah wants to make sure Preston can attend her birthday party in March. If not, she'll change it to another date that works for him."

By now, Sam and Samantha were standing beside me excited at what they heard. I tried to write down the date, but my eyes had become instantly overwhelmed with a new joy this unexpected surprise brought, so Sam wrote it for me. This was not only Preston's first birthday party invitation, but we were so utterly moved by where Sarah was holding it. They lived in a two-story house, so they decided to have the party at their church, which had a wheelchair ramp. Sarah told her mom, "I want Preston to be able to go wherever I go because he's one of my best friends. And my party cannot start until Preston gets there."

After I hung up the phone Sam and I hugged each other then laughed at how happy we were for a simple birthday invitation that felt more like a miracle. Who would have imagined it would take eight years to get invited to a birthday party?

We then joined Samantha who was already sitting beside her brother with a smile that took up her entire face, exclaiming, "Pres, you just got invited to Sarah's birthday party! What do you think of that, mister?" Samantha started clapping her hands while chanting, "Preston's going to a birthday party, Preston's going to a birthday party!"

He began kicking his legs so hard he kicked them right off the mat, followed immediately by his dolphin-like squeal of delight. Looking at them I couldn't help but think that even though inclusion took a lot of work; it was the right choice for both of our kids. Our hearts were fuller than they knew how to be. This Friday night would go down in the record books, not for the temperature but for the miracle of friendship.

Life is cyclical. Birthdays are cyclical, milestones are cyclical; and for us, parents of a child with severe disabilities, hospitalizations and surgeries were cyclical. We came to accept that the unexpected and undefined, defined our days.

Preston's body was as good at forecasting the weather as any meteorologist. His tight tone was a barometer of impending changes in weather patterns. The winter had been cold, damp and intolerable for him. Some days his rigid body felt as if it were going to snap in half as Sam persuaded it into his wheelchair, which, at times, was about as easy as threading a teeny needle. Physical therapy could only do so much and with his hip issues and constant sitting; he required hamstring muscle release surgery.

Going to the hospital became familiar the way Sunday turns into Monday.

We had not one ounce of control over it, but what we were determined to control was how we still remained us while in the hospital. The unfamiliarity of each surgery, procedure, diagnostic test, and emergency run stressed us beyond what we were aware of, at times. But the only comfort we clung to was of the human kind—where nurses commented on a new hairstyle, or how much Preston and Samantha had grown. Where they asked what his joke of the day was and he teased them while grinning from ear to ear until a nurse begged him for the punch line. Then everyone laughed for a brief second like we had all forgotten our assigned roles of doctor, nurse, patient and parent. Preston's humor and their compassion allowed our minds a light-hearted breath. Doctors and nurses who knew him; the ones who took the time for a few minutes of shared humanity in their busy world of too many patients were like precious gems amongst a mountain of rocks. These people who Preston knew and liked added a soft layer of comfort he desperately needed in an otherwise scary, sterile world.

Hospitals were our second home. Seeing familiar faces that knew our family always felt like old home week. I think your soul makes it so. So you can survive. Finding a speck of humanity in a sea of sterile white saved us.

I imagine if worry were a color it would be sterile white. The kind of word that makes your heart race when you hear it. Not because hospitals are horrible places where nothing good ever happens. Countless lives are saved every day. But because of a time less forgiving we keep lodged in our memory place—when nothing worked and a life was lost. These are the captured images our hearts can't let go, the ones that jump in your way when you walk in to a hospital, settling in that place deep inside where you feel the tightness of sterile white constricting your throat.

As far back as the NICU, no matter what hospital we were in, nurses always marveled at how close Sam and I were. At first it seemed like an odd comment. Of course we were close, isn't that what's supposed to happen? We eventually came to understand why, as the marriages of several couples we knew who had children with special needs unraveled. It was true; we'd been through everything together that was crafted by odds makers to completely break us into little pieces, rather than meld us into a solid cohesive unit. Not only did we have a son who was disabled and in and out of hospitals and doctor's offices faster than we could say STAT, we had the unique balance of specially loving our precious little girl. That duality was as easy as breathing.

We didn't have it all figured out, far from it, but what we did know was these moments in our lives that were meant to tear us apart bit by marital bit were the ones that made us who we are. I don't know why it was that the more we had thrown at us the stronger and more in love we became. Maybe it was all the years we spent together as friends that gave us such an enduring love. What I did know was that we had seen the darkest scenario possible and we continued to remember the lightness we felt eight and a half years ago.

Perhaps it was as simple as that—not forgetting the lightness.

It would be silly and downright fanciful, however, to think we skipped through life with flower bouquets in hand, the sun shining down upon us, accepting of everything as we gazed lovingly at each other during a hospital run. Oh no. The secret of our deep-seeded love came from being ugly, scared and honest with each other. Allowing one another to be ugly, scared and honest without judgment or analysis. Sometimes stress, worry and fatigue worked its way through each of us in different ways, at different times. And when it did we were often impatient with each other. We felt so overwhelmed at times we weren't capable of loving each other thoroughly. Thoroughly required two sets of eyes and arms that were often preoccupied in the daily giving of care. And every so often they were just too heavy themselves to lift another soul. We each meandered through the day as our newest raw truth dealt with both of our souls separately. We came to accept, without guilt, that we couldn't always love thoroughly, but we could always love enough.

Most of the time we managed to twist and turn out of the confines of a problem. It rarely meant our problems were solved, it just meant they dimmed a bit in each other's arms. I can't explain why, unlike so many couples, we didn't turn away from each other. I suppose if it were that easy it wouldn't be called love.

On most nights though, when we fell into bed, our bodies still knew how to love and our lips still longed to kiss. What we felt in each other's arms was more powerful, more forgiving and more loving than any negative force around us. Most days.

This was Preston's eighth surgery. We were hospital veterans. We'd become adept at spotting the people spent from being here awhile. Their faces fresh as a splash of cold water would allow, where the smell of unwashed hair found us after they passed by. We had learned to cope, as they would if they stayed long enough.

I had a ritual of washing all of the clothes after a hospital stay. Whether they were dirty or not, it didn't matter. Somehow the practice calmed my soul. To me everything smelt of sterile hospital air. If I breathed them in too long I could almost smell metal and plastic mixed with alcohol and starched sheets. Though they probably lingered louder in my memory place than the actual smell. Hospital stay by hospital stay—they existed like chronological file folders my mind's eye couldn't unsee. The intense smell of illness conjured up pieces of things in my mind.

They were all there: scratchy white sheets, clattering of bed rails, silver colored trays containing meds and syringes, nonstop intercom noise, alarms and beep, beep, beep, iv's hanging from poles connected to patients bruised arms, a sense of always being cold, hours passing like days, the anticipation of long white coats who held our world in their hands, the parade of eager interns, a tedious dialogue of patient history, sleeplessness and sleepiness at once, scary questions that clinked together like metal hooks on privacy curtains, ominous test results that bore the weight of an elephant, and the insinuation of isolation. I would wash them all away.

These were the routine things not specific to anyone or any outcome, yet most specific to everyone.

I was so thankful to be home. In this soft place between the washer and dryer, my fingers felt the smoothness of the chrome wash cycle dial. It's choices clear and consistent.

Preston was resting comfortably in bed with splints on both legs. A brown teddy bear with a red heart on its chest that Laura L. gave him for Valentine's Day rested on a pillow beside him. Samantha was happily at school now that we had returned home. Sam had gone into work early this morning to catch up. And tonight we would all be home together for a celebration dinner of spaghetti and meatballs. In no time, with the push of the normal cycle button, the specific generalities were gone. My pliable mind had the power as I watched our clothes whoosh and swoosh the hospitalness away.

Our life could continue again—until the next cycle.

Samantha came home with a cassette tape full of get-well messages Preston's friends made for him. When he heard each one of his classmates tell how much they missed him, or how they couldn't wait to sit with him at lunch, or play on the playground, or work on the computer together he looked like he would burst out of his skin. His face looked surprised by all the friends who were talking to him through a small silver speaker.

He reacted to different voices, pausing for a favorite voice then attempting to kick his legs or talk back to them as if they were right beside him. Sometimes his hands stretched out like he wanted to hit his switch to respond. His eyes sparkled, bouncing expectantly back and forth as another voice spoke to him through his boom box.

He listened to this tape without end. Each time belly laughing, again and again, till I thought our hearts would well over with joy. The gloriousness in the surrender of his unabashed joy crawled into my Mothers Being and took hold.

It was so free and pure and wild in its joy. I wanted to buy stock in how he could be so wildly joyful. There was righteousness in Preston's joy that owned the entirety of his soul. Watching him, I wondered, is it possible to well over with joy or is joy so boundless it just feels that way?

Maybe it was joy on top of gratitude on top of seeing our son happier than he's ever been in his life. Have you ever gotten to that place you once imagined in your mind only to find its reality even more breathtaking? That's where we were. At the place where goose bumps and silly tears mingled happily with each other as we watched Preston explore all the places he could travel within himself—with a little friendship, love, acceptance. And joy. Another realization.

Chapter 12

Raising Expectations

MISS STEPH COULDN'T WATCH PRESTON FOR A PLANNED disability-free day out with Samantha before the start of a new school year. I called family and other possible caregivers who knew him, but no one was available. Next I called the ARC who kept an official respite care list on hand. We felt lucky that up to this point we never needed to use it.

Betty, a registered nurse and respite caregiver for ten years, came to meet him the week before our trip to a theme park. She had big green eyes that went well with her short brown pixie cut. Her colorful red glasses along with the playful tone of her voice suggested she knew how to have fun. Preston looked her up and down as usual, his eyes digitally scanning the unfamiliar. At first he was quiet, testing her to see if she would work for his attention. We spent several hours together so they could get to know each other and, equally, so that Sam and I would feel comfortable leaving her alone with our son. Preston eventually warmed up to her and we thought with her experience everything would be fine. I wrote two pages of instructions on feeding, seizures: likes, dislikes, positioning, emergency phone numbers. You name it; it was all there tightly squeezed onto paper. I realized, once again, how remarkably blessed we were to have Steph—she didn't need instructions and we didn't need reassurance.

It was of utmost importance to Sam and me to not only honor Preston's presence in the world by taking him everywhere and anywhere, but equally, to uphold and honor Samantha's presence by allowing her to once in awhile experience the world without disabilities and every inconvenience it entailed. There would be no going back to the van so Preston could stretch his legs. No getting out of the sun because he could no longer tolerate the heat. No separating so one of us could walk around with him while she rode a ride. No stopping for a seizure or muscle spasm or headache. The three of us would spend an entire August day at an amusement park doing whatever delighted our sweet daughter, while we expected Preston would be entertained and cared for by an experienced respite caregiver.

Betty arrived at seven am. Sam carried Samantha to the car with her pajamas still on; her prized pink and white snuggly blanket tucked safely under her arm. I tediously went over each instruction until he called from the back door for me to hurry up. I couldn't figure out why I was so worried—was it the fact she wasn't Miss Steph or was my Mothers Being trying to tell me something? On our kitchen island were four brown prescription bottles, extra bandanas, his special drinking cup and a bottle of sunscreen. In the corner of the family room I staged his favorite toys, movies and tapes on top of the wooden toy box, making note exactly where I placed them. Looking down at this specific arrangement I wished I were more trusting, but I'd inherited this trait from my father. I didn't see it leaving me anytime soon. I reminded her the way an overly anxious mother does, saying, "Remember to stretch him and put him in different positions so he doesn't get uncomfortable. Plleease *do not forget* to put sunblock on him if you take him outside. With his Irish skin he burns in the shade. Seriously, he does."

She smiled, waving her hands toward the back door saying, "Don't worry we'll have a lot of fun together. Go. Enjoy your day."

At eleven pm Sam came in the door carrying Samantha; her sleepy head lay heavy on his shoulder from too much fun. Light brown ringlets from her pigtails fell to the side of her rosy cheek. Her little six-year-old body had ridden every ride possible including the roller coaster twice. She ate cotton candy, ice cream, burgers and fries. We had a wonderful time doing all the things a typical family does without a wheelchair. After we kissed her goodnight we went in to check on Preston. He seemed to be resting fine. After Betty left we noticed a note on the dining table saying what an angel he was, even bragging that she had time to read her book. As we read it our eyes scrunched together at each other, thinking what an odd comment it was for someone who was being paid twenty dollars an hour.

Preston woke up at five am, yelling loudly. Sam looked concerned as he carried him over to our bed saying, "He feels pretty hot; we better take his temperature."

I turned my nightstand lamp on, horrified by what we saw. Preston's face, arms and legs were badly sunburnt. Like a hound in pursuit I sniffed from the top of his head to his toes, not smelling a trace of sunblock. I should have called Betty and woken her up with a start like Preston had, but I didn't. At eight o'clock I called her demanding to know what happened, holding the phone out so Sam could hear. Her dumbfounded voice sounded so fake it made me sick. "What? Well I just can't believe he got sunburnt. He was having so much fun laying in the grass," she assured me.

"Wait, what did you say? You laid his skinny little body on the hard ground? Where?"

"Oh in the backyard in the grass next to the patio," she answered.

"Let me get this straight—you laid our son in the grass with no blanket, out in the open where there are no trees to protect him from the sun? He didn't even have sunglasses or a hat on! Well that explains the bite marks on his legs. I'm sure the ants had fun crawling all over them as he lay there unable to swat them away. How could you do something so careless? I will make certain you never do respite care again!"

As soon as she told us where they were we went outside to look around. A wicker chair from the screen porch had been placed just outside its door on the brick patio. In the afternoon, shade from the porch building would have provided ample protection for her. And I'm guessing that's where she sat reading her book while Preston fried in the bull's-eye of the sun as the grass tickled him and ants feasted on his legs on a heat laden August afternoon—completely defenseless and at her mercy.

We didn't want go to that place in our minds where we wondered what he must have been thinking—wondering why mom and dad left me here with her. How helpless he must have felt. But of course we did—guilt yanked us there. It didn't make a damn bit of difference that we had checked all the boxes, done everything correctly. We felt guilty, angry and foolish that we expected she would care about his happiness and wellbeing.

We called the ARC to lodge a formal complaint and request our money back. Shortly after, they eliminated the respite care list from their services. These were the moments that made us feel desperately worried for our son's future and for his safety.

There would, unfortunately, always be people like her ready to take advantage of the fact that he couldn't do a damn thing about it. The words he needed had been lost to CP, and she knew it.

This year's in-service didn't involve sending the receiving teacher to Colorado or anywhere else for that matter. There was no official staff training planned by the county administration at all. It was done at our house on the Saturday before the start of the new school year, implemented through Nancy. Her leadership and constant support as principal continued to serve as a catalyst to Preston's success at Myersville. Without a trip to a conference on inclusion, local or otherwise, we were on our own. With my access to inclusive practices through MCIE, educational conferences Sue and I had attended, along with our community advocacy and as luck would have it, now Tess was pursuing her master's degree in inclusive education. We were well equipped in every imaginable way. If I special ordered a special education teacher it would be Tess. She was compassionate, smart and someone we highly respected. We were very lucky. And we were about to get even luckier.

The first time we met Debbie her voice sounded exactly like you would imagine for a third-grade teacher. It was soft and caring just like her grayish blue eyes. But on the edge of her voice was a sharper, deeper tone that said "nothing gets by me." I smiled when I heard it, sensing we could be friends.

Sam and I decided to host a brunch for the new team. Nancy, Tess and Debbie attended along with Carol and Mary who had started to job share the position of instructional aide. We felt blessed to have two amazing women who now helped him through his school day. It was probably the best thing—having everyone at our house in a more relaxed environment so Debbie could observe all aspects of his personality.

She carefully watched as Preston chowed down his breakfast in his usual manner, always shocking everyone that such a skinny guy ate so much.

She saw Samantha and her brother sitting in the beanbag chair, removed from his wheelchair, watching cartoons and laughing. She got to hold him; feeling the different ways his tight tone worked for and against him, while Carol and Mary shared their tidbits of wisdom from the previous year. And Tess interjected just the right amount of information at just the right time.

I could tell that Debbie was pleased seeing the different relationships Pres already had with Tess, Carol and Mary. Preston was sitting on Debbie's lap looking comfortable the way a child looks with someone they know. Debbie was telling him she was excited to have him in her class. I watched as Preston looked directly into her eyes smiling his heart smile. I could tell by the way his eyes held hers; even though he was still a mystery, she knew that he knew. We were already starting out on far less shaky ground than last year. It was such a relief not to have to make a case for why our son deserved to be there. Even though Debbie had no personal interaction with Preston, she had the privilege of observing him from afar during his first year. After a mere hour with her we were convinced she had been chosen due to her overwhelming ability to empathize and to teach.

Little white bowls filled with orange sections and grapes sat at each place setting. Egg strata, bacon and a linen lined basket of cinnamon rolls graced the center of our oak dining table between two lit pewter candlesticks. Around it sat caring human beings laughing with each other as they passed food back and forth, then as the laughter faded, serious conversation about how to build on last year's lessons while fresh coffee refills were poured and one more person's heart was about to be reshaped into a different remembrance. What a feast of kindness and wisdom. Our village was being reconstructed once again as we welcomed another member.

"Mom how much longer until we can go to Grammy and Poppy's house?" Samantha begged. The kids were excited; Gram and Pop had invited us for dinner—one of their favorites—roast beef, mashed potatoes, gravy and carrots. They had been away on vacation for two weeks visiting my sister Julie in Las Vegas. Dad was sitting on the front porch blowing smoke rings with his pipe in hopes that a hummingbird would flit amongst them as they floated in the air, one after another in front of him.

Hummingbirds were attracted to his pipe smoke and would zip right up within inches of his face like an animated character in a Disney movie, sometimes hovering in his exhaled smoke rings for almost a minute.

Samantha ran over to her Poppy's waiting arms while we got Preston out of the van.

Growing up I never quite knew where my father's temper ended. Now I did. It ended with his grandchildren. Every time he saw either of them his eyes lit up and his face softened into a marshmallow version of his former self. Watching him with the kids I thought: *this is the Dad I could have had*. There were parts of him I remembered as though I was connecting with a long ago friend. Mom opened the door so Sam could lift the wheelchair over the stoop. In the kitchen she turned to Preston excitedly, saying, "Well there's my favorite redhead."

Preston lifted his chin in the air turning it indignantly away from her, sticking his bottom lip out as far as it would go. He had learned to use his pout as efficiently as he used his infamous smile. He was insulted that his precious Grammy had left him for so long and made sure she knew it.

Going out in the world had become easier in many ways. We still got awkward stares once in awhile, but more and more we ran into familiar faces. And with Pres able to use his communication devices. He could say "hi" and tell a joke if he wanted. But still we were often told certain things that were hard to hear. Comments like—"You have a very special child," while we stood with both children by our side. Our response was always, "Thank you. Actually, we're lucky to have two very special children." It concerned us that potentially because of others' comments, Samantha would ever think for one second she wasn't as special as Preston. So to compensate for the voices of others that might be in her young impressionable head, we frequently told her how special she was to us. I never quite understood how an adult could stand in front of two young children and call one special.

People say the strangest things—like, "God certainly knew who to send Preston to." Or, "I don't know how you two do it. We could never do what you do." Or, "He's lucky to have parents like you to take care of him," all in front of our son! The last one always sent the little Irish redhead in my brain spinning wildly out of control as I stood smiling saying, "We're the lucky ones. And I'm sure you do whatever you have to for your children, too."

Though he was still the kid who had to be strapped in his wheelchair so he wouldn't fall out, still the kid whose wheelchair tray created a physical barrier. Now he was as free as a bird to laugh and learn beside his non-disabled peers. Watching Debbie sit in the back of the room with Preston in front of her looked so normal. And I *hate* the word normal, but it truly depicted what it looked like—like it was screaming, why wouldn't you sit in a beanbag chair with a kid whose usually in a wheelchair so he can make a physical connection like other kids. His classmates sat in a semi-circle in front of them while Debbie read a book. If Preston started to tighten up one of the kids, would tap their knuckles on his tray to the tune of Shave and a Haircut, which always made him smile and loosen up. It was all so freaking normal because it was what Debbie normally did. It was her way of letting him know there were no physical barriers whatsoever—one of her many ways to model total acceptance for her students and anyone who passed by her open classroom. Most importantly, along with the kids, it was their way of saying: of course Preston should be here. They showed everyone that what was normal was also natural.

Perhaps it was the fact that Preston was mentally and physically disabled that gave him a differently-abled energy. He couldn't rely fully on his body or his mind so he called on his spirit and his soul always, and in all ways.

I think it's one of the spiritual entities that come with having a child with special needs. Up until now we were the interpreters of his needs when he became trapped inside his body. But now he had friends like Laura B., Laura L, Ian and Angie who could reach into his soul with their eyes and feel connected to him. I was preparing for a presentation and asked a few classmates to write what it meant to have Preston in their class. I was expecting comments like, 'I like his smile.' Or 'He's funny.' I got those along with Laura's B's heartfelt declaration:

"When I hold Preston's hand it makes me feel wonderful inside. When I talk to Preston it makes him talk better and it makes me feel better inside. When I talk to him he listens to me. It doesn't matter who you are on the outside, it matters what you think and feel on the inside."

Preston was tactically defensive. He didn't do hand holding—Laura didn't know. She only knew their souls connected when they held hands . . . and so did Pres. Their friendship liberated them both to be who they were meant to be. It released within them an intimacy of trust and understanding that never left.

Tess often worked with Pres in her the resource room so he wouldn't be distracted. She set up his Language Master, (an auditory card scanning device) and laid beside it a set of color cards.

At the top of the pile was a purple color card with both the color across it and the word spelled out. She started to pick up the cards, then remembered she had left something in the back of his classroom. "Preston, I'm sorry, today has been crazy, I'll be right back." She returned only to realize she left her glasses in Debbie's classroom, too. "Preston I can't believe how disorganized I am today. Now. Where were we; oh, we were talking about colors." He looked at her, and in a tone that said, I'm tired of staring at this purple card, and spoke, "Purple," the way any other child would say it. Tess looked at him; her eyes and mouth flew open together. When Preston saw her shocked expression he laughed at her with his ornery laugh that told Tess how amused he was that he had surprised her. He had made it clear once again—there was more in there than what we knew. Another realization.

Mary became ill with Guillain-Barre syndrome, making it impossible for her to return as Preston's aide. Mark, Carol's twenty-one-year-old son had brown eyes, olive skin and an athletic build. His face was as handsome and friendly as his voice was deep and thoughtful. Preston loved having a guy to hang out with. And while he never suffered in the cute girl department, now, with Mark by his side he was even cooler than before.

At recess Mark and Preston played kickball, running the bases together while everyone cheered them on. The wild-eyed wonder on our son's face as he whizzed by was a sight to behold. It was yet another affirmation that our expectations of what was possible were widening before our eyes.

During another surprise observation I watched Preston and Melanie sharpen pencils together. As Pres hit a switch that turned on the pencil sharpener Melanie inserted the pencil. Then Mark stood him in his prone stander for the pledge next to Angie, the miniature flag from last year sat on the stander's tray. Today Pres operated his switch to say the Pledge of Allegiance with his classmates, sometimes verbalizing along with them. Ian helped him use his name stamp in handwriting. In spelling Mark worked beside him and through an eye gaze/pointing system, Pres identified words. Debbie always put him close to her so visually they could connect—and connect they did. But Debbie was the kind of teacher who connected with all of her students; Pres just happened to be the one who happened to be in a wheelchair.

The Maryland State Planning Council on Developmental Disabilities contacted Tess. They invited Preston and three other classmates to give a presentation at their upcoming conference co-sponsored by the MD State Department of Education, MCIE, and the ARC of MD, called Creating Inclusive Schools. Clint, Laura B and Lindsey went with Preston.

Norman Kunc opened the conference with: "When you segregate kids with disabilities you tell them explicitly you do not have the right to belong. You systematically prevent learning by forbidding them the opportunity to belong."

The kids talked about the much-coveted position of peer buddy for the day. Clint described Preston as his friend saying, "Preston smiles a lot. He lets you know what he likes and what he doesn't like. He likes to play kickball."

It was clear the kids were developing a depth of caring different from what they had previously experienced. Building on last year's experiences, they were learning that appearances could be deceiving, that the soul and the power from within are so much more that what you can see. It seemed watching Preston try so hard to overcome his weakness gave them the courage to overcome theirs.

For Preston, knowing how much they believed in what he hadn't yet done gave him the courage to try. Like holding hands and playing kickball. Courage wasn't a big superhero with a puffed-up chest, it was a typical kid being a friend to a not so typical kid. It was the quiet child in the corner who could now help Preston and in turn feel more confident too. And it was all so natural.

Courage happened every time their souls saw through to each other.

In early spring NASBE (The National Association of State Boards of Education) invited Debbie, Tess and I to speak at a Congressional Study Session. We each discussed our roles as vital team members: regular educator, special educator and parent/advocate of a child with special needs. Our presentation went well, but even better were our many conversations with attendees in the hallway afterwards.

Finally. Whether you were a regular or special educator, or a congressman, inclusion was becoming a natural topic to discuss. Over the last few years little Myersville Elementary had gained notoriety for the successful inclusion of several students. Visitors had to be scheduled at intervals so as not to disturb students and teachers too much.

To wrap up the year, Debbie, Tess and Nancy planned a celebration. Students, educators and representatives from the Frederick County Board of Education gathered at Myersville for a Celebration of friendship, teamwork, and genuine appreciation for everyone's accomplishments in inclusion. Each student wore a pin with his or her picture on it labeled Myersville Inclusion Specialist. Indeed, each and every student had become an important part of Preston's achievements. Without them it wouldn't have been possible. They were his mentors, teachers, tutors, but most importantly his friends.

Sam and I listened through laughter and tears as each student shared proudly in telling the audience about Preston's accomplishments as he demonstrated his newfound skills with a friend. His friends had every reason to be proud for they were equally responsible for every spoken word, every movement. Every milestone. Watching them together it was clear that not only had they been right beside him for all of his accomplishments, but also for every smile in between their laughter.

At the end of the evening the mother of one of Preston's classmates thanked me for letting him come to Myersville, saying,

"My son used to be afraid of people that are disabled, but because of his involvement with Preston he has become a strong advocate for how hard Preston tries and how much he has learned. Fear is no longer a part of his vocabulary."

The little Irish redhead leaned over, quietly tapping on my brain saying, *Whew, if only she knew what it took to get here.* I smiled while fighting back tears and replied, "Wow. Thank you; I'm so touched by that. Kids have such strong, powerful connections, don't they? No matter how good a teacher is it can't replace the potential that comes from the natural gift of friendship. I want to thank you and your son for giving that to Preston. What they've shared can't be defined in an IEP."

Her kind words made it clear once more that all children need to live, learn and play together in order to stay together as adults in their communities.

In coming together to celebrate this phenomenon called inclusion that had been so arduously fought for, we were really coming together to celebrate our humanness. Our likeness and our diversity. By recognizing our diversity we found in each other's souls, likeness. Two moms with drastically different boys found a common ground called community (Inclusion). Her son no longer feared a person with disabilities but instead considered one a friend. We were now neighbors without borders.

Because of P.L. 94-142, because of a redheaded boy, because of an incredible group of administrators, teachers, parents, and ultimately, because of the unfiltered brilliance of children—Ignorance and Fear had been replaced by Love and Courage.

In looking back at the five core values that drove us, it's astounding (but not really), how any the descriptive words can be interchanged with one another.

Community . . . kinship, likeness, commonality

Friendship . . . familiarity, closeness, understanding

Inclusion . . . admittance, embracement, involvement

Love . . . appreciation, friendship, respect

Courage . . . bravery, determination, spirit.

And maybe that's the point.

Because the minute we shun diversity we separate ourselves from each other.

differently/dif-(e)-rentle/ ~

in a way that is not the same as another or as before, in varied ways; diversely

Origin ~

from French different, from Latin differentem

abled/a-beld/ ~

having a range of physical or mental abilities as specified

Origin ~

English back-formation from disabled

differently-abled ~

proudly owning being a rockstar

celebrating the uniqueness of ones abilities

Chapter 13

Samantha's Workshop

THERE ARE TIMES WHEN ADDING YOUR VOICE ONLY dilutes others. When something is so pure and true in its original form it defies description.

Such was the case when I came across seven-year-old Samantha's presentation for a sibling workshop at the Parent Information and Training Center's Conference. I realized that our daughter's presentation needed to be showcased in its original form in a way that only an incredibly special sibling can.

When preparing for her presentation we sat down together and broke it into various topics of her choosing. I then wrote down her exact thoughts. She asked that her presentation be on construction paper saying, "It will make it brighter and more fun, mommy." After I wrote her words on the construction paper in magic marker we read them together, then she added some things she'd forgotten.

Samantha had seen me give a few presentations over the years and wasn't about to take this whole speaker thing lightly. Half an hour before her presentation started, Rosemary, the Director of Support Services from the Frederick ARC, who facilitated the workshop, took her to the front of the classroom where she'd be speaking. Samantha turned to Rosemary and politely asked where her glass and pitcher of water was.

I loved that she was modeling what she had seen, but more than that, I loved that she asked for what she wanted. The best we could do was a paper cup filled with water from the fountain in the hallway.

There wasn't a dry eye in the audience as our little girl spoke lovingly with such conviction about her big brother, barely looking at her notes. Sam and I sat in the classroom watching her with great pride; realizing in amazement she had memorized the whole thing.

She didn't do this presentation because we urged her to. She did it because she wanted to, because she was proud of her brother. Because she wanted others to understand him the way she did. She knew, at seven years old, what some adults didn't yet know. That with understanding comes kindness. With kindness comes compassion. And with compassion comes wisdom.

She was wise beyond her years for all that she had seen and heard, for all she carried in her sweet little soul; but most especially for what her and Preston's spirit and souls had exchanged with each other.

This is my brother Preston. He is 10 yrs. old and we go to Myersville Elementary School. Preston is in 4th grade and I am in 1st grade. Preston has Cerebral Palsy and uses a wheelchair.

I like Preston and ME being at the same school because I have alot of good friends and I can see that Preston does too. It is important to me for Preston to have alot of good friends.

Things that are different

1. Preston has to be fed

2. Can't walk, so he has to be carried from place to place. I help Mom and Dad with his mats and pillows.

3. He has seizures sometimes and I help him to not be afraid. He smiles as soon as he sees me.

4. He wakes up at night because he has musole spasms.

5. We can't always go everywhere we want because his wheelchair can't go up the stairs. I don't like it when we have to split up our family.

6. We can't go to some stores at the mall because the security system bothers his ears and he screams. I don't like it when preston Screams because poeple stare at preston.

Things We Do Outside Of The House

1. Sledding - my Poppy made a special sled for Preston, my poppy also makes Knives.

2. Swimming - Preston loves the water because it makes his muscles feel good.

3. Take Walks together inthe fall; spring and summer. Summer.

4. Swing together. He has a special swing my Daddy made.

5. Attend school activities like the BlueGrass Festival, eat Chiken Bar-Bo-Q, Do Picknics.

Things We Do Together

1. I read to Preston
2. We listen to music on his tape player
3. We watch movies together
4. Play instruments
5. Get silly
6. Bounce on the bed
7. Work on Preston's computer
8. Play baseball
9. Run wheelchair races
10. Just hanging out together is fun!
11. Preston pulls my hair!

How Preston Communicates

1. He says uh-huh for yes and oh for no

2. He has a Powerbook Computer he makes choices on.
   - Yes/No
   - Picking numbers
   - Reading spelling words
   - Talking to friends

3. By looking at what he wants

4. By pointing to what he wants

Facilitated Communication Story

Last year Preston learned to talk by pointing to letters on a keyboard. One night after dinner we were all laughing and telling jokes. All of a sudden Preston looked at me and pouted and his eyes were filled with tears. Mommy asked him what was wrong. He started to move his finger and typed out Du Yu Luv Me? I said I that's a silly question Preston. I love you to bits and pieces. Then he smiled a great big smile.

Just because Preston has a disability doesn't stop us from being together as a family and having fun. Even though Preston can't do everthing the regular way doesn't mean he can't join in, we always find a way because he's a neat brother!

Chapter 14

Lost Words and Lost Weekends

*A*LL THE LOST WORDS PILED UP ONE ON TOP OF ANOTHER, precious word after precious word grew breathless and heavier with each passing year. Trapped inside a body that didn't work, like a bank vault stuck shut.

Though Preston lost most of his words at birth it seemed as if the energy of those words remained in his soul. According to many who knew him, he had a way of speaking without talking. Though it wasn't always crystal clear, often enough, he got his message out one way or another. And in the trying, sometimes it took a hundred times. I wonder how much energy it took for him to express just one thought? It must have been exhausting for him to reach down with restricted limbs and pull from that, just one message with all the lost words. Many times I've tried imagining what it must have felt like to be misunderstood due to your mind miscuing your body or short-circuiting all together. Holy crap, it's easy enough to be misunderstood with all things firing properly. How much physical, emotional and intellectual energy did he use up just getting a word out? How much endurance did his differently-abled energy need to exert to move his arm across his wheelchair tray to the correct square on his Tech Talk? Was it like running ten miles, climbing the steepest incline then back again?

His energy was like a rocket launcher that burst a few lost words out of his mouth, or through his telling facial expressions, or into his rigid limbs that often resisted like the wind.

Some days Preston seemed exhausted beyond repair for no specific reason, but for every reason. Do you know how many tons of energy it takes to launch a rocket ship? I ache thinking of this, but not for the reason you would imagine. I'm remembering all the times; due to too much worry or stress, too much this or not enough that, when we forgot what it took to launch a rocket ship.

The students and staff at Myersville Elementary found a way to do what we had not been able to do. They enabled him to literally speak a couple lost words. At first we wondered why he spoke those accurate and appropriately timed words so clearly at school. Usually it's the other way around; parents of children with special needs have to convince the school they really can do something they've been doing at home. It made perfect sense though; they had already exchanged oodles of unheard words with their secret language only children know.

Our son was part of a collective community that walked and talked and moved about freely as a means of a God-given set of miraculous gifts. To be able to tell someone what's inside of you is a freaking miracle.

And to have them understand you is an even bigger freaking miracle.

To speak and be understood was another privilege our old life had assumed was a birthright. Preston speaking was his miraculous gift to the people who had gifted him so much. Another realization.

And when he didn't have his words or verbalizations, when his hands were too conflicted to hit the correct square on his communication device, his silence was his language interpreted by the hearts of those who loved him.

I can't say for certain what the magic was. All I know for sure is that whatever entity presided over us at Myersville, we experienced it together. We, a collective band of unique individuals, had expanded Preston's village beyond the boundaries that had been dictated to us.

We celebrated, succeeded, failed and brainstormed as a team—students included. With Preston's differently-abled energy, the staff and students, the particular times and the unique blend of people, humanity was breathed into every lesson. And though sometimes we were all frustrated students; friendship, trust and acceptance seemed to be graffitied into the walls of our neighborhood school.

We would forever remain a community of friends brought together because of a boy. If I were to write a play about inclusion the cast of characters would read—a remarkable special education teacher who goes on to pursue her master's degree in inclusion after meeting Preston, a principal as smart and real as they come, who set a gold standard for all to follow, a second grade regular education teacher who was as compassionate and innovative as she was scared, a third grade teacher who went on to sit on the board of directors of the ARC—whose teaching ability rivaled that of her humanity. The instructional aides, tentative at first, who came to treat our son like family. They were his other teachers, friends, and caregivers and all-around magnificent human beings. There is no conceivable way we could have succeeded without them. And though not all the teachers were huge proponents of full inclusion they were always kind and conscientious in their teaching and interaction with Preston.

That's the reality of inclusion; not every teacher is going to be jumping for joy over it for various reasons. Looking back it almost seems to make it more believable, more real. Like life. Though I'm biased, it's almost illogical to expect every teacher to believe in inclusion the same way it's almost illogical to think every person you meet will become a friend. Almost.

I realize, too, that school systems need to consistently and fervently train and support all teachers in their endeavors to educate all children. Not almost support them, almost all of the time. Hopefully, one day, inclusion will not have to be spelled out with a fine tooth comb, then examined under a microscope as if this inclusive teaching thing is a new and bold concept. Hopefully, one day everyone will realize it doesn't take a special teacher to teach a special child. It takes only one human being to teach another human being. What a wonderful world it would be to fully trade our unique gifts with each other, teachers and students alike, by simply including and supporting everyone. Not almost everyone.

The most important cast members were, of course, the children.

The beautiful friends, who, in their unfiltered wisdom and brilliance, became the teachers, and the teachers their students. But most of all, they were Preston's true and real friends. By learning in two different ways together, playing, laughing and hanging out together, they made Preston accountable for his actions in a way only they could. They inspired each other.

It was Saturday. The weekend had arrived. The two days at the end of the week allotted for mowing the grass, running errands, catching up, going out, watching movies, and relaxing. Weekends for us meant all the usual things along with taking Samantha to a friend's house or a game, or shopping with me. It also meant taking care of Preston and seeing to it he was entertained. For Sam and I, weekends never meant rest and relaxation, they meant being on call for the two days others used as a typical weekend.

Our son caused us to live life caring over every detail of each minute of the two days called the weekend. For us weekends meant feeding him three meals, lifting his body up from his wheelchair and onto a recliner or mat—making sure he changed positions several times a day, entertaining him, massaging his legs, taking him out in the world and making sure he had fun. Most of the time we did so good naturedly, exchanging minutes and hours with each other. But at times, we did so begrudgingly, when in our humanness our souls felt tired, stressed or craved a break from caregiving. "I'll watch him for the next two hours so you can work on the car, then can you come in so I can fix dinner?" we would say. Or, "I'll feed him dinner so you can play a game with Samantha afterwards. Okay?" We bartered back and forth like two swappers at a flea market. Trading time like the precious commodity it was, was all we knew.

For Preston, Saturday meant riding in the van with his buddy. He was a daddy's boy, and guy time alone with his best friend meant everything to him. He lived for Saturday afternoons with his dad. Each time they left the house looked like the first time as he excitedly kicked his legs back and forth in his wheelchair, squealing his dolphin-like squeal of delight or verbalizing his enthusiasm non-stop. Whether it was for a couple hours or all afternoon, Saturdays always began with a Frosty and fries at Wendy's.

I need to be clear with what I'm about to say because the gentlest man I've ever known did this without fail, precisely and tenderly. Every Saturday through every season, whether he was overwhelmed, tired, behind on house chores or client files—he lifted his son's body into his wheelchair, fed him lunch, and drove around with him for hours. Every Saturday. Sam did so with such great and tender love that at times it took my breath away. They enthusiastically went on scenic rides, ran errands at Lowes, got haircuts at Pete's barbershop, listened to loud rock 'n' roll, ate things they weren't supposed to, kept secrets and laughed the way guys do with each other. Because that's what a gentle man does.

Even more precisely and tenderly, I know this gentle man did this not only for his son, but for Samantha and me, too.

Samantha stood on a chair by the island ready to roll out dough for biscuits. Her curly hair was pulled up in a high ponytail that fell into one ringlet and her sleeves were pushed up past her elbows. She loved helping me in the kitchen. I could already tell by her ease she was a natural. For me, cooking was a way of expressing love, and kitchen moments with my sweet girl were everything to me. It's where we exchanged life recipes with each other and bonded over the preparation of food. The minute the guys came through the back door a distinct earthy scent of cigar smoke overpowered the smell of beef Guinness stew cooking on the stove. Samantha blurted out, "Eww, you guys stink!" Sam winked at Samantha and me.

My eyes bounced curiously between them as I approached Preston, "Um, was someone smoking a cigar in the parking lot again?" I asked. Preston, the great defender of his dad, looked away from me, his expression purposely unreadable. Then he pushed his joke button on his Tech Talk as if changing the subject. He hit the punch line continuously, laughing his ornery 'huh, huh, huh' laugh in a way that said the joke was on me. I played along. It was on me as far as Preston was concerned; he and his dad had stealthily tricked me once again. And that's all that really mattered.

Looking back I know our weekends weren't really lost. We had fun family nights watching movies, so much fun that Samantha hated to miss them when she had a sleepover at a friend's house. We popped popcorn and ate pizza like a typical family.

We grilled and sat on the back patio in warm weather. Good friends visited. We laughed. Preston teased Samantha by verbalizing loudly when her favorite movie was on. She would ask him to quiet down and he would laugh at her like any other brother. We played ball with our dog and the kids laughed at his antics. There were slumber parties galore with late nights and later mornings, still. Of course, amongst the constant, there were leg braces, meds, special equipment that had to be hauled to wherever we needed to go which meant extra time to set it up and pack it away, heaving a bag that looked like something a SWAT team would carry, everywhere we went. Then massaging cold legs from poor circulation, or a seizure, or headache, or muscle spasms would occur. All of these separate and conjoined entities kept time with the typical things a weekend brings. It was the ability to be carefree that was lost to our weekends. For us, sometimes weekends felt like two days banded together like siblings that didn't speak—tense and tiresome. But once in awhile, if we were lucky enough, and we were, they felt like a great family reunion.

From the kitchen window I saw Preston's bus turn into our driveway. Then I heard the familiar crunch of gravel underneath its big tires. Suddenly everything in me felt crowded knowing that in one minute I'd possibly be dealing with another temper tantrum. Standing at the edge of the grass watching the wheelchair ramp lower him to the ground I inhaled the lilacs behind me by the side of the house. I tried to capture the attention of their soothing scent in hopes that today would be better than yesterday. But as soon as I wheeled our redheaded boy through the back door his whole face yelled angrily at me. Just like his laughs and smiles, he had several ways of yelling "I'm uncomfortable," "I'm bored," "I'm tired," "I'm in pain," and the last one bore the nasty tone of a short Irish temper like his grandfather's. I went through the regular after-school motions the way parents do without even conscientiously thinking about them, grabbing a pudding snack from the pantry while asking him how his day was. More yelling. I picked up his tape recorder from the kitchen island then reached in his backpack for the cassette tape while trying to encourage him to verbalize something other than a scream. I put his round, red switch on the tray and hooked it to the tape player. Instead of sitting passively while I read a note aloud, he operated the tape recorder; he was in control and loved 'talking' about his day by playing his messages. What a joy it must have been to control something. Anything. Often his voice could be heard in the background talking along with his friends as they recorded what they did together.

Afterward I fed him chocolate pudding and milk. The second he swallowed the last spoonful, the entire unpleasant configuration of his face screamed at me again. This was nothing new. His Irish temper often reared its ugly head when he became impatient at waiting. A behavior we continued to work on both at school and home.

I walked to the kitchen sink, taking a deep long breath to calm myself. For a second I closed my eyes; the warm water running through my fingers felt good against the yelling. I couldn't remember taking such outrageous pleasure in things such as this before becoming a mother.

I smiled with the silent breath of an inward laugh. Staring through the window I could see wildflowers growing along the stacked limestone wall that ran the length of our front yard: Queen Anne's lace, miniature daisies and something that resembled a tiny purple aster popped up in happy random bursts.

Maybe Samantha and I would pick some later. She loved to surprise me with a bundle held tightly behind her back until she pronounced with outstretched arms, "Here mommy, I picked these for you!" What a wondrous and curious thing is motherhood. My cells had morphed simply by birthing two children, like they had grown antennas that could now feel the luxuriousness of warm water in a way I never had before, while flowery things I once regarded as weeds were now worthy of a vase.

I stood in front of Preston's wheelchair tray, close enough that its wooden edge touched my thigh. I stood tall flattening any emotion from my face, then looked him straight in the eye and firmly said, "As soon as you stop yelling I will get you out of your chair." He'd been yelling out more than usual, and we feared we were losing valuable ground. Sometimes his behavior was his way of controlling his environment in a constructive manner, most times his behavior meant something, and other times he was just being disagreeable like any other kid. Trying to decipher between them was, at times, frustrating as hell. Today I felt like I was staring at a vintage map whose directional cues no longer made sense. No matter how hard I tried, I couldn't make the puzzle that was Preston fit together. Today I was inefficient, impatient, and stressed.

All this stress made me feel thick in my head, like ten thousand channels had converged into my brain at once. I felt emptied of all things wise, funny or curious. I wasn't where I was supposed to be. Or was I?

I asked him once more to calm down so he could get out of his chair, but he yelled at me again, this time louder with a wildfire raging in his eyes. "If you don't stop yelling you're getting time out in the corner," I warned. His eyes shifted back and forth. It was a standoff and he was determined to get his way. In the corner he went, yelling even louder as I turned him to face the wall, then silence. Glorious splendid silence. I watched the time on the kitchen stove count down two minutes then pronounced, "Good job mister, now that you're calm I'll lay you in your lounge chair so you can watch a movie." His eyes, minutes ago fiery, now looked past me reticently.

I had recently been asked to speak before a congressional subcommittee regarding the reauthorization of IDEA from a pro inclusion standpoint, and today I'd been feverishly working on my presentation. Given the fact that introverted me didn't do public speaking so eagerly, I was a basket case at the prospect of standing before this esteemed audience. Nope—picturing them naked wouldn't help. Between that and Preston's bad-tempered yelling all 45 miles of nerves within my body had risen up like antagonistic gremlins.

I prepared chicken enchiladas for dinner while Samantha and Preston watched Raffi together.

The sounds of laughter and music filled the house once more—the lightness. Soon Sam would be home. For now I would forget about the yelling; somehow we would get through this. We would figure it out. Sam and I had long ago left a singleness of mindset regarding our day—our life.

With the chicken enchiladas cooking in the oven, I chopped cilantro and scallions and thought about the running water and flowery things. Mindlessness and mindfulness—that was motherhood. A pulling away into ourselves so we don't go insane, and a pulling into our heart so we can love insanely. Such a balance of extremes I was growing into and between, a softening of my heart muscle like when Samantha was born, and a healthy selfishness that made my soul expand into a different knowing. Losing myself so I could find myself. Our children were lifting my guardedness daily. I could no longer relate to the person I used to be. I was evolving and so grateful for that. Another realization.

love/luhv/ ~

a profoundly tender, passionate affection for another person. a feeling of warm personal attachment or deep affection, as for a child, parent, or friend

Origin ~

Old English lufu, of Germanic origin;

Love recognizes no barriers. It jumps hurdles, leaps fences, penetrates walls to arrive at its destination full of hope. Maya Angelou

love ~

the embodiment of courage

a hug, a helping hand, vulnerability

kindness

the opposite of indifference

a willingness in your heart to open all chambers

Chapter 15

Conversations

*W*E LAY IN BED ENJOYING AN EXTRA FIFTEEN MINUTES of sleep. Outside a solid spring rain pelted down on the house. Neither of us wanted to get out of bed, as though the constant shroud of water pressing against the windows was actually a pouring of intention to stay in bed. Sam rolled over to hug me once more saying, "You stay here; I'll get Preston." Seconds passed; I didn't hear the usual: "Good morning buddy," from Sam. Then all of a sudden I heard, "Preston! Preston, are you all right? Hey buddy look at Dad."

I ran into his room; he didn't even react—bile and blood had dried around his mouth. His stomach was distended twice its normal size. He started to wretch again. I sat him up while Sam ran to call his doctor. He was as limp as a rag doll, lifeless and ghastly pale. His pining eyes looked up at me begging to be relieved of whatever horror this was. I kissed his clammy forehead telling him, "Don't worry, you're going to be fine," not certain of what I said. My mother came over to stay with Samantha. We couldn't make her go to school, she was too worried about her brother.

Dr. Fairborn's voice was loud with bad news, "You have a very sick boy. I think we're looking at acute pancreatitis. I've already sent his blood work STAT to the hospital lab. We'll know more shortly. Let's get him admitted and stabilized." We'd seen that look on other doctor's faces and knew without knowing how extremely sick he was again. Luckily the hospital was across the street from the doctor's office. Preston was given IV pain meds and hydration to help stabilize him.

It took three days to get him well enough for travel. When Dr. Fairborn told us how painful his condition was, I couldn't help but wonder how long it had been brewing inside of him. AI DuPont sent a special team skilled in IV's to transport him to Delaware.

Samantha stood in the doorway of Preston's hospital room nervously watching as the team quickly maneuvered around her brother. His IV's kept blowing. There was talk of a central line. She had witnessed this scene before. For her it was a cyclical part of our life. As soon as I picked her up she started to cry. I wiped her tears away from her little face with my thumbs. Then she asked me the way she always did, with her blue eyes meticulously inspecting mine for the slightest discrepancy, "Mommy, is Preston going to be all right? He's not going to die, is he?"

I took her in the hallway and said, "Your brother is still pretty sick, that's why we're taking him to DuPont, the doctors there have more experience in helping kids like your brother. They already know him and they're going to do everything they can to get him better. That much I can promise you, sweetie." It broke my heart not to be able to tell her he'd be fine, but Sam and I always told her exactly what was going on so that when we told her he was going to be all right, she believed us.

We dreaded saying good-bye to Samantha. I really have no words to express what it feels like to chase one sick kid's ambulance and say good-bye to the other kid being a crying, inconsolable seven-year-old girl. Our heart and hands trembled along with hers. She had seen enough hospitalizations to know that this one was more serious than others. No matter how much we wanted to—we couldn't tell her otherwise. The only comfort was in knowing she was in the loving care of her Gram and Pop. I imagined a chocolate milkshake in her very near future.

Sam stayed with us until the following afternoon; he had to drive back to Maryland to work and be with Samantha. Preston's enzyme levels were over three times the normal range. An endoscopy was ordered to determine the best treatment options—he was still extremely ill. Given the fact that he was way too young and didn't drink alcohol it made no sense that he had developed pancreatitis. Eventually we discovered that his seizure medication was the probable cause. That's what happens when you need to take multiple medications—it's a great big gamble. You hope and pray that the side effects of the drugs you're taking to treat you won't be worse than the ailment itself. In Preston's case it seemed as if it was a colossal coincidence of calamities.

Carrying photographs from his endoscopy, Dr. Vale, his gastroenterologist, walked into Preston's room pulling up a chair beside mine by his bed. After saying hi to him and getting a faint, "oh" back she hesitated, like she was trying on a word that didn't fit. "I don't know how this young man has been able to eat the way he's been eating. It was difficult to read his endoscopy. Let me try to explain: if you took a rag and twisted it several times, then folded it over on itself—that's what Preston's stomach looks like. There's something else. He has a condition called Superior Mesenteric Artery Syndrome, (SMA).

"It's rare, but basically the first part of his small intestine is compressed between two arteries—the aorta and the superior mesenteric artery. I'm afraid it can cause a lot of pain, so that explains why he's been so uncomfortable along with the pancreatitis. We'll need to schedule exploratory surgery to see exactly what we're dealing with. There is a slight chance that he may not be able to eat by mouth again. We won't know for sure until we get in there, though."

I sat in a stupor, staring through her as she spoke of the newly discovered stomach disorder. *It can cause a lot of pain, cause a lot of pain, a lot of pain*, shouted at me from every corner of the room with sirens bright—the spotlight pointing at me. All I could see was me. Horrible me—putting him in the corner for yelling—telling him to control his temper. Due to the stress of juggling life I missed his signals. I forgot to look for what, at times, couldn't be seen through the cloak of cerebral palsy.

Huge tears, the kind that form when you're mad at yourself, did a free fall down my face, mocking me as they fell. Ashamed of myself, I quickly swatted them away. I was supposed to know. I was his mother—the giver of comfort. My Mothers Being had failed me, and I in turn had failed Preston.

I put his bedrail down and hugged him then kissed his cheeks a ridiculous amount of times. "Hey mister, mom needs to tell you something," He looked directly at me—I had his listening eyes. "I'm sorry I didn't pay attention to your signals, pumpkin. I'm sorry I didn't see the pain in your eyes. I thought it was your temper, but I was wrong. Boy, you must have been frustrated that you couldn't make me understand what you were trying to tell me. And you must have been really mad when I put you in the corner for being in pain, right?"

He laughed a single 'huh.'

"I'll look closer next time, I promise. Can you ever forgive your mom?"

He smiled his crooked smile at me and said, "Um mum mum," opening his mouth to give me a kiss.

My Mothers Being shook me hard until I realized I would make many more mistakes being Preston's mom. I would make many more mistakes being Samantha's mom too, though my verbal dialogue with her allowed me clearer signals. Unlike Preston, Samantha spoke in punctuated syllables put together into whole words with a child's animated body language to guide me in case I needed more help. Now my Mothers Being, along with Pres, was teaching me the power of forgiving myself. Something I wasn't so good at.

I was reminded that the person we allow the tiniest margin for error is our self. Another realization.

Sam and Samantha arrived. Seeing my sweet husband's handsome face immediately transported me to a warm, safe place inside. And seeing my adorable Samantha run down the hallway toward me awakened in me a second breath. I could feel my Mothers Being flourishing within me, helping me to be lighter and fuller in myself. I felt stitches bursting inside of me—the ones that melt away as you're healing.

This moment felt unkind in the most generous way. Preston's forgiveness helped to heal me. Sam and Samantha's presence helped to heal me. And *I* helped to heal me.

Preston's face lit up at the sight of his dad and sister. His eyes were like effervescent bubbles floating through the air toward them. We sat on his bed together catching up on each other's week. Joy wiggled and giggled its way through his body and onto the bed. Past the sheets, down to the floor, then leapfrogged onto the walls until it sat in the large window basking gloriously in the late-afternoon rays. It nudged the already upturned corners of Samantha's mouth even more, then coaxed Preston's hand onto his Tech Talk to tell a joke, and without delay it drew the silly, light fluttering sound of laughter resonating out of our voice boxes.

The room of our bodies couldn't contain the joy we felt at being together. After the uncertainty of the last few weeks . . .

This is who we were . . . still.

Love was what we had . . . still.

We were us . . . still.

Real and messy and alive . . . still.

Happily together again for the weekend. In this moment I felt my entire being pounding in my chest, telling me I was exactly where I was meant to be. Another realization.

After the second week of sending Sam and Samantha off, watching our little girl cry in her Daddy's arms as the ding of the elevator warned of the door's closing. I stood waving and smiling like an overly enthusiastic cheerleader telling her how quick the week would pass, blowing continuous kisses until the elevator doors shut—leaving an impenetrable wall between us. My heart counted five nights and four days until I would see them again. The tears I'd captured inside until Samantha's precious face disappeared from view now made themselves known as I watched the red, down arrow light up. Rounding the corner to walk the long hallway back to Preston's room stood a nurse, like my newly appointed best friend, waiting with a Kleenex in hand. "This week will go by quickly, that handsome redhead of yours is going to feel better real soon," she reassured me.

Her presence surprised me, though her act of kindness did not. After eleven years of hospitalizations this wasn't the first time a nurse had gone out of her way. There's an undeniable tenderness when another human being does something kind knowing they will never receive any recognition beyond a thank you. Nurses' covert acts of kindness reached around every corner; they waited behind every door, held every nervous hand, and comforted every worried heart.

That's what nurses do. They humbly and heroically take care of everyone. They don't get paid extra for it. But they do it anyway.

They stand in hallways, sit in patient's rooms, offer warm hugs, bring tired parents a cup of coffee on their break, chit chat with worried parents, stand watch so mom and dad can take a ten minute break, and beg for a joke from a red-headed patient when they really don't have time, but act as if they have all the time in the world.

They are friends, secret angels, fellow moms, pseudo doctors, counselors, administrative assistants and detectives. They are stealth observers who monitor human nature and the hospital environment as a whole. They're the caregivers of all hearts and souls. That's who nurses are. Kindness is soft and powerful. Receiving even the smallest act of kindness cushioned the edges being in a hospital can create. And we couldn't have survived one hospital visit without the kindness that a skilled nurse offered to our entire patient family.

If you're lucky enough to receive VIP status due to length of stay you get moved to a deluxe suite with a real sofa that feels like down after sleeping on the standard hospital cot. Charlie, an adorable nine-year-old boy who looked younger than his years, was Preston's next-door neighbor at the end of the hall. Like Preston, he was small for his age. His elfin grin almost made you giggle; he was that kind of cute. His once brown hair was growing in dirty blonde, which only served to highlight the warmth in his brown eyes, that, when I looked into them, made me think of a glass of iced tea dappled with lemon. He and Preston had become hospital buddies when, several weeks ago, Charlie's nurse brought him into Preston's room to say hello.

After Charlie greeted us, Preston struggled to push 'Hi' on his Tech Talk—he was excited and his CP tried hard to lock up his arm, but finally he hit the right button as Charlie patiently watched like he knew he could do it all along. Preston then followed with an enthusiastic "Oh," picking his head up off the pillow, looking directly down at Charlie in his hospital wheelchair. He was intrigued by Charlie. It was clear that being fully included at Myersville had tremendously improved Preston's ability to interact with other children. I explained to Charlie that because of his cerebral palsy, Preston couldn't say the word 'Hi' and 'Oh' was his way of saying hi.

"Cool," Charlie exclaimed, "Cause 'hi' makes us friends."

"Uh huh," Preston said in a low tone. "Now does that mean yes or is that in Preston's other language, too?" I smiled once again at the unfiltered brilliance of children, this child in particular. "How observant of you, Charlie. That does mean yes."

"Preston you speak two different languages: your made up one and mine, so I'll speak yours too! OH!" Charlie yelled out as if he was about to burst into song. Preston laughed at the way he said it. Charlie laughed back.

Since we'd been moved next to Charlie, this had become their routine. It wasn't like they were great friends or knew each other well. And sometimes, depending on who was more worn out from a procedure or general malaise, not many words were spoken, just a quick exchange of smiles. That and Charlie's curiosity about Preston along with his excitement for the new Joke of the Day was really all they needed.

With his wicked sense of humor our son's jokes were an important part of who he was. They were the right to his left, the heart of his heart and sat always at the core of his sprightly soul for someone to beg a joke off him. Not one humorous moment was wasted. He understood sarcasm and deception, like when he hid his cigar-smoking dad from me. It had become standard practice for us to carry at least one joke book in our travel bag. I had to be on my A game since recording the joke on his Tech Talk was normally Sam's gig. We felt it was important to have a male voice speaking for Preston whenever possible and he clearly preferred hearing his dad's deep voice to mine.

When we left for our walk around the grounds the following morning, Charlie's door was closed. I leaned over Preston from behind his wheelchair quietly saying, "Shhh, he must be asleep. We'll visit later when he wakes up." Preston responded with a hearty "uh huh" and the usual stretching out of his arms and legs that indicated forward motion and excitement. Returning from our walk I discovered Charlie's room had been emptied of all his baseball pendants and get well cards that hung from a huge paper baseball bat his mother made. After putting Pres back into his bed and getting him situated with a tape on his boom box, I went to the nurse's station to inquire what room Charlie was moved to. Our nurse, Lynne, came from around the counter, her dewy eyes told me everything I didn't want to hear—"Charlie died, suddenly, through the night," she said in a hushed hospital tone.

Children die. Beautiful soulful children like Charlie. One minute he is laughing at Preston's Joke of the Day and the next damn minute he is gone. The world had been emptied of an endearing little soul.

I didn't tell Preston when I went back to his room—I couldn't. It was all too real and senseless to comprehend. Not even my Mothers Being could make sense of this. Death was our next-door neighbor last night while we peacefully slumbered. Death chose Charlie. Not Preston. Not the blonde haired little girl on the other side of us. But Charlie.

The next morning as we set out on our usual walk about, and as we passed Charlie's room that was no longer Charlie's room, Preston yelled out when we didn't stop. "Charlie went home," I told him. Charlie went home." It was easier to tell him that then to try to explain death. We didn't know if Preston understood death; we thought it was perhaps too much of an abstract concept for him to grasp, but I knew he understood home. Whenever we were told he was being discharged we didn't dare tell Preston he was going home until the very last minute, because as soon as he heard the word home—he was ready.

I don't think Charlie was.

The afternoon was generous with sunlight. The bright blue-sky overhead showed off a patchwork of young, billowy clouds that looked like a dance. I sat on a bench by the sidewalk in front of the hospital sipping my cappuccino, watching people come and go. It was stunning to be breathing warm air that hadn't had the life sterilized out of it. Red and yellow tulips planted in a pattern of all red then yellow, decorated the parking lots perimeter. Once in awhile a slight breeze gently tipped them towards me. It's funny how I was so completely entertained by tulips swaying as if their sole purpose was to amuse me.

Nurses reporting for the three o'clock shift passed by me in groups. It felt good to be outside experiencing the real world hearing people talk in real life language as they glided by. Their steps felt light, their tone even lighter, like what they were saying was the heaviest thing in their life. *Bob had to ask off early so he can take Nicholas to his first baseball practice,* I heard, *Pat's coming over to help me weed the flower gardens tomorrow,* sounds like fun I thought, *We're having weekend guests and I'm going to be prepared this time, so I'm making two pitchers of mint iced tea tonight,* ohh homemade iced tea, what I wouldn't give, I smirked. That's right, it was Thursday. All the days have different names in here—surgery day, procedure day, test result day and pre-op day.

Standing to go back in, suddenly the overheard conversations pushed hard into my soul; so much so that it physically hurt, like when you have to put a pair of heels back on after having freed your feet. I needed so badly for us to be home as a complete unit, for Preston to be all right so we could name the days of the week again.

How I'd forgotten what a privilege it was to be able to say, "Today is Monday and I get to do the laundry, tidy up and cook dinner for my family."

Preston and I had been here for four weeks and for us today was "the day before we see our family" day. I didn't dare tell him yet. I had learned the hard way at the mention of Dad or Samantha's names he either pouted a lot or got angry at the wait. Mom and dad were helping take care of Samantha and couldn't come to visit this week, which made it feel longer than it deserved.

A new resident was assigned to Preston. He caught me coming back from getting fresh sheets and towels off the rack in the hallway. "Hi, I'm Dr. Miller; your son's blood work came back. I'm sorry to say that I need to put the NG tube back in again."

I felt suddenly hot, almost nauseous hearing him talk about the reinsertion of the tube. Preston fought having the tube put in which made it harder to insert, then tried to pull it out afterward. The doctor walked into his room, smiled and said a dutiful hi; his eyes looked in Preston's direction but never found him, making it clear he wasn't anticipating a response as he began setting everything up. I waited for him to stop and explain to Preston what he needed to do but he didn't. As he pushed the tray toward him, finally I stepped in, "Dr. Miller, you need to tell my son what you're going to do." He looked at me like I was off my rocker; you know, some unrealistic mom who couldn't deal with the way her son was. "How do you want me to do this?" he asked perplexedly. "It's real simple. Stand beside him, look him in the eye and tell him the way you would tell any other child," I answered.

He was polite enough but by the mixed-up look on his face it was clear he thought he was being asked to talk to the wall. He began in a vacant tone that said he expected nothing back, "Preston, I need to put the NG tube back in your nose." Preston's eyes grew big with real fright the moment he heard NG tube, so did Dr. Miller's eyes—his with shock.

Preston then looked at me with his round, terrified eyes, yelling um mum mum for me to save him. It wasn't one of my best moments. I started to cry. I was tired and stressed. Worried beyond reason that he would never be able to eat by mouth again. And seeing his desperate eyes, knowing I couldn't save him sent me completely over the edge. This moment will forever be in my memory place for all the wrong reasons. Mothers are supposed to be strong. We're supposed to be the epitome of courage. All these moments had chipped away at my courage leaving me wrecked—the resident thinking Preston was as aware as a blank wall, the tube again, Charlie, the sleepless nights, missing Sam and Samantha, worrying that one of his biggest pleasures in life might be taken away forever—it overwhelmed me.

I asked Dr. Miller to step outside; tears dripped onto my face, "I can't watch this again, I can't look at his terrified face as he's being held down, wondering why I'm allowing this. So you can call a nurse in to help you. I'll be right around the corner. I just don't have it in me tonight. Sorry, I'm not usually like this, you can meet the better me tomorrow." I gave Preston a kiss and said I'll be right back. "Please don't fight it this time, pumpkin. Help Dr. Miller, okay?"

In the hallway I paced back and forth feeling guilty as hell, questioning what I had just done. Lisa, one of our favorite nurses was on duty and I was so grateful. She stopped to give me a hug I felt unworthy of. "I'm going to make sure Sam takes you out for a glass of wine this weekend, 'cause you need it girlfriend. Hey, don't worry, I've got him," she reassured me. Leaning against the wall outside his room I could hear muffled sounds of struggle but not as bad as the last time. *Deep breath in and out, then another,* I reminded myself.

Growing up I thought courage was something so immense it couldn't be contained. Perhaps I was right. Maybe courage happens the minute you realize you can't contain your fear and you release it and it becomes your courage. A stripping away of layers to reveal your innards whatever they may be. In my case it was a stressed out mom naming what she couldn't handle, recognizing she needed help and asking for it.

Dr. Miller came out of the room, with his right arm pressing against the wall, he looked down at his shoes, "I don't know what to say—today was a really busy day. I still have four patients to see but that's no excuse. Thanks for letting me get to know your son. He's pretty cool. He even told me a joke on that thing, so I felt honored. By the way, I think he's got a crush on Lisa." We both laughed. "Seriously though, I'm going to remember this: what I initially thought, what your son taught me. I will never again assume someone like him doesn't understand. Had you not stepped in I wouldn't have seen it. He's lucky to have such a strong advocate.

"My wife is pregnant with our first and I would expect nothing less for our baby." He started to walk away, then turned and said, "Just so you know—I think I already met the better you. See you tomorrow."

Preston was finally strong enough for surgery. It was a success. His stomach was sutured to his abdominal wall and he would once again be able to eat by mouth. A g-tube was permanently installed for nutrition when he was ill, and a j-tube was temporarily installed while he recovered.

All the conversations—the ones I overheard, the ones I participated in, and the ones I had with myself had all schooled me in one-way or another. Lessons come in all shapes and sizes—residents and nurses, sick boys and a scared little girl, overwrought moms and dads, tulips and sunshine, and love and kindness. One more conversation was heard: my Mothers Being spoke to me in her whisper-thin voice,

Most often the greatest lessons are learned in the heart before the mind knows what it knows. Keep leading with your heart. Remember when I told you the rest would follow? It still holds true, my darling. It still holds true.

When wrapping up the loose ends of an overwhelming day, sometimes I felt like an awkward two-year old whose fingers aren't quite nimble enough.

The strings still fall away. But I practice, still. And I'll try to remember the easy days that laced themselves together when I wasn't looking.

I shall strive for too many of these. I'll be more careful with my unruly thoughts—tendering the conversation I have with myself.

And when the day feels broken apart, I'll whisper inwardly so my heart can feel the vibrations of its words.

Chapter 16

Wayward Marbles

F WOULD LOVE TO BE ABLE TO SAY THAT WE HAD THIS DIS-
ability thing down every day, but we didn't. And I'm not even talking
about the days Pres had a surgery or emergency. I'm talking about the routine days in between that seemed to scream at us when I'm sure they were
quietly speaking. Some days gratitude succumbed to stress. Some days pos-
itivity got wrapped up so tightly our entire being felt bound. Some days the
sheer physicality of lifting his helpless body was exhausting beyond what I
can ever tell you, especially on those days when we didn't feel well ourselves,
or we plain just didn't feel like doing anything at all. Some days worry crept
up from behind, scaring the shit out of us. Illness had created so many folds
in the crevices of our souls, we worried about every imaginable and unimaginable thing we could find to worry about. We worried he would be ignored,
we worried he would be stared at. When he was well, we worried he would
get sick. And when there was nothing tangible to worry about, we worried
about worrying too much. Some days the contrasts of having two vastly
differently-abled children swallowed us whole, humanness and all.

At times, the skin and bone of our life felt stretched and broken beyond
repair.

Usually the wisest thing to do is to fold into the unknowing, softly, the
way a meringue is folded into a batter so it won't collapse. At times we
weren't that wise; our human selves wouldn't give way past the tight borders
of our knowingness.

And all the worry collapsed in on us. In our utter humanness we made all the human mistakes. We cried when no one was looking. We yelled. We took it out on each other. We retreated inwardly. We lied, craftily pretending to Samantha we weren't worried or stressed rather unconvincingly I'm afraid. She watched us like actors in a movie, studying our body language. Our eight-year old daughter was quickly learning to see through our simulated smiles by the way we carried our shoulders so high they almost touched our ears. She sensed worry's energy hanging flatly in the air, like an unresolved fight, the way children always do.

Children are such insightful, smart creatures. Without our realizing it she saw when we were stuck invisibly inside of worry, at the other end of nowhere. That's where worry takes you; it is also where worry leaves you.

Worry. The singular, most negative force that often consumed us. Not everyday, not all the time, but when it did, it did so completely.

Worry is torture—a slow poison quietly leaching into your soul.

History was telling us to be prepared for the next bad thing. The omen of worry lived with us. We had long ago been taken to a place we never knew existed, and because of that we couldn't go back.

At twelve years old, Preston had averaged a surgery or two a year and several other hospitalizations. Every time our dear boy needed another surgery or got sick we unconsciously deposited another coin in our worry bank. So how then, could we function as human beings without being stressed or worried beyond what's reasonable?

What, really, is reasonable anyway?

Our reasonable was horrid to most people, but our reasonable was wonderful to someone whose child was dying from cancer.

A corner of our brains had become indented from worry's heavy baggage being left there too long. Sam and I learned to carry worry well on the outside, aloft in the treetop of our persona. An imperceptible groove to our family and friends, it hung in the shadows just out of sight. It was so hidden, that few people knew of his precarious beginnings. We were always happy, positive, laughing and smiling no matter what had happened; problem solvers from the get go. But when no one was looking we let escape one of our biggest worries: that he would outlive us. Not a typical way for parents to think about their child. Sam used to joke about when we were old and gray how we would hobble around taking care of Pres. Even though

I didn't realize it in my conscious being, most of the time it felt improbable to me that Preston would be in this world for any great length of time. This feeling followed me around the way something catches the corner of your eye and you turn to look, but there's nothing there. Not convinced, you turn to look again, still nothing. And yet, all your senses light with curiosity, and you wonder if there ever was something there—an apparition or material being. I have no real explanation to offer other than the whispers I heard in my sleep and my Mothers Being layering his story so it wouldn't crush me all at once.

Other than Sam, my friend Sue was the only other person I allowed myself to fully worry out loud with. She and I often talked about how a good day felt more worrisome than a bad day, sarcastically saying that a day this good was sure to be followed by a day that bad. It's what our brains knew. If we were prepped and ready to roll then a medical emergency couldn't sneak up on us like a past life we couldn't shed, while we were in the middle of living a brilliant day. Dare we tempt fate and enjoy a day too much?

I suppose it's only natural to be consumed by worry when your world is a succession of challenges—when as soon as your son gets over one crisis he is hit with another. But, still, we always remembered the truly sick kids, the ones too ill to go outside to feel the warmth of the sun on their face, or to know the anticipation of sleeping in their own bed again swaddled by bedroom walls painted their favorite color; around them mementos of friends, hobbies and sports warmly gazing back to help them greet the day.

Whether it was educational or medical, a questionable day thickened so big inside of us there wasn't an inch of space left for anything else but worry. Was worry then an immovable obstacle—a mountain towering shadowlike over us? Or could it be culled from the air in our house and thrown out with the trash?

Inwardly, worry felt like solitude stuck inside a dark bubble. And what prey tell do you do with an entity you can't see to defend yourself against?

Outwardly, worry felt like a thousand wayward marbles spilling onto the floor. And how, I ask, do you chase all the marbles?

There's always that one marble you know you didn't get. You can't see it, can't prove it, but you know it will appear again one day and possibly trip you up. It remains there, tickling the back of your mind just enough to interfere with your precious day.

That's worry.

courage/ker-ij/ ~

the quality of mind or spirit that enables a person to face difficulty, danger, pain, etc., without fear; bravery

Origin ~

from Latin cor "heart" which remains a common metaphor for inner strength

Courage is not simply one of the virtues, but the form of every virtue at the testing point. C. S. Lewis

courage ~

wings to fly

the grit that lies quick beneath the shining of your soul

what releases love unbound and unfurling into the hearts of human beings

swiftly. quietly. before a knowing soul can intervene, the beginning of an internal evolution

Chapter 17

Clear Signals

PRESTON BEGAN A SPLIT DAY SCHEDULE FOR MIDDLE School so PT, OT, speech and vision services could be delivered at Rock Creek. It wasn't ideal, however, it made sense—middle school in the morning and the segregated school in the afternoon.

Middle school is different, a far cry from elementary school. The kids are different. For one, there were more of them—a conglomeration from feeder schools, now all together. For another, puberty had struck every one of them and there was no cure for the way they were at odds with themselves. They were now a mixed bag of full-on emotions and no emotions: yelling, screaming one minute, sulking and silent the next.

And now there was Preston.

So what did we do? We began at the beginning, because for the staff of Middletown Middle, it was the beginning. There had never been a multiply handicapped child at their school.

And now there was Preston.

We started by in-servicing the sixth grade staff. I'd been hired by our school system to run a parent/educator training center, which provided advocacy for parents of children with disabilities and resources for teachers and parents on everything from disability information to curriculum adaptation. I stood at the podium looking out onto a classroom full of squinting eyes, crinkled foreheads and mouths unable to turn upwards. By now I was used to telling my Preston story of how he fought so hard to be here to get to this place of now. It was an honest story about being human and disabled at the same time, a growth chart of his accomplishments, a raw examination of CP and specifically what it meant for our son. I spoke truthfully of his meager developmental level, hoping they would understand that inclusion is not about catching up. Our county now had inclusion specialists for primary, middle and high school. Our middle school specialist talked at length about curriculum adaptation, how it worked at Myersville and how it would continue at Middletown Middle. Another staff member spoke further about the benefits of inclusion to all students.

We shared examples, philosophies, real-life success stories, disability awareness activities, and the paramount role of his instructional aide. Shirley, the inclusion specialist pledged ongoing support for the entire staff. The three of us all but stood on our heads for them.

A teacher raised his hand. I don't remember his name, but I can still see his face—annoyed, like I was taking up too much space in his day. His question was for me, "What is a kindergartener doing coming to my sixth-grade classroom?" *Not really a question, so much as a statement,* I thought.

The little Irish redhead in my brain wanted to jump straight over the podium at him. Straight over. She wanted to get all up in his face and ask: *Have you not heard a single freaking word we've said? Do you not care enough to try? She wanted to stand on a desktop, wave an inclusion flag and say to him, Hey! Guess what? You don't get to tell my son where he can or cannot attend school because you're entirely ignorant of the process and of him!* Well that felt good. Thank you, little Irish redhead. My face remained serene and studious as I answered his question, "As we mentioned, inclusion is not about catching a student up to grade level. It is about adapting curriculum to their learning level. So a kindergartener won't be coming to your classroom; a human being named Preston will be coming." Next question.

Question after question after question made it painfully clear to the three of us, this wasn't going to be easy. I was worried. I couldn't get their questions out of my mind. They weren't good 'I don't understand, but I want to learn' questions by any stretch of the imagination. I couldn't get their sullen faces out of my mind either. I dreaded telling Sam we had another battle on our hands. *Such protest for a measly half-day,* I thought.

After our presentation, walking down the hallway scantly rimmed with teachers felt like long ago when we fought for our son's right to learn at his neighborhood school. It felt like I was back to being the advocate spelled with a capital T. Shirley and I said polite goodbyes to aloof profiles.

My skin felt cold, my mind spun a thousand scenarios of how to fix this, and my heart broke all over again for Preston. We'd made such progress at Myersville Elementary. We'd arrived at this point standing tall on a mountain of success stories and achievements. So many collected moments had taken our breath away; not one of which seemed to stir the hearts or minds of the sixth-grade staff. Even the Myersville teachers who didn't believe in full inclusion believed in a human being named Preston and welcomed him as a significant part of a whole in their classroom. But sadly, our neighborhood middle school felt nothing like community. It appeared they didn't want to learn about him, didn't want to get to know him, didn't think they could remotely connect with him. They just plain didn't want him in their school. The sense of community we experienced at Myersville was lost on them. We had been dropped into the icy waters of them and us again.

Like always, I stayed away for the first month, promising a scheduled observation first, then a surprise one. I wish I could tell you several stories of profound student interaction and creative adaptions like at Myersville. I ate lunch in the school cafeteria with him. Angie sat by him chatting with a long table of very talkative kids, once in awhile glancing at her buddy and whispering something to him. Laura B. whizzed by, quickly brushing the top of his crew cut for good luck. She said a fast, "Hi buddy," to him. Preston's face lightened for a second, but before he got his 'oh' out she was gone. Then as if darkened by a dimmer switch, I watched his eyes go dull again.

Several other Myersville friends came by to tap on his wheelchair tray to say hi. They moved like they were being timed for the fifty-yard dash. Middle school was fast as wildfire.

And now there was Preston.

Joanne, Preston's aide, did an amazing job adapting whatever she could for him, seeing to it he was well taken care of emotionally, educationally and physically. However, on the surprise observation I was the one surprised. I went to the class Preston was scheduled to be in. He wasn't there. I went to the health room to see if he needed to lie down. He wasn't there. A bad feeling came over me while I walked hurriedly to the front office, "Hi, I just went to the class Preston was scheduled to be in and he wasn't there. Do you know where he might be?" The school secretary looked down at a piece of paper that had been scratched through several times and said, "Oh, yeah he's in music class."

"Why is he in music class? I asked.

"They've been trying out different classes to see if he likes them."

I hesitated then replied, "Ok. Thank you." I could feel my face getting hot. I could hear my brain starting to assume things. I reminded myself what I always told the parents I advocated for—"Don't get emotional. Don't raise your voice. Do you want to be remembered for the content of your words or an emotional outburst, cause I guarantee you won't be remembered for both? You'll just be another emotional parent. Save your emotion for when it's really warranted, then they'll pay attention to both."

Walking into the music room I saw Preston and Joanne across the room in the back corner. Another student, a girl I didn't recognize, was half turned around and staring at him periodically. But worse than anything, I saw our son's blank expression as if he'd been plunked down into some unfamiliar world. Looking around the class I didn't see anyone I knew. It was also clear the class knew nothing about him. After talking briefly with Joanne and Pres I stormed back to the front office asking to speak with the principal immediately.

He explained as nonchalantly as you explain switching cereal brands that they had put our son in multiple classes to see if he liked them. There was no disability awareness training for the kids who'd never met him before, just classroom hopping. I sat looking at him as his mouth moved confidently, almost boastingly over his words. I paused, taking a deep breath in, not moving a muscle in my chair and said, "I want to make this perfectly clear to you. You are not to move Preston around like a token on a board game ever again without our approval. Do you understand?"

"Well yes, but in our initial meeting we discussed how we'd experiment with different things to find what worked, like you did at Myersville," he said.

I snickered; I couldn't help it. "When *we* talked about experimenting we meant educationally, as in adaptations, positioning of his arms, communication methods. Come on, you know better. Teachers need to be prepared, students need to be prepared, *Preston* needs to be prepared.

"Change is not easy for kids with disabilities. So that was your first mistake before you even began. And experimenting was not something we did haphazardly at Myersville, ever.

"Whatever was done was always done as a team with everyone's consideration in mind. What you've been doing here for the last several weeks has not created purposeful learning for Preston, and it's most certainly not inclusion."

Sometimes things just don't work out. Or perhaps they do, just not the way we envision them. Middle school is hard. Extremely hard. And as much as everyone tried or didn't try, Preston didn't like middle school. He yelled out to the universe the day his split schedule began. I think we were still high from breathing in the luscious oxygen from our elementary school experience, thinking it would continue on, convinced we could make it work. But Preston was not convinced. His friends that had time for him before had less time due to classes quickly changing as hallways became a sea of frantic students rushing to their lockers, and the myriad of adjustments their middle school bodies and minds were undergoing was an additional challenge. No bond at all was formed with the kids who didn't know him. His differently-abled telepathy picked up on the negative energy from people who didn't believe he belonged there. And while some teachers did try, our school system wasn't yet where it needed to be for including children with severe disabilities in middle school. So far in fact that Pres was beginning to regress in certain skills at Middletown Middle, while at the same time making great progress at Rock Creek.

Like my Dad, the fixer, I was determined to fix this. Along with inclusion specialists, I participated in extra teacher training thinking this would do the trick. How frustrated our son must have been waiting for mom and dad to pick up on his signals. Our non-verbal boy made certain though, his signals were heard loud and clear when he began yelling loudly as soon as the wheelchair ramp was lowered each morning arriving at the middle school. Contrasted with beaming smiles and legs kicking excitedly while getting off the bus at Rock Creek in the afternoon.

I remember our last IEP meeting at the middle school in November. Sam and I listened as both schools gave their starkly variant progress reports. Even their tone of voice was vastly different. Finally, I looked at the middle school principal and asked, "Can you tell me why it sounds as if we're discussing two completely different students?" His silence was loud.

It was time to talk to Preston.

Sometimes, separating my heart and mind on behalf of Preston was a difficult task. Considering I was a sensitive soul who also thought with my heart and loved with my intellect at times, made it harder still. My Mothers Being sorted through thinking and feeling like a great conveyor belt, leaving the divided things for my mind's eye to see. I looked closely at the two divergent piles.

One left me thinking all our inclusion-community work had been for nothing. The other told me it didn't matter what we'd done or for whom we'd done it for. It only mattered that we'd done it wholly with a pureness of intention. And in the end there was no choice for Sam or I to make.

We wheeled Preston into the family room parking his wheelchair beside of us. Sam and I sat on the sofa explaining that we understood his recent actions and that he needed to help us decide what to do. His blue eyes seemed bluer today, more intense. He wore his comfy Saturday clothes, his favorite gray sweats and sweatshirt with orange and maroon "VA Tech" letters running down one leg and a maroon bandana to match. His auburn cowlick still looked Saturday morning ruffled. He sat absolutely still as we spoke; we had his listening eyes. There was a distinctive stillness the way he seemed to take hold of each word and breathe it into his skin as if every muscle gently held his body at attention. His body wasn't fighting him as much today, I thought. Or maybe the importance of his message, maybe his sheer will overpowered his cerebral palsy just for this day.

We stood in front of him explaining the two choices on his Tech Talk as we demonstrated where they were. A half-day at each school, his current situation, or a whole day back at his segregated school meant no more inclusion. This was what we'd worked for, for years: the right to choose.

Now, watching Preston as he reached for his Tech Talk button, his eyes followed his out-stretched hand intent on the yellow square. This was one of those rare, beautiful days when two parts of his body worked in tandem with one another like they actually belonged in the same body.

I suppose my Mothers Being already knew what I was about to hear. I don't remember breathing, only his bright-eyed laughter as he repeatedly chose to go to Rock Creek all day. The excitement in his eyes overrode any hesitation we had. Watching him wiggle from side to side as he joyfully kicked his legs knowing that mom and dad understood was further proof. In ten succinct seconds my heart and mind had been ushered into separate rooms to listen to our son's message. And outside in the hallway, standing quietly still, waiting to embrace them was my Mothers Being who gently whispered, *I've been waiting here a long time for you. Welcome to this knowing. Don't worry; he'll be all right. Just look at him, listen to his laughter.* It was true; his laughter contained the ebullience of a million tiny bubbles dancing in the air.

It was one of the most bittersweet days of my life. Sam and I witnessed the empowerment of our non-verbal boy. Our unconditional love had given his voice the depth of tone and power it seldom experienced over his world. His joyful, dolphin-like squeals filled the room. He chose Rock Creek School. He chose to be with other children like him. He chose less chaos. He chose less judgment. Above all else—he chose. His choice was not our choice, but now, his choice had become our choice because we loved him unconditionally. Our souls had come together in the most exquisite way.

They met in the center, in the still space between our mind and our heart where unconditional love abides.

I think if Preston could have spoken aloud he would have said, "Inclusion is not solely a place, it is the empowerment of a person to choose their place in society. Thank you mom and dad for paying attention to my signals. Thank you even more for respecting my choice."

And we would have answered, "You're welcome precious boy, you're welcome."

The writing was on the wall and Preston had written it. For a mostly powerless human being, he had powerfully told both schools what he wanted by his contrasting behavior. What we mistook at first as a transitional adjustment period was our son simply and irrefutably deciding what he wanted.

One of the most loving and respectful things you can do for another human being is to listen. And listen well. Another realization.

I don't have all the answers when it comes to inclusion and the acceptance of diversity. As a matter of fact, after all we've experienced, I have more questions than answers. Maybe that's the key. In the asking we keep a conversation alive by refusing to accept status quo. Throughout history asking questions has broken down barriers. Questions like—*why can't women vote?* Or, *why can't I sit in the front of the bus?* Or *why can't I marry someone of the same sex?*

Hopefully one day our future children will ask their parents: *Why did kids with disabilities have to be separated from us?*

Through the years Sam and I have found that the exceptional doctors, nurses, teachers and administrators never minded being asked questions. They say that knowledge is power; well perhaps that's the root of the problem. Everyone is walking around with their perceived knowledge so busy trying to acquire it. I think rather, that curiosity is power, is what fuels wisdom. Without wisdom we are all just walking encyclopedias talking at each other.

What proving ground have we left for the next generation of kids with disabilities? They won't stop coming you know. What will we tell their parents? That we tried, succeeded and did nothing with it? That we stood fresh on the summit of much achievement then turned our backs on learning more?

How easy it is to say it won't work without ever having tried. It sails out of mouths propelled by vague winds so high no one can reach them.

And why do children with disabilities need permission to belong from the people in their very own community as if they and they alone are the rulers of the kingdom? Inclusion, if done properly, brings with it a sense of belonging, a community for all. What then makes a community? A community isn't a community simply because it holds within it's borders neighbors living side by side, the same way a family isn't a family simply because everyone is related. Likewise, inclusion isn't inclusion simply because a child with disabilities attends their neighborhood school. Like being part of a community or a family, it requires a lot of things great and small: like hard work, respect, openness, forgiveness, equality, humanity, acceptance and some love.

Inclusion is not a place or placement. It is a mindset, a belief and a practice. All day, every day—for all children. The best of the best, the worst of the worst and the ones that fall in between our ideals.

I don't know how else we get by in this world without applauding diversity. Why is it so hard for some to accept? Diversity is what helps us celebrate each other's soul. It's what we believed on Preston's first day at Rock Creek, through his years at Myersville, his brief stay at Middletown Middle and what we believed as he returned to a new and improved Rock Creek School.

Diversity is humanity's heartbeat. Without it what a flat boring, vanilla line we would be.

If I were in front of a classroom of teachers, again I would say to them, "I want for my child the same thing you want for your child."

The simplest, most miraculous things—to be healthy, happy, loved, accepted and understood, to have friends, to be given every possible opportunity to think and to grow and to breathe and to love and to learn something. Anything. So excuse my loud voice, for it comes with all the echoes of children who can't speak enough to be understood. Though I've never raised my voice in an educational setting, my message is loud so the people who said he wouldn't live, or smile, or see, or learn beyond his label of severely and profoundly handicapped deemed can hear me now. And whether it's at a school, around an IEP table, in a mall, or in a hospital: I make no apologies if my advocacy makes you uncomfortable.

Inclusion was a tremendous amount of work, especially in its infancy. It was like a life learning lab on wheels that challenged us every single day. It took me in directions I'd never imagined, and on the road to acceptance and diversity I stopped at many unexpected places and found myself.

Although without my best friend of a husband by my side, without his consistently wild love and involvement, without him watching the kids so I could go to a CHAMPIONS meeting, or give a presentation after working a long day himself—this would have never been possible.

And if we had to do it all over again—the research, the presentations, the headaches, the advocacy, and the outreach—we would. With one exception: next time we would stand taller and raise our voices higher for the kids. All of them.

Chapter 18

Chop Wood, Carry Water

THIS MORNING SNAPPED US AWAKE WITHOUT BENDING into the day. No soft introduction into what was to be.

It was Sunday, exactly one week before Christmas. Our bedroom was directly across the hall from Preston's, so before going downstairs to put coffee on, I did what I always did—peeked in on him first, then tip-toed down the hallway to Samantha's room. How I loved watching them sleep.

I almost screamed, but my Rapid Shock Process grabbed it and held it inside. Our son was a grayish, bluish kind of pale that suggested he could possibly be dead. Vomit and bile had washed up over his mouth. He was close to being nonresponsive. I laid my head on his chest to check for a heartbeat. Sam heard me gasp and came running. Just then Preston seized again. He apparently had several seizures in the early morning hours and aspirated while seizing. We quickly rolled him on his side. Sam called for the ambulance, then for my mom and dad to come help with Samantha and start the emergency phone tree.

I had to wonder if most bad things happen in the wee morning hours when the day is too shy to forbid such things.

I remember Sam's face being a confluence of something off a Scared Straight poster and "Don't worry honey, we got this," as he stood holding Samantha by Preston's bed telling them he was going to wait for the ambulance at the end of the driveway.

Samantha held Sam's face in her hands and asked, "Preston will be okay, right Daddy?"

His Rapid Shock Process held his fear in too as he told her, "We're going to make sure the doctors do everything they can to make him better, kiddo." Then he kissed her cheek.

I heard the back door open, it was my dad. Samantha yelled excitedly, "Preston, Poppy is here!" as if his presence changed everything. She ran to the top of the stairs to wait for her Pop. Dad gave Sam a reassuring tap on his shoulder the way men do, as they passed on the stairway. Their eyes met and left each other quickly. In that moment I realized there's nothing as tender as watching two grown men trying not to look scared. Each of their eyes cast off each other's, afraid of what might show in their strong fatherly façades. The look in their eyes said we the men are girly scared. And the tap on Sam's shoulder said, I want to hug you, son, but that would show my fear and release yours.

My dad had an enormous amount of respect for Sam.

He often said, "I don't know how that man does what he does." And he showed his respect by mowing our grass before Sam got home, or helping him work on our cars, or anything else he needed without ever being asked.

"Does this mean we can't get our Christmas tree today?" Samantha asked through tears emanating from a scared, disbelieving place in her innocent, young heart that said,

Not today, not at Christmas Time, as she called it. Her eight-year-old soul had already seen so much. I had to wonder how old all this actually made her. I agreed, *Not at Christmas Time*.

Samantha was too young to understand the ridiculousness of today. This was her normal. We were supposed to pick a damn Christmas tree, tie it to the car roof and drag it in the house just like in the movies so it's pine scent could officially start our holiday. Then I would prep our Sunday dinner of roast chicken while running back and forth between kids and our holiday to-do list, while Sam cussed while artfully finagling the tree into the stand. He would string lights on it, inevitably a few bulbs were burnt out so he'd frantically look for the little white box of extras that was somehow always in the bottom of the last box. We would make hot chocolate and play Christmas music while we decorated the tree and field intermittent whining because it was taking too long. Preston's talking Christmas tree would sit on his wheelchair tray and say, "Merry Christmas" in a robotic voice when he hit its switch. And we would all laugh. Then eventually we would lay him in the lounge chair beside the tree so he could watch us and relax while Mickey's Christmas Carol entertained us. It was Preston's favorite song that always had to be played first or he got mad. His legs would kick wildly, and he would laugh out loud as he heard various parts he knew all too well. Then his body would pause like an animal ready to pounce as he anticipated the chorus line, letting loose the joy from his body and mind. And we would all laugh again. Sam was supposed to lift Samantha over his shoulder so she could put our gold, hand-painted angel on top.

Then both kids were supposed to beam smiles that rivaled the sparkly white lights of our newly decorated tree. All in that order just like in the movies except for the bloopers of our real life. And then after putting the kids in bed Sam and I would collapse on the sofa and sigh a deep breath for having finished one more holiday task.

Our imperfect holiday preparations sounded so perfect to me right now.

Instead, Sam was nervously standing at the end of our long driveway so the ambulance wouldn't miss us again. Our house was on a gravel back road off what would be considered by most to be a back road. The last time we called an ambulance they drove past our house. Our medical experience told us we didn't have a minute to lose. Samantha stood in her one-piece purple fleece pajamas next to her Pop, holding tightly onto his big hands. I stood with my hip touching Preston's bed, his hand in mine in between sitting his limp body up when he vomited.

At Samantha's request Pop lifted her up to give her brother a kiss on his forehead. She told him, "I love you Preston; feel better, okay?" Her ok trembled off into the room making it hard to keep our fright hidden. Even she could see how awfully sick he looked. Conversational sentences about when we would get the tree and how we would finish getting ready for Santa's arrival were batted around the room half-heartedly while I watched to make sure he was still breathing. My eyes communicated with Dad's in a silent Morse code so two innocent beings wouldn't know how scared we really were.

We were adult scared.

We'd seen this look before and no amount of positive thinking could shake the terrified feeling that was making our hearts race in our throats. Even the air smelled strange like the metal hospital smell had already injected itself into the room.

Diagnosis: Aspiration Pneumonia. Luckily, feeding could be administered via his g-tube. Once antibiotics were safely on board and there was no sign of a fever for twenty-four hours we were discharged, as they knew that Sam and I could provide the necessary care at home. Magically, when we pulled up the driveway, leaning against the side of our back door was a Christmas tree Poppy the elf had gotten for us.

Once we knew Preston was stable, we joked with him about pulling a fast one right before Christmas. And we all laughed. Believe it or not, we honestly did laugh a lot in hospitals. All kinds of laughter: inappropriately, the way you laugh at funerals, and genuinely to remind ourselves we're still human, our bellies pressing outwardly toward whatever was pressing in on us. Laughter said that our human family was stronger within than the things around us. Those things didn't have a heart, or the strength that comes with having a heart. But mainly we laughed for Preston and Samantha's sake.

Laughter said everything would get better somehow, someway. Laughter said this didn't break us beyond repair.

Being in the hospital was always a fascinating study of the human spirit—a world within a world. Groups of people: secret societies often moving in contrast to one another and energies colliding. Yet we were all here for the same good, weren't we? To heal or be healed. Our souls had been rubbed raw by tragedy or illness. Or if we were lucky enough our souls had been buffed and polished by a miracle. I could only imagine that if thinking and praying, wishing and hoping could be physically seen; what beautiful auras I would witness. Maybe seeing everyone's thinking and praying auras over their heads, like captions in a comic strip would cause human beings to practice being more human. Maybe then there could exist empathy without effort—thought without judgment.

Routine was everything to our redheaded boy. His power. Control. His right against all wrongs. His deep long breath.

In our brutal, delicate space known as caregiving, loving Preston and all of his differently-abled conditions brought us into a stillness we'd never known and probably would have never known without the daily rituals his condition allowed. There's a Zen saying: *"Before enlightenment, chop wood, carry water. After enlightenment, chop wood, carry water."* Three times a day we fed him, our hands making the same repetitive movement bringing food to his mouth. We chopped wood, carried water.

Every evening we bathed him as we laid him in warm soothing water washing his long, skinny body. We chopped wood, carried water. Everyday we dressed him without even thinking about what to put where. We chopped wood, carried water. Every afternoon and evening our hands ran the length of his feet and legs massaging better circulation back into his lower extremities as we religiously watched Wheel of Fortune and Jeopardy, listening to him talk the answers out loud while flirting with Vanna White. We chopped wood, carried water. Every night we laid his body in bed to rest. We chopped wood, carried water. And with the ritual of revolving hospital doors we saw others so much more in need. We chopped wood, carried water.

We were sent back into the world with a unique knowing. We found choices, extraordinary choices that appeared to some to be very few. The ritualistic manner in which we lived our lives sent us into a state of grace or panic depending on the day, but still, we chopped wood, carried water. And what with the chopping of wood and the carrying of water, there's no choice but to step outside of yourself which eventually; if you chop enough wood and carry enough water, you come back to your center.

Day after day, night after night, we performed our caregiving tasks and held our breath that this was the worst we would know. And we told the universe that no matter how physically tied down; we were extravagantly free. The lightness we vowed never to forget.

We had the choice, we always do, to see these continual tasks as a spiritual opening or closing in our lives—we can participate or shut down.

To see his body go limp like it was floating on a cloud and his eyes gaze at us from a place of healing and relief and to see a smile wash over his entire being because we eased his discomfort reminded me that we were the lucky ones. The givers of care to another human being.

These reminders were the spaces that sprung up like gushing wells in between our life, a life that was itself a metanoia. And oh what we would have missed had we not experienced each and every one of them fully. Another realization.

advocate/ad-ve-ket ~

a person who speaks or writes in support or defense of a person, cause, etc

Origin ~

Middle English advocate, from Anglo-French, from Latin advocatus, from past participle of advocare to summon, from ad- + vocare to summon, from voc-vox voice

Happy is he who dares courageously to defend what he loves. Ovid

The following sentence was part of a note given to me by someone who worked with Preston.

"Your devotion to advocacy for Preston's rights set an example, which I will follow as best as I am able personally and within my profession."

advocate/advocacy ~

defender

mover of mountains

to enable others to see what cannot be seen

to summon the power from within to affect a cause or person that is without

to be empowered, and to empower others

Chapter 19

Wee Birds and Vast Dreams

PHYSICALLY, HE BEGAN RIGHT BACK WHERE HE STARTED. But this time things were different. He wasn't returning to the same school. Gael, a new principal was now at the helm, and she was current on state-of-the-art educational practices and open to new ideas. And Preston wasn't the same child who left five years before. He was no longer the child who kept his head down, or had never been asked to high five a friend, or attend a birthday party, or run the bases at recess. They had enlightened each other with their brilliance that only children know.

And now Preston had chosen to go back to where he began. It's funny how life takes us in circles. Just when we think we're moving away from something, life teaches us that we travelled in one great, big circle. Hopefully, if we're open enough we learn that we can begin again from wherever we start.

This morning did feel like a weird loop, like the first time we put him on the bus to Rock Creek a lifetime ago. Preston's body had stretched a few long inches. Now his long lanky arms and legs gave him the appearance of a kid who didn't eat enough. He was so excited, wiggling from side to side in his wheelchair and kicking his legs. And when we told him he would be able to see Miss Steph, his joy let out a dolphin-like squeal.

Ironically, my office was located at Rock Creek, so I too was back at the beginning. Even though I had accepted Preston's choice, my inclusion-minded brain was still battling it out in my head. My heart still broke for what might have been. The concept of an inclusive community taunted me. It was hard to hold back the reins on my ruminative brain from going over what we missed and could have fixed.

On Preston's first day back, Gael, my boss, walked into my office saying, "Hi. How are you?" I heard it with my ears at the same time I heard my father's voice saying: *Don't ever cry at work. They will see you as a weak woman.* My heart received her simple yet complicated question, and the only way it knew how to answer was to bleed out some tears. Deep down where I couldn't quite get to right now, I knew this wasn't a regress but an egress into a new beginning. The two unsettled halves of my heart and mind needed one more meeting out in the hallway between the separate rooms that contained them so they could catch up to Preston.

My Mothers Being already knew this. I could faintly hear her, somewhere between the obscurity of our failed middle school inclusion experience and now, warning me to be careful of what my heart and mind saw. *Do not see failure. See lessons. Begin again. Simply begin. Just look at your son—he already has.*

So once more for old times sake, I cried tears of sadness for thinking our inclusion trailblazing had led nowhere as I answered, "I'm fine."

I was fine; it would just take some getting used to. New beginnings always do.

We knew Preston liked his new instructional aide, Connie; by the way she could make him laugh so hard he snorted. She was a natural—able to look and see what was in front of her, quickly seeing how normal his abnormal is. Sometimes the two of them went casually around the school either by wheelchair or gait trainer telling his Joke of the Day, stopping in classrooms having impromptu conversations critical for cause and effect in the most natural way. Connie didn't stand by him, telling him what to press on his communication device; she let him figure it out only stepping in if need be. And it was clear from the beginning Preston didn't mind looking at her pretty face either. We bonded with her, and eventually she offered to come sit with Pres when Miss Steph wasn't available. Another kind human being had joined our village.

She was known for her scrambled eggs and salsa, which Pres loved. And together, they were known for making fun of my list that I always left on the kitchen island. Connie would say to him, "Let's look at Mom's OCD list and see what it says this time. Nope we're not doing any of that—Mom's crazy." At which he laughed his head off. Having a stream of aides was commonplace in our world of special education. We began anew each time another new person stepped in. We were lucky though, the exceptional instructional aides were not only Preston's friend, but ours as well.

When I worked Tuesday through Thursday, Mondays became Maintenance Mondays. I did the laundry, cleaned the house, washed dog bowls, then usually fixed a quick meal of salmon and broccoli for dinner. My parents never stopped by on my days off, knowing I needed to finish everything.

But on a day when the sky was so full of its blue self, when the temperature charmed me to go outside and bask in its fall glory, something unforgettable happened. It remains in my memory place, vivid as the blue sky that day.

On Monday morning my father knocked on the back door. I knew it was him before opening the door. His cherry pipe smoke filled the side porch and snuck in under our door. He was holding a plastic grocery bag with its handle tied into a bow. His eyes looked every bit like that of a little boy, his smile whimsical. He was wearing a red and black plaid shirt, black pants and his tweed hat.

He handed the bag to me and said, "I know you're busy but I thought you might need these babe. I'm not coming in. I've got to run into town. I just wanted you to have this."

"Can I open it now?" I asked.

"Open it later when you have time."

"Okay."

"Well. All right then."

"Thanks Dad, for whatever this is," I said. He had already stepped off the porch onto the brick sidewalk. He turned around once more, "It's just a little something." His voice trailed behind him alongside the rings of pipe smoke as he walked down our gravel driveway, across the road to his house and out of sight.

I placed the bag on our dining table and opened it immediately, still wondering why he didn't want me to open it in front of him. My father was observant when you didn't know he was. He'd seen me looking at small wooden birds in a folk art catalogue and surprised me by carving five primitive birds prettier than the ones I saw. He painted each one in muted colors of blue, white, green, burgundy and gold. I thought it was odd that he brought them over since I would see him Thursday night for dinner, but I surmised he was too excited to wait.

Wednesday night I had a vivid dream that I had to cancel my hair appointment because of a funeral. I woke up telling Sam of my silly dream. He said, "How weird." I agreed. We both laughed.

On our way out the door Thursday morning Samantha already had her backpack strung across her shoulders, my purse and workbag hung from my left arm. But when I reached for the doorknob something made me pause and stare at the dirty crockpot, its cord dangling in front of a full dishwasher I was too tired to empty last night. In the sink were four bowls, salad plates, silverware, a wooden salad bowl and cheese grater from our chili dinner. "Mom should have done those dishes. If it wouldn't make us late I'd do them now; you know how I hate that," I complained to Samantha. While I'd thought that plenty of times when I was too tired to clean the kitchen, or when catching up on sleep or cuddling with the kids reigned superior to washing dishes; I'd never stopped to verbalize it out loud the way I did that morning.

But for some reason they were calling out to me like an early warning system. I guess that's what intuition is. A light beacon we have only to look for to see.

Mary, Gael's administrative assistant, had just gotten up from her desk to find me when I came around the corner. Her face looked scared; I could tell she was trying to keep her mouth from being open the way you do when you hear something bad. "Hey Karen, I was just coming to find you; let's sit down," she said as she took my arm and guided me to the mailroom beside her office. I knew Preston was okay, I would have heard an emergency call for the nurses or an ambulance. She continued, "Karen, your father has been rushed to the hospital and your mother needs you to come immediately."

I drove as fast as I could. Approaching the steep hill by the hospital, the radio played, "It's All Coming Back To Me Now," by Celine Dion. I felt melancholy, not panicked, which I thought was odd. Just then I saw my mother's car driving down the hill away from the hospital. I did a fast

U-turn all the while laying on the horn. My mother finally stopped and pulled over by a red brick office building. It was clear she was in shock. "Oh Karen, they took him to the wrong hospital. What am I going to do? The nurses wanted to know if someone could go with me, they said he didn't do well in the ambulance."

I put my arms around her and took her to my car, saying, "It's okay Mom, I'll drive you," In that moment I somehow knew my father was dead. My mother didn't know though.

Her mind couldn't take her there just yet, she was still too busy hoping and praying. On the way to Frederick Memorial Hospital my mother talked about the possibility of him already being rushed into the operating room and wondered what care he might need afterward.

I walked my mother in to see his body. White skin against white sheets against white walls—that's what I saw. Lifelessness everywhere. The wisdom was gone from his mind. The love gone from his heart. The space his presence took up in a room would forever leave a gaping void. My mother yelled, "No, Joe. No!" sobbing in my arms. I stood holding her, staring at his dead body in disbelief. I heard my father's voice telling me to be strong. Then I felt it: suddenly, knowingly, all the untidiness of the world emptied into this day. And so too, into me.

My father died of a heart attack on Thursday morning before the ambulance pulled out of the driveway. He died on his mountain that he loved so much. Why did he say he thought I would need the birds? Did he know? He was right. I did need them.

This man I knew so well and not at all, this man I feared and revered was dead. And I didn't know what to do.

The kids . . . my God, how would we tell the kids their beloved Pop was dead?

The bringer of milkshakes and surprise treats. Fixer of broken toys. Maker of furniture and lamps and toboggans. Inventor of handicapped toys. The reader of books. Teller of tales. The giver of a special brand of gram pop love had died. All of these infinite people in our children's minds was gone without a word.

In this moment their childhood was broken.

Miss Steph took Preston with her from school and arranged for the bus to drop his wheelchair off at my mother's house. Then afterward, picked

Samantha up at Myersville and took them out to dinner, telling them Sam and I had been delayed in Frederick with Gram.

It was dark when Miss Steph pulled into the driveway with the kids, eerily darker than it ever seemed before. We could see Samantha leaning forward looking at several strange cars that were parked in the gravel area beside the carport. She barely let the car come to a stop before she jumped out and ran around to Sam and I, asking why Miss Steph picked her up and whose cars were parked at Gram and Pop's house. She already possessed the intuition gift. Sam and Miss Steph entertained Preston while I struggled with words in my mouth I didn't want to use. With everything she'd witnessed with her brother, still, she had never heard dead, and now she would know the pain a nine-year-old shouldn't know. The exact minute she heard me say, "Poppy is dead," she burst from my arms running into the house and down to his workshop thinking the way a child thinks, *He must be here hiding; he has to be here. My poppy wouldn't leave me.*

Sam and Steph brought Preston in through the front door so he wouldn't see anyone before we could get him in the living room off the foyer where it was quiet. Sam went in to hug Samantha and explain that we needed to tell her brother.

We were about to be reminded that what we thought we knew needed to be relearned. We didn't think Preston would understand such an abstract concept; even his very bright sister was struggling. We wheeled him into the center of the room in front of the big picture window. One single candle was glowing in the glass against a black starless night sky. Miss Steph stood in the corner. Sam and I stood directly in front of his wheelchair. His perfectly still body and his listening eyes told us that like Samantha, he knew something was different.

I began, "Pres, Poppy got sick this morning, so sick that the ambulance came to take him to the hospital. He had a heart attack." His eyes started to look panicked, bouncing between Sam and I as though they were looking for a way out, but his body remained still, so still it startled me. Looking at him, a disheartening sadness attached itself to his entire being, unlike anything I'd seen in him before. All of a sudden I couldn't continue. Sam went on, "The doctors did everything they could, but they weren't able to save him. I don't really know how else to say this buddy. Your Poppy is dead. He is in heaven with God."

Just then a sad vibrational lament like I've never heard formed from his trembling pouted lips, "Woooh, woooh, woooh came out in painful, tear-filled streams—a mourner's declaration of love for his Pop.

"Well I'll be damned," Miss Steph said softly from the corner of the living room, like the words had involuntarily fallen out of her mouth. The three of us stared at each other in amazement without staring too long. Right before our eyes his heightened awareness was unwinding itself like a tightly coiled light beam in between the darkness of this day.

Once in awhile we were allowed absolute proof of our son's vast understanding. Our expectation for Preston's potential was limitless (within the confines of reality). It was also mysterious and vague. And as we came to learn from our silent teacher, reality was only what you could conceive of up till now based on past experiences. Perhaps, like when Emory died, my Dad's passing had opened another gateway of possibility. We now had confirmation of his capacity to understand abstract concepts. Another realization.

After coming home late Thursday night from my mother's, I had another dream. At five-thirty in the morning, drenched in tears, the vivid, stunning beauty of this dream woke me. Me, Sam, Samantha and Preston were flying over Ireland with my parents; literally flying like birds as though it was our natural state. My father was flying out in front.

We swooped down almost touching the ground several times, close enough to smell the earthy greenness of the grass, close enough to touch the rough texture of the stonework. We flew over what looked like the Cliffs of Moher, over castles surrounded by rolling fields so vividly green it took my breath away. Then, down the cobblestone street of a small town lined with brightly colored buildings and cottages with flowers in window boxes. Dad was smiling the way he smiled when he was full of himself, turning back to us, pointing out various landmarks. He was happy and safe.

Because of an angel visitation of some kind, I had been to Ireland. This was my first angel encounter. There would be more to follow. It was unexplainable in its clarity, but I suppose that's what angel encounters are meant to be.

Why don't we talk about dreams and coincidences and angel visitations like they are real instead of something imagined or improbable? It's exactly why I didn't tell most people, not even my mother; I didn't want any of it stolen from me by a dismissive reach. I wanted to enjoy it where it lived close in my heart, then store it in my memory place forever.

I was beginning to tap into my intuition in a way I'd never explored. Intuition helped me to see in the dark. The mysterious coincidences started becoming less mysterious and more like a visit from a sage of a friend. The kind of friend I could have an exchange of listening with. Another realization.

A month had passed since Dad died. I missed this simple and complicated man who valued family above everything else, always instructing us siblings to stick together and take care of one another. But now that he was gone, my oldest sister took aim. Though it was clear she'd always taken pleasure in causing upheaval. With our father's death came a new and foul vengefulness from a desperate soul.

Preston began as an extraordinarily beautiful baby boy. Then he became a sick baby, an extraordinarily sick baby. Somewhere between being born, fighting like hell to be in this world and now: he became a generic glob of the disabled, an SPH student, and a conglomeration of defects to some. As his parents we knew early on that he would be judged by his defects first by a feeble few. But what we never supposed is that a family member would judge him even more harshly.

Helen sat facing me on a dining chair she'd situated in between the kitchen and dining area while I prepared roasted butternut squash salad at the kitchen island. She looked at me as if I were the defendant and she the witness for the prosecution. That sums up our relationship. I was always on trial for something her mind perceived I had or hadn't done correctly. Over the years she had gone to great lengths letting me know what she would have done if she had a child like Preston. She made it her mission to prosecute him for living and me for loving him. Foolishly, I defended him, time after time, hoping some way or another she would get it. But I knew deep down in my Mothers Being that one day she would go too far.

As usual, she spoke arrogantly as if I needed special gear to reach her lofty level of intellect. I was chopping squash when I heard the question. I knew this was why she had come.

"So tell me Karen, what does Preston contribute to this world? He's nothing but a future tax burden for me. What right does he have to be here?" she demanded.

"What? How dare you question his right to be here! But just so you're clear I'll tell you. He deserves to be here because God put him here, because he brought him back from the brink of death for a reason. Because he exists. Period." I spoke passionately knowing all too well that trying to make my sister understand was like coercing a green leaf on a tree in the dead of winter.

I am at a loss for having such a sister, whereby love and understanding cannot penetrate her thick Irish skin. Because tolerance is a muscle she'd never used. She misunderstood me in every way, from conjecturing what I thought and condemning my mothering skills, down to critiquing my physical being. The entirety of me was so egregiously misinterpreted by my oldest sister. She did so purposely in order to fill some wicked plan in her head. She needed to make him fragile and weak. And me even weaker. If she had looked at me with something other than her narrow-minded lens, she would have seen that I was growing into myself. That my cells were ripening before her eyes. But she didn't look at the exactness of my being with any sort of wide-eyed wonder, only scorn and jealousy.

She didn't have a clue I was becoming who I was meant to be.

After trying one last time to explain Preston and to justify his right to be in this world to the stranger called my sister, I caught an almost evil, twisted smile in her eyes, and in that moment something in me stopped caring whether she understood or not. Maybe it was no longer having Dad whisper *family* in my ear.

What a sad vessel she appeared to be: sitting smugly in her chair unmoved by my words, long ago hollowed out of any ability to love without terms, now, casting stones at her disabled nephew. I watched her for the last time with any fondness or respect. She failed to understand how Preston demonstrated that whatever form we come in, whether or not we can walk or talk, whether or not we are dependent on others. As long as we have the wide breath of love that speaks from our soul into the soul of another: we matter.

"Hmm, well there you go on your disability tirade just as I anticipated," she said.

The harshness of her tone matched the stare in her eyes that watched for the slightest sign of duress, but all I could do was feel sorry for her. She was like a junkie looking for a quick high of injecting pain and hurt into others. I think, too, it was all the love she could neither input or output that scared her so.

"You really don't get it, do you?" I asked. "He's entitled to take up the same space in this world as you. You are no greater than him. He is no lesser than you. And your thinking so doesn't make it so. Now get the hell out of my house."

Naturally, Sam and I took our responsibility to nurture Preston's differently-abled soul seriously. Where there belonged an innate sense to discard anyone who refused to respect the space around his being. By Christmas I would disown her, then allow her back in our lives, then disown her again, then allow her back . . .

I'd made a promise to my dad, but now with him gone I struggled to keep it.

I think she would have loved for me to hate her, for some horrid, lowly emotion to disrupt my every day, but I don't; that would give her significance. And I can't—hate her, that is. In the muddy breath of words slung back and forth it is like arguing with a stranger, one full of hatred and emptied of love. I step away because I was never really close. It is easy and hard. Just one step. By law she is my sister—that is all.

Chapter 20

Defying Gravity

ONE SYNONYM FOR THE WORD ADVOCATE IS PLEADER, AND a synonym for plead is beg.

Preston had been ill with what we thought was the flu. By the second day though, his extreme lethargy was peculiar. His eyes looked distant and it was difficult to keep him awake for any length of time. Sam called his doctor while I sat the head of his bed up and lay beside him talking, trying to keep him awake. We suspected he might be in shunt failure. The device in his brain responsible for keeping him alive had been working efficiently for eleven years now. It was unusual; most kids we knew with shunts had already had multiple revisions or total shunt replacements.

What we knew about shunt failure was that it could happen slowly and safely over days, even weeks. It could also, depending how and where it was failing, happen quickly leading to coma or death.

It was two months to the day since dad died, making the possibility feel strangely ominous.

His doctor called in a STAT CT Scan order to a local imaging center. Preston's usually tight body was like a limp noodle as Sam put him in his wheelchair to leave. At the center we waited twenty minutes before his name was called. We kept talking to him trying to wake him up. He'd open his eyes for a mere second, then they'd close as though he wasn't controlling them.

A grandfatherly looking gentleman with a head full of white hair sat in the row of orange chairs across from us. Out of the corner of my eye I could feel him watching. Each time we attempted to wake Pres up the expression on his face read, "For God's sake, why don't they let that poor boy sleep?" He didn't know that our Rapid Shock Process had already kicked in. He couldn't know we were in our fight or flight mode. All he could see was a very sleepy boy and two parents who kept interrupting their son's sleep. Perception.

After waiting half an hour, Sam walked up to the front desk pleading with the receptionist to speak with the person in charge. A technician came out asking, "What can I help you with, sir?"

Sam began, "We believe our son is in shunt failure. Typically his tone is tight, his legs and arms active, but for the past hour we've watched him literally dissolve into his chair. He needs to get to Hopkins where his neurosurgeon is, immediately."

"I'm sorry you've been kept waiting. As soon as the radiologist gets back from lunch in about twenty minutes, he'll read your son's scan."

Sam pleaded again, this time more assertively, "My wife and I know what a bad CT Scan looks like, so please, I'm begging you: let us look at his scan. I don't think we have a minute to wait. We know our son. This is different from what we've seen in the past."

I sat holding Preston's limp hand that I could've picked up and dropped to his side without resistance, watching Sam plead with another human being to believe us, and thought: *what is known or seen to us as parents is not necessarily apparent to others.*

For all I knew they assumed he looked this lethargic all the time. Or we were overreacting or unrealistic parents. Perception.

As parents, advocates—we beg of others to believe and trust us. To not assume what is perceived by their unlearned eyes when beholding our child, but to turn to us with their eyes and ears. And listen very well.

The technician looked at Sam like he was crazy, then over at me for further verification, pausing for what seemed like an awkward forever, but eventually said she would talk to her boss. Seeing the skepticism in her eyes, the way it wore her body, made me angry. I was tired of explaining Preston. And now, irony of all ironies, we even had to prove he was as sick as we were saying. Was there anything we didn't have to prove when it came to our son? This aroused the little Irish redhead in my brain. She wanted to stomp her feet with both hands raised in the air, eyes bugged out wide, and ask, *"Do you think we want to be here? Do you think we're in a zippity-quick hurry to get to the hospital for the fun of it, lady?"* I sat politely looking at her as she examined me for any signs of instability thinking of how the Irish redhead had saved me once again. Minutes later we were escorted into a room to look at the scan while two technicians looked on.

I remember hearing Sam say, "His ventricles look like lakes." Preston was quietly slipping into another world; any trace of coloring was gone from his face, we had to pry his eyes open. Once again we pleaded with them to call 911. They did.

We were told they would have to transport him to the nearest hospital, triage him, then call another ambulance to get him to Hopkins. Sam called a private emergency transport, but was told that they were forty-five minutes out.

We looked at each other, our Rapid Shock Process in full operational mode, and without discussing it Sam said, "I need to make one more phone call to Preston's neurosurgeon at Hopkins, then we're going to take the scans and our son to Baltimore ourselves. We don't have time for anything else." We were no longer asking or pleading or begging. I was already turning his wheelchair around and heading out the door.

Crazy or not, we, his advocates, were leaving with our son.

Sam raced down I-70 to Baltimore clocking 95 miles an hour; pushing our van as fast as it would go. I sat in the back beside Preston, talking to him non-stop, lightly slapping his face and shaking his arms and legs attempting to keep him from slipping away. Halfway there we passed a state trooper with his speed radar gun pointed straight at us. For the first time in our lives we were happy to see one, begging the universe for him to pull us over and give us a police escort to the hospital. But he remained right where he was and watched us fly by.

At Hopkins we were immediately taken into triage. In our rush to get him into the ER we'd forgotten his bag. Sam ran back to the parking deck to get it.

Dr. Wright, a neurosurgery resident quickly examined Preston while IVs were being inserted and nurses called out a medical checklist to one another. He looked across the stretcher at me and said, "We will have a nurse tell you how he's doing after we get him up to the OR."

I was surprised that a resident was going to operate and told him, "I'm sure you're very good, but we'd rather wait for his regular neurosurgeon, Dr. Rosen."

The nurses had already started quickly pushing the stretcher into the hallway. Dr. Wright moved along with them like he was attached. He turned back towards me and said, "I have fifteen minutes to open up your son's head or he could die." Just then Sam reappeared. I frantically motioned for him to follow and we jumped in the service elevator with the OR team.

Knowing there was no time, in the elevator, we bent down once more saying our I Love Yous formed from magnificent smiles as white knuckles gripped the guardrails of his stretcher, then prayers as he disappeared past the double doors of the operating room. The shunt replacement surgery was his eighteenth surgery. Over the last several years his body and spirit had endured another hip osteotomy, bilateral adductor releases, biceps lengthening, pronator releases and several other surgeries. Most times, watching Preston rebound from a surgery or illness we marveled at his resiliency. Every once in a while, when I thought of the people who said he was too fragile, my head automatically started shaking from side to side. If only they knew. If one of their children had endured half of what our son had, what a better understanding they would possess.

I remember one Christmas after several close calls that year we bought *Flubber* themed toys and a sweatshirt, telling him he was as bouncy and resilient as a piece of flying rubber that defied gravity. I wish I could say it got easier with each successive surgery. It didn't. We simply got better at practicing sending him off with as much positive energy as we could muster. We learned to reserve our falling apart moments for the real deal. These little practices spared our hearts.

I don't know why we didn't fall apart. Maybe it was our Rapid Shock Process holding us up, or the fact that he was at Hopkins. Sitting in the waiting room Sam and I talked about the state trooper not pulling us over; all of a sudden with a fast, involuntary gasp, it dawned on me: the time it would have taken to stop and explain may have been one minute too long. Another realization.

Dr. Rosen walked toward our glass-paneled waiting room with such an extremely serious look on his face; we gulped down fear with each step. Noticing the worried look on our faces he hurriedly said, "He did great. He'll be just fine. I'm so sorry; I'm intrigued by this device that was in his head." A puff of exhaled relief and a sense of euphoria quickened within us.

He held up what looked like a miniature funnel then said, "I've never seen anything like this before. Do you know anything about this?"

Sam answered, "No, all I know is that his surgeon wasn't a pediatric neurosurgeon: Preston was his first."

"Well I'm going to hold on to this and do some research on it if you don't mind. There must be something to it for your guy to have gone this long without a full shunt replacement," he said smiling.

One of the added perks of brain surgery is that Preston got to rock a badass Mohawk upon returning to school, compliments of Pete's barbershop!

It was Saturday night and Samantha was at a friend's house. With Thanksgiving a week away we were in a celebratory mood. We decided to host new friends for dinner. The family room glowed with warmth from the flames in the fireplace. A bottle of cabernet sat breathing on the kitchen island beside a wooden serving board of pate and crackers. I made coq au vin and served it with mashed potatoes and Caesar salad. I fed Preston while Sam ate, then as soon as he was done we switched chairs and he finished feeding him. Our friends talked with Pres, telling him they couldn't believe how much he ate; as usual he proudly smiled and verbalized back to them. When I finished eating I got up to get milk for Sam to give to Pres, then went in to the family room to make sure his lounge chair was reclined properly. Sam lifted him out of his wheelchair onto the lounge and burped his g-tube while I put a movie on and covered his legs with a blanket.

Returning to the kitchen, Sam made cappuccinos for everyone while I served chocolate cake. Preston could be heard from the family room talking to his Winnie the Pooh movie. Diane commented, "Boy he loves Tigger doesn't he?"

"He sure does, he thinks he's funny." I answered.

"Karen, do you mind me asking about his verbalizations? Are there any that you understand? He sounds so happy; I just love it."

I told her, "No, not at all. We always appreciate it when people ask questions because they want to understand him better. He has a few words that he can consistently say; otherwise, CP jumbles his words and they just come out they way you hear them now. But, nevertheless he still enjoys using his voice to talk."

We sat down to find Rob smiling and staring at us with a pleasant but bewildered look. He leaned across the table, extending his left hand beside of his plate like he was reaching toward Sam. Then asked, "Can I share an observation with you guys?"

Sam and I looked at each other curiously and said, "Sure, observe away!"

"Well, I've never seen anything quite like it. Watching the two of you silently exchange places and duties was like watching a trapeze act. One partner swings hard and fast in preparation for catching the other. Then they both swing through the air together. Then as freely as a feather flies, one partner is released, landing gently on the safety net below. That's what I saw watching the two of you take care of Preston. There were no words exchanged, just bodies in motion, one helping the other. I've never been around parents of a child with such special needs as Preston. And I have to say I was quite moved by it. "

We both laughed at the thought of us looking anywhere near as effortless as a trapeze act. Sam replied, "Well I can definitely relate to the whole circus theme! I never thought about it that way, but I guess we do." Sam looked at me; putting his hand on my leg and gave it a squeeze. "We've been doing it together for a long time now. It's all we know. I promise you though, it's not always as calm as it was tonight."

It was true. We did approach everything inside and outside our home with a tactical mindset. With Preston, the threshold to our world was accessed through handicapped parking spaces wide enough to fit the girth of our vans large wheelchair lift. By a second wheelchair with tires rugged enough for bumpy nature trails he loved to go for walks on. Through our eyes inspecting sidewalks for uneven concrete slabs or other rough surfaces that made pushing his wheelchair difficult or dangerous. Through ramps that burgeoned from buildings declaring us welcome. When visiting friends with stairs too steep for his wheelchair; subconsciously our brains calculated the succession of tasks needed to get him into their house: carry lounge chair and egg crate foam cushion in house, set up folding lounge chair, lay foam cushion on it, bring in boom-box, CDs and bag, lower wheelchair, lift Preston from wheelchair, carry him up the stairs into the house, lay him in lounge chair, then lift his wheelchair up the stairs with the help of a friend.

I thought about Rob's observation of us. Initially I laughed because I'm terrified of heights and would never swing that high up, not even with Sam! But we did do a lot of things silently without needing to think them out loud anymore. We had our unspoken designated roles that separated, and then came together. Sam and I were partners holding on to each other for dear life; releasing one another when we had no strength—most of the time. Some days, it felt like the hands of the clock had been stripped bare, leaving us fully in a state of grace and patience, like when Rob and Diane came. Then there were the days that came at us hard, when it felt as if the minute and second hand crashed together every hour in a calamity of chaos. That's what they didn't see.

Everything we did, as givers of care to our son required us to move as a team or allow the other to rest. It was the only way we knew to survive so both our children would thrive. And on most days we were each other's safety net. This was our normal as we moved in tandem without words.

A synchronicity only we knew.

perception/per-sep-SH(e)n/ ~

a way of regarding, understanding, or interpreting something: a mental impression

Origin ~

"receiving collection," from Latin, seize, understand

And those who were seen dancing were thought to be insane by those who could not hear the music. Friedrich Nietzsche

perception ~

a judgment based on outward appearances

a surety of knowing

Chapter 21

Songs of the Spirit

OUR SPIRIT PROVIDES THE ALCHEMY THAT BRINGS OUR human bodies to life. It's the sunshine that wakes us up. It possesses no gender, form, creed or color. Every human being has a spirit. If you drew three rings to represent the trinity of spirit, soul and body, our spirit would be in the center, surrounded on one side by soul and the other by body.

Preston's imperfect vessel of a body that contained a damaged brain and war-torn muscles and bones was home to him, to his unflinching spirit. His spirit, or the idea of it, was always busy working through his soul and out of his body, electrifying his eyes and his smile, so people could see through to the truest part of him.

By all accounts, he was not an ordinary child with disabilities. I don't really know what makes a person or a day ordinary; I think it lies in our perception of ordinary or more than that, which hastens us to be in an iterated need for extra. Why do we often search for extra or more, when in reality they're overwhelmingly and ordinarily right in front of our eyes?

Preston was severely disabled, yet profoundly aware. He was differently-abled, which meant that he caused most of us to look at things differently. He visited death closely, not just as a baby, but several times throughout his life.

Because of those touches with death I think he brought back a differently-abled knowing, the kind that made his spirit so on fire and alive. The kind that only, almost-angels know.

With Preston there was no singleness of spirit. He came alive through so many venues. His bandana exemplified this—bright and multi-colored. His wheelchair tray bore stickers from moments with friends, his book bag slung over the back of his wheelchair with his name boldly embroidered on it showcased the spirit of individuality. It was clear watching him listen and joyfully react to music with the whole of his body and voice that it enlivened our spirits. His humor and the daily telling of a fresh joke were as necessary to him, and everyone around him, as breathing. Humor was the spoken language of his spirit.

Being non-verbal and non-ambulatory only meant that his multiplicity of life energy escaping at will through his soul and his body couldn't be denied. No matter what.

Routine was necessary for his spirit to thrive. It was his prayer, meditation and constant companion. And when something was missed his spirit withered or yelled. To have little control other than a scant few things meant that if any of those things were missed, then he must demand they never be missed again. We had to regularly remind ourselves, this was not bad behavior—it was an expression that a need had been missed, overlooked, or misunderstood.

One of the things our redheaded boy's spirit demanded was watching Wheel of Fortune and Jeopardy every night without fail. Once we tried recording the weeknight shows so he could watch them on the weekend too. But as soon as he realized he had already seen them he yelled.

Sam and I were taking Samantha for a non-disability night out and Stacie came over to hang out with Preston. They met while she was interning at Rock Creek and clicked instantly. Stacie said that the first time she saw him smile it melted her heart and his warm, inviting presence just sucked her in. Being the chick magnet that he was, Pres quickly became enamored with Stacie's pretty face and long blonde hair. When we arrived home Stacie couldn't wait to tell us what happened. She began, "It was time for Jeopardy and I was sitting beside his recliner. I don't remember the question, but I yelled out my answer—which was wrong. And before Alex Trebek even said my answer was wrong, Pres flat out looked at me and laughed. Like actually laughed as if he was thinking, 'Come on, is that really your answer?' Then within a few seconds the correct answer was announced. Again Pres looked at me, smiled and laughed."

Together, we laughed about his great sense of humor then it got quiet until finally Sam said what we were all thinking out loud: "I wonder just how many answers he has in that brain of his, you know."

In the months following my father's death, I'd been feeling frustrated that I wasn't remotely doing a good enough job meeting everyone's needs. I was stressed from family issues that hung relentlessly over my head, not giving me enough space to grieve properly. So much so that I ended up in the ER thinking I was having a heart attack. Yet it seemed like forever since I had cried. Really cried.

On my first birthday without my father the weather outside contrasted with my internal mood. The sun was bright for a late February day and the temperature smiled mildly at me. Sue was taking me out to my favorite spot in downtown Frederick for breakfast. The restaurant was long and narrow. Brick walls lined the length of it. We sipped coffee while I filled her in on the latest family drama. We ate heartily, ordering creamed chipped beef on biscuits. As usual, we talked about advocacy and inclusion then chatted about anything and everything.

We were in the middle of a conversation when his eyes touched mine, freezing me. Sue and I, the only other patrons, sat on the left side by the large picture window that afforded a view of the sidewalk and passersby. The restaurant's big glass front doors were on the right side.

He wore a light beige jacket, a plaid shirt, brown pants and a tweed hat. He was my father's age. With him were two petite women; one had short black hair like my mother, the other had long blonde hair like my sister Julie and was carrying a baby in an infant seat that appeared to be the same age as her baby.

This is unexplainable in the ordinary sense, but if you believe in angels it is extraordinarily explainable.

These beings that represented my mother, father, youngest sister and brand new niece all looked similar in size and age except for one. The being that represented my father looked exactly like him. Exactly. He dressed like him; he carried himself like him. And what he did convinced me beyond any reasonable doubt that I had had an angel visitation.

He looked over at me again as they walked to their table and tipped his hat the way my father used to, never once looking at Sue. They sat on the opposite side of the restaurant in the middle, positioning themselves facing the street so I could look straight at them. Sue and I didn't panic or startle, but remained in a state of peaceful awe. We stared at them the entire time in a way that would be considered extremely rude. Not once did they look up or acknowledge our elongated stares. They had come to be stared at. My sister Julie, who I was very close to, lived in Las Vegas. We talked every week, sometimes twice and were connected through the universe, both of us knowing when the other was in need. I'd been thinking of her more than usual, so it made perfect sense that a being representing her was present. I was worried I wasn't doing enough for my mom and was just plain worried about her since my father's death. He brought with him the two people in our family who were in the forefront of my mind.

Sue and I drank cup after cup, continuing to blatantly stare, discussing what this was and what it meant, marveling at the uncanny likeness to my dad and the remarkable representation of the three other family members. The more I looked at the face of my angel dad the more relaxed I felt. I remembered how my breath slowed to a meditative state. We were in our own world. A vaporous, warmhearted air had ensconced us. We were dreamily calm and still like we'd been given a mild dose of laughing gas. No one else came in—it was just the angels and us. We wondered if the others were actual angels since they were still very much alive or if you could craft an angel if you needed an extra. Not even then, when we laughed loudly, did they look. We contemplated going over and saying something to them, but something stopped us. Something told us to stay and be still. And for once we listened.

After almost an hour they got up to leave. The woman and younger daughter with the baby left, walking a direct line from their table out through the big glass front doors, never looking back for him. To this day, what happened next still makes me cry. My angel dad walked toward our table. I honestly thought he was going to say, *Hi babe,* in my father's voice, but he stopped just shy of us, never acknowledging Sue, and smiled at me like he did when he was proud of one of us. The way his eyes beamed happily as he tipped his hat to me once more left me motionless and speechless. It remains big and warm and blissful in my memory place where it will remain forever, waiting for me to abide with it. I had an angel visitation.

He came to help me to be still, to grieve, and to let me know I was doing a good job. And for whatever circumstance of reasons: to see him once more.

Immediately after they left, the restaurant filled with people like they'd been waiting outside in line to get in. After the angels left it was as though Sue and I came up for air, gasping, "What just happened? Why didn't we ask any questions? Why didn't we go talk to them? Why didn't I talk to my Dad? Why didn't I try to touch him to see if he was real?" We ordered more coffee. If you could get drunk from coffee we would have been seriously intoxicated. After another forty minutes of suppositions and translations we staggered out into the bright sunlight feeling its warmth on our faces, back into the reality of the known world.

Some things don't require explanations—they exist solely to bring us peace and joy. People almost always require an explanation. Especially people like me. But sometimes. Just sometimes we need to be still and know that, it is the explaining that diminishes them.

For months after my angel visitation I didn't tell anyone but Sam and Julie. I wanted to keep it just the way it was, before I heard others diminish it with their rational explanations. Some things, most things in truth, are more precious left in their purest state.

I hung out of the upstairs bedroom window yelling good-bye once more. Preston was sitting in his wheelchair on the brick sidewalk below outside the back door. "Mom loves you, pumpkin. Be good for Dad, okay."

He smiled, muttering back one more, "I uv oo." It was June and I could tell by the way the late morning air already felt heavy with heat, summer was here.

Pres wore light khaki shorts that made it hard to see where the shorts ended and his pale legs began. Maybe it was the strong summer sun, but from above, his royal blue and white striped polo shirt and bandana made his red hair look even brighter against the backdrop of green grass. Seeing the continuous motion of his arms and legs, I knew he was excited to be going on a road trip with his Dad.

Sam loaded his wheelchair into the van then looked up at me and blew me a kiss and said, "Take it easy. I mean it. Don't worry; he'll do just fine.

We'll call you girls as soon as we know." With my head propped lazily in one hand I leaned out a little more to look down at the pink pentas and yellow coreopsis that edged the black-eyed susans we had just planted, but not even my flowers could cheer me up. My spirit sagged as I watched the van pull out of the driveway, fighting back tears as they drove out of sight.

Sam and Preston were on their way to AI duPont without me. I was recovering from a hysterectomy and couldn't travel. Samantha was out with her Gram so I could rest, but instead I felt restless and alone. My emotions were all over the place from surgery, which only seemed to compound my mother's guilt. I sat on the edge of my bed indecisively fumbling through magazines while the fishnet canopy hovered above my head like a mantle of guilt. My arms stationed by my side ready to propel me out of bed away from my own restlessness. Having been warned by my doctor not to use stairs for a few days, three bedrooms had become my territory.

I walked down the hallway looping through the bedrooms like I was on some monotonous treasure hunt until my stomach cramped up, reminding I just had surgery.

Just then the phone rang. "Hey sissy. I don't know why, but I got this sudden urge to call you. Are you okay?" Julie asked. Most times, for either of us, all it took was hearing the other one's voice.

"I'm finnnne," I blubbered. "Of course you called me now; Sam and Pres just left for Delaware."

"I knew it. Something told me to call you," she added. My sister was my person in this vast universe, who, when I looked at the night sky, saw the same shining star.

"Sorry to be so emotional. It's just that this is the first time I haven't been at the hospital with Pres. I'm worried with how busy Sam is at work, that he has way too much on his plate. And I can't be there to help him, Julie. I feel so guilty. What if the baclofen trial doesn't work? What if it doesn't help his spasticity? What then? Countless more surgeries and pain. Whew. I don't know; I just feel everything right now. Every little, big, ridiculous, stupid thing; its all right there, large as life."

Julie's voice went deeper into a soft, warm tone, "I know, my sissy. I wish I were there to give you a great big hug. We would watch a movie in bed and relax with a glass of wine. I'd hug that little niecey of mine and we would laugh ourselves silly. Try not to worry, okay. I have a good feeling that shortly after they inject that drug into Preston's spine his body is going to respond very well, and he'll qualify for baclofen pump surgery. It's all going to work out."

Just then I heard Samantha's sweet voice outside yelling, "Mommy, we're back. Guess what we brought you?" and my heart exploded with joy. She ran into the bedroom holding flowers to make me feel better, then ran downstairs to help Gram heat up dinner. I leaned back against my pillows; closed my eyes and took a deep breath, telling myself—Sam was going to be okay. Preston was going to be okay. And no amount of worrying was going to change the outcome. I had my girl to snuggle with tonight, and tomorrow was going to be a great day. No matter what.

My sissy was right. Preston did qualify for baclofen pump surgery.

A device the size of a hockey puck was permanently implanted under his abdominal muscles and took up a good amount of space on the right side of his skinny stomach. A small catheter was inserted through a needle into the spinal fluid and threaded upward. The catheter was then tunneled underneath his skin to the abdomen and connected to the pump that's filled with baclofen and programmed by a computer to continuously release a particular dose into the fluid surrounding his spinal cord. He was now bionic.

Some days dealing with the unexplainable, unknown entities that rise up in the course of a day is hard. It deflates the spirit. Maybe our spirit and soul grow the second we accept the things we cannot change. The messy and real, the cracked and worn: all the perfectly imperfect things of life. I imagine then, if we celebrated a love for things, as they already exist; our spirits would soar to unknown heights and our insides, well, they would breathe without compromise. It's called peace. Another realization.

Chapter 22

Heartbeats

*E*VEN THOUGH WE HAD LONG AGO BECOME SETTLED IN OUR unsettled routine, Preston still disturbed the sedate and normal places in us. He roused them up like a fox listening for low frequencies as they hunt their prey. Typical thoughts on a typical day were Preston's prey. He set our thoughts on a different path, the one we began on when we burst from the realm that felt thick and unyielding, never to return again. And as well, he set our ears to be sensitive to certain spoken words.

One word in particular made the entirety of our beings clench with anger.

"Oh, don't be such a ree-tard," Linda told Susan who was sitting next to me.

Susan laughed, "Well I'm not trying to be I just don't understand what you're talking about."

I was sitting in the middle of several tables that'd been put together to create one long table, having lunch with a large group of ladies from church. But at that particular moment I might as well have been sitting alone. One word had isolated me from any sense of camaraderie. My heart pounded angrily when I heard her vile word; it pounded even more when I heard their collective laughter. They knew Preston. Saw him almost every Sunday, laughed at his jokes, were intimately aware of his many challenges. Yet no one budged when this word was spoken.

Not even me.

I hoped to God that in my isolated silence there remained a spark of wisdom. I sat looking down at my salad, randomly skipping a fork through it, feeling anything but wise. Instead I was ashamed: ashamed for not speaking up, ashamed of the ignorance of my friends. My Mothers Being shook her head at me in disgust. I know, I know; I know better, I silently told her. I had the opportunity to speak up and educate people, yet I chose silence, not what a good mom should do when hearing a word that mocked her son.

Today silence was easier. Not right or honorable. Just easier. One word had mummified me, traveled me miles back into myself while lighthearted laughter echoed off-key around me. I felt hot, a sudden rush of blood to skin, clarity of guilt. Mother's guilt.

Lisa looked down the table at me, tilting her head slightly as if to say, "You all right?" I smiled a half-baked smile back to her then started chatting absentmindedly. Right or wrong that's what I needed. I didn't feel like getting on another disability bandwagon when all I came to do was talk and laugh about typical things with my typical friends. Inside my head, the little Irish redhead's heart beat with outrage.

I've been told I'm sensitive. I've been told I'm guarded. Both are true. I don't think it's possible to be intuitive without being sensitive. And I don't think it's possible to hear with your heartbeat all that a parent of a child with disabilities hears without stealing a part of yourself away.

I'm reminded of several lines from a story I once wrote called "The Warrior and the Human," which was about the writing process, but in essence applies to how I've lived my life as the sensitive, vulnerable human and the guarded, strong warrior. The warrior has broad strokes written with a steady hand the human won't always attempt. The human's hand is shaky, written with a depth of emotion the warrior can't afford. Still, they walk hand in hand. One walking closely behind the other as if to receive strength or vulnerability through osmosis.

That's what we are as we walk through this one life of ours—humans in warrior form—warriors in human form. Here's the thing—both are real. Both are necessary. Another realization.

Sadly, I've heard the word ree-tard used by ten-year-olds and fifty-year-olds alike. Every time we laugh or remain silent after hearing someone use ree-tard as an insinuation of another's stupidity we give breath to this vulgar word. Even though the user of the word doesn't necessarily mean to target people with mental retardation by pushing them down to an inhumane level, they are—by creating a visual image aligned with indignity.

Allowing it is like wiring our brains to declare the worthlessness of a person with mental retardation. Not intentionally, but until we stop the acceptance of this disrespectful language: somewhat knowingly. Unless we stop the user of this word and embarrass them, casual disrespect towards people with mental retardation will never stop.

Oftentimes I felt woefully disconnected from my friends with typical children, not because they weren't lovely, understanding, considerate people, but because there was no way in hell they could understand. In the last few years alone, Preston had been in the hospital for seizure med toxicity four times, Kawasaki syndrome, a Dilantin toxicity that almost put him in a coma, and an impacted bowel three times.

Sometimes when asked how he was, Sam and I just smiled and said, "Fine." It was easier that way. And when we did I thought about the mom in the support group whose daughter died. I now understood exactly why she had come. For a cup of ordinary.

Once, when a friend expressed concern about her child's elevated fever, then quickly stopped, saying, "Oh God, I'm sorry. That was so insensitive of me. You just got Pres home from the hospital." I told her what I always said, "Look, it's all relative. If worrying about your child's fever is the worst health problem you've ever known, then that's a big problem in your world. I'm here for you, so tell me all about it."

There is no greater pain, lesser pain, greater troubles, lesser troubles in raising children. All parents worry about their children. We are all the keepers of our children's struggles and cheerleaders of their successes. What is different is the intensity and consistency at which parents that have children with disabilities or health problems experience them while still balancing all the other entities of life.

It is a cold night and we both need to tend the fire. I would compare it to having your hand directly over a fire or standing beside the fire feeling warm and cozy. We're both standing by the fire dreaming as the flames flicker and dance. Both of us see beauty. We're both hoping it doesn't get out of control. We're both hoping it burns bright for a long time. We're both hoping its sparks never hurt anyone.

The difference is that one has the freedom to stand there longer, considerably longer than the other. Standing calmly amongst fire takes a certain undoing.

With Samantha being an active middle-schooler, our long jaunt from on top of South Mountain to Middletown required more and more strategic planning. And with Preston's long skinny legs dangling dangerously between mine as I carried him upstairs, we began looking for land.

We built a handicapped accessible house in Middletown just five minutes from Samantha's school campus. Now I could easily run to pick her up as well as coordinate with other moms for carpools.

Mom left the mountain too; it wasn't the same without Dad. She moved to a senior living community closer to Glenn, whom she'd been dating for awhile. It was good to see her happily participating in life again.

Our new home would be a shelter from the inconvenience of disabilities. Our main living space was now on one floor. Hallways and rooms were open and wide enough for Preston's equipment and a hospital bed if necessary. Off of his room was an adapted tub with a lift that made bath time easier on our backs. An indoor pool complete with a hot tub for therapy was just off the hearth room's French doors. A guest suite over the garage was built for a future live in caregiver. Our house had wonderful energy. From the day we moved in it was like Preston knew it was built with all of his needs in mind. For a while he was happier, with a Zen-like calm, different than before.

With a media room in the basement, it was not only nice for watching movies on the big screen as a family, but with Preston's hypersensitive hearing it came in handy when Samantha wanted to have friends over. The boxes were all checked. Everyone was happy. We bought Pres an adjustable Tempurpedic bed both for comfort and convenience. I thought he liked his bed as much for the relaxation it afforded his wound, too-tight body as he did the privacy it gave him. Whenever we laid him in bed a blissfully peaceful look fell over his entire being. His eyes thanked you by the way they looked happily medicated and his body joyfully loosened. Bedtime—the only time he could be completely alone with his thoughts and his own body, something CP had robbed him of. I think that possibly the vulnerability of having his body bathed by someone else, being fed and dressed by someone else's hands. His body carried and positioned by another human being— always entrusting that this body of his would be respected and well cared for enabled Preston to teach the most beautiful lesson of love and humanity.

Lessons can't be just learned in the mind. Sometimes they need to begin in the heart. Sometimes they sit in your soul simmering until you're ready to learn them. The most profound lessons lie in the stillness in between your heartbeat. When you go quiet and all your senses light up at once, then you know. Children change the way in which you react to the world, forever altering the way in which you hear heartbeats.

Children teach us how to see the world through their innocent, curious eyes. Ultimately, how we see the world is really up to us. It's in how many entities we allow ourselves to collaborate with when looking at another human being. When seeing do we allow our hearts in, our compassion or empathy in? How often do we allow our grace, emotional intelligence, book read knowledge, or kindness to connect with our vision? How much light do we let in? I remember once years ago before our son was born, I saw a disabled man in his twenties severely limping along the sidewalk, his body rail thin, thinner than Preston's. His arms contorted like a twisted branch about to snap. His face struggled in time with his body as he dragged one leg that appeared to weigh a ton, laboriously behind the other.

I remember thinking to myself in what I thought was an empathetic manner, "That poor guy."

Years later, with a much older Preston and Samantha in the back of the van eagerly anticipating getting cupcakes from a bakery, crossing the Key Bridge into Georgetown, I saw another young man struggling along the sidewalk with a limp almost identical to the first man, this one slightly more severe. He was halfway across the bridge. Bright, multi-colored spots of kayakers on the Potomac River passed underneath him and ribbons of people, some turning to gawk, walked hurriedly around him. This time I excitedly shouted out, "Wow, look at him go guys!" We all watched him limp in such a severe manner his whole body plunged to the right with each step. But to our heartbeats, with Preston strapped into his wheelchair his head against the headrest, his upper torso strapped tight so he wouldn't fall forward, his hips buckled against the back of his chair so he couldn't kick his way out of it, it wasn't the dips we saw—it was every time his body rose after each plunge to take one more step that our eyes lighted on. The way we saw the whole of the world had immeasurably changed. Sam and I smiled softly, exchanging enlightened looks that said, "Yeah, who would've ever thought we'd get excited for a man limping across a bridge one day?"

I didn't say it to anyone that afternoon, but my memory place took me straight back to years ago, to the woman I used to be, to how two awkwardly burdensome-looking bodies now looked like the bodies of finely tuned athletes. For I knew what stamina it took to take just one step. I smiled inwardly. Preston had humbled me.

I felt wiser, happier. And even though our world was so uncertain the way it dipped and plunged like both of the young men's bodies. We had within us, still, the lightness we vowed never to forget.

lightness/lit-nes ~

lack of pressure or burdensomeness, an ease and gaiety of manner, style, speech, etc.

Origin ~

Middle English; Old English lihtness

lightness ~

embracing life's uncertainties

a bright attitude in dark times

a recognition and celebration of what is

a long breath

levity

a smile

looking up

Chapter 23

Two Worlds

SOME YEARS, NO MATTER THE SEASON, IT SEEMED TROU-
bles poured from the sky with no letup in sight but not this year; it
was a landmark year for our family. For the first time since his birth, Pres
had gone an entire eleven months without a surgery or illness. Months
passed defined only by seasons. It felt like a miracle being able to breathe
in autumn's brisk air and watch crisp leaves fall back into the earth without the unease a questionable day always brought. Winter's snowfall took
us outside: Pres in his hand-made sled with an adapted seat and Samantha in her custom toboggan, both made by Pop. Then inside, huddling by
the hearth room's big fireplace sipping hot chocolate with Pres lying in his
lounge chair watching the fire and Samantha sitting on the floor with Buck
by her side. Spring brought the emergence of the hundred some perennials
we transplanted from our flower garden on South Mountain, Samantha's
lacrosse games and the promise of Disney World in June. This must be what
it feels like to be a typical family, I thought.

Slowly, all of a sudden, something we never had control of had freed us.

This was to be our last summer vacation with Pres. With him being
almost as tall as me, bathing him in a small hotel tub was becoming difficult even for Sam and carting him around the beach or pool had become
exhausting for all of us. He didn't tolerate the heat well. In fact we usually
spent more time transporting him and his equipment to and fro then we
did lounging or playing in the water, then separating while one of us took
him back to the room to rest. And there was Samantha to consider.

A vacation is supposed to be a retreat from the ordinary—a rejuvenating, exciting getaway. Lately it was anything but that. Initially Sam and I felt extremely guilty for even considering such a thing. We supposed that we would always be able to blend our disability world into our vacation world. He had always done whatever we did. But now, none of us were having any fun. How could we not include Pres, but how could we not consider Samantha's needs and wants? She deserved a week of carefree. And so did we. After this vacation we would gather his village of givers of care, love and friendship, and together we would plan an amazingly fun time for him. In looking back, I suspect he fancied himself a bit of a rock star—with everyone out of the house he had all his women at his beck and call along with throwing mom's lists out the window.

We brought Miss Steph with us to Disney World. We supposed that Pres would be able to hang with us for the morning, but then due to the excitement and heat would be tired, and she would take him back to our condo to lie down and rest. Then in the evening we would all go back out for dinner and a little walk-about, then once again she would take him back to put him to bed. I imagine in Preston's head, this was probably similar to all the times doctors stood by his bedside proclaiming what would happen next as he lay there listening and laughing inside saying, "Oh yeah, well you're about to be punked!"

We left the first morning with spare clothes, diapers, g-tubes, meds, spare everything in his wheelchair bag. We bought yellow Disney ponchos for everyone, even for his wheelchair, ready for the sudden bursts of rain that Florida brings. Our pit crew was ready.

First lesson: seeing Disney World with a child in a wheelchair is basically like Disney on crack! Their personnel are trained to spot a wheelchair quicker than you can say Mickey Mouse. As we approached a ride or show, a cast member would take us to the front of the line or seat us in the front row. We heard Samantha repeatedly saying, "Thanks mister!" to her brother. He smiled back or said, "Uh huh!" His arms and legs were in constant happy motion that said, "Off to the next adventure." For once being in a wheelchair meant we were boundless instead of bound.

Second lesson: who says you only go around once? After surviving stares from the hundred some sweaty people waiting in line as a cast member opened the entrance gate and shouted, "Come right this way please."

We boarded the Kali River Rapids ride. Sam, Preston and Miss Steph sat on one side while Samantha and I were told to sit across from them for balance. We had the raft all to ourselves. When we came to the dock to get off, Preston and Samantha were still laughing. The cast member looked at the kids and asked, "Do you want to go around again?"

We shouted, "Yes!" But because most of the weight was on Sam's side, when we got to the waterfall where they got a little wet the first time; the three of them got completely soaked from head to toe. Steph and Sam had to buy new shirts. Luckily we had a change of clothes for Pres.

Third lesson: Never, and I mean never, suppose what Preston is capable of. The first day we thought he was just wound up, but would eventually crash. Nope. Up until the next to last day our redheaded boy hung with us the entire time. Towards the middle of the week Miss Steph remarked, "You call this a vacation? I'm worn out."

She looked at Pres and asked, "Come on can you give me a little break here, beanhead?" He just laughed.

Fourth lesson: Don't put a child with severe physical disabilities on a roller coaster. Not even one that appears calm. It's called Big Thunder Mountain for a reason! Once again Sam and Miss Steph sat with Pres in between them while Samantha and I were seated in the car in front of them. As our train began to move, quickly picking up speed seeing the steep hill in front of us, all I remember thinking is, *he's going to break his neck*. We survived—the adults that is. The kids loved it!

Fifth lesson: Remember all the rules of the real world, then forget them. You're in Disney World.

Like all his other instructional aides, Ann was at first taken aback by Preston's overwhelming disabilities and list of medical notes and problems. She felt scared and intimidated. But she said it was his crooked, joyful smile that won her over. She didn't consider herself a patient woman, and yet, because of a redheaded boy, she became one. Once again we happily welcomed another human being into our village.

Ann and Preston bonded immediately. Once when visiting the school I found them in the gym roller skating. Yes, roller skating. Ann had asked the physical education teacher to help Preston to skate. He was strapped into his walker, strapped into his skates, and while music played Ann and Pres laughed and carried on making loops around the gym. She was no longer scared. One year for Halloween they dressed as Pat and Vanna. Preston looked so handsome in his suit and tie and Ann went all out wearing a long blonde wig with a fancy royal blue dress. Sam and I crafted a Wheel of Fortune spinning wheel behind his headrest so everyone could see it. We made a word puzzle for his tray, then programmed his Tech Talk with phrases such as, 'Would you like to buy a vowel?' They had a blast going around the school playing Wheel of Fortune with staff and students alike. With graduation in the near future it became even more important to get him out in the community as much as possible, so together, Ann and Pres were greeters at a senior living facility.

Preston's after school mentor program was on Thursday. I loved Thursdays, yet I felt guilty for loving them the way I did. I picked him up once in all the years he attended. Walking into the gym I couldn't see him for the large cluster of high school cheerleaders that encircled him. As I reached the group of uniforms and pompoms I said, "Hi girls, I'm Preston's mom. Well hello, mister!"

His expression went flat as soon as he saw me. He immediately turned his head away as if to say, *Mom, can't you see I'm busy here.* When I asked if he was ready to go home he turned his head away again. I laughed to myself and told him, "Okay. You can have five more minutes, then we need to go." I stood in the back of the gym waiting and watching our suave, redheaded guy's energy hold the attention of an entire cheerleading squad with smiles, laughter and his joke of the day.

Other than that day, Sam gifted me an afternoon off and always picked him up, then often took him for a ride, ran an errand or went back to the office. For me that meant no getting him off the bus, feeding him a snack, giving him a drink, changing his diapers, massaging his cold legs back to warm, no deciding what after school movie or music he wanted. On bad Preston days it meant no listening to screaming or running back and forth from the kitchen to family room ten thousand times because he had a headache or muscle spasms or a seizure or cantankerousness. Thursdays meant girl time with Samantha. Today I would pick her up after lacrosse practice and treat her to Starbucks.

But every now and then this duality felt like being on the wrong end of a lopsided see-saw that would never right itself. At times I felt guilty for wanting a break from disabilities, guilty for wanting time alone with Samantha, guilty for letting Sam pick him up.

For Sam and I, sometimes traversing two worlds felt like a long, tiresome flight. But that night, as I lay in bed beside Sam hearing what fun he and Pres had and thinking of how Samantha and I laughed together at Starbucks, I knew I had done what felt right for me, was what I was capable of at that moment. And it was okay if once a week I wasn't capable of being excited about disabilities. Sam kissed me goodnight and thanked me for making his favorite Chicken Divan casserole. Then said, "I'm glad you girls had as much fun as us guys. Goodnight my dear."

Life is such a precarious balance. Some days you need the warrior and other days you need the human, I thought. I smiled, rolling over into Sam's arms and heard my Mothers Being gently whisper: *the human won today, you know. After all, the warrior is lying beside you.*

I needed to find a way to somehow unburden myself from what is, I'm guessing, ingrained into every female at birth—*guilt*. Guilt for doing too much. Guilt for not doing enough. Guilt, guilt, guilt for everything and anything. For appearing too together. For appearing too disorganized. This unhealthy dose of mother freaking guilt needed to leave my body once and for all.

It was time to retreat to my breathing space when the day was tired and my soul felt bound in its weariness, when I didn't understand why Preston was sick or in need of another surgery after he just recovered from one.

When worry or guilt wouldn't release their hold, I retreated upstairs to my meditation space. Our guest suite over the garage had become a spiritual place for me. Like my own personal Irish wishing tree where ribbons of need and hope hung in the breeze—that was my heart. Even though I didn't get away, I traveled very far in my mind.

Just as I could no more walk around constantly open allowing every hurt in, I couldn't walk around constantly closed either. Our bodies are such wonderful teachers of how to lead a well-lived life.

Hearts pumping open and shut, open and shut, always moving, never dormant. Warm blood coursing through veins always moving, never dormant. Even our bones have hinges that allow the hardness of their very being to bend. And the bones that cannot bend, serve to protect that which is soft. I would listen to this masterfully made body—opening, closing, bending and protecting. I practiced my ritual whenever my body and mind felt incapable of doing what it was made to do. It was in this space not far away from my reality, yet so far removed in my mind, I expanded the space inside my being.

I questioned. I thought. I got angry with God and the universe.

I forgave. Myself included.

I breathed in my yoga breath, figuratively throwing worries and stress out the window.

Standing in my usual spot upstairs, close enough to touch the window that allowed a bird's eye view of South Mountain, where I grew up and where Sam and I grew into parents. This precise spot is where I always stood watching shape-shifting clouds loosen into imaginary animals like a free rolling circus before me.

I stood looking at the vastness of the universe and the mountain with great incredulity. *What was it about the mountain that made me come alive and rest at will*, I wondered.

It knew such pain and joy and never told a soul.

Watching its separate personalities emerge was a lesson in living well. Its cold aloofness turned inward as it stripped bare to the bone of winter to rest like a lone wolf at its crest. Then it danced its way to the most resplendent spring green to enthusiastically present its fertile blooms with outstretched branches like open hands. The stillness of summer's heat showed off its resiliency to endure a quiet pain and still stand tall. Then as if flaunting its abundant fortitude, knowing what had been and was to be, it boldly emblazoned itself with all the colors of a sunrise and sunset, letting go of each leaf when it could no longer hold on.

Holding on and letting go, what a show off our mountain was.

I watched its display of grace season after season and thought: *If the mountain can do it then so can I*. Breathing in and out I watched in awe each season's philosophy of beauty. This leafy and bare boned creature in all its diverse personas released the knots of worry from my gut and ceased the spinning top of my brain if just for a bit.

How wise the mountain to give up what it held, I thought. And in doing so revealed its true, natural gifts. I breathed in one more long breath, then turned toward the hallway and walked back down the stairs into the heart of our home.

Replenished by the mountain.

Today I fell a step behind. Breathed. And discovered how far I can go.

Graduation was upon us. We had attended many graduation ceremonies over the years, watching the graduate's parent's smile through tears. And then joined them in celebrating the completion of high school or college, a moving on to a higher level of education, or being gainfully employed. A new destination loomed brightly on the horizon for the graduate.

Life's milestone moments have a way of reminding you of everything you have and everything you have not. For the first time in our lives we hit a wall.

It was hard and unyielding. It hurt. As proud as we were of Preston and all his hard work, deep inside our parental souls we realized that there was really nothing that he was graduating to. We heard a loud, harsh horn blowing through our hearts that yelled *Preston will never go to college, he will never be gainfully employed at a job he loves, he will never marry and have a family.* While we knew it all along and had been working closely with the school in preparing his transition plan, we were the ones that were having trouble transitioning.

Life for an adult with severe disabilities in the real world looks drastically altered. After leaving the protection of the public school system there are no more entitlement services. His rights to a fair and appropriate public education were gone. Vital special education services he relied on like speech, physical and occupational therapy would soon be gone.

I talked to Gael about not attending graduation, "What was the point?" I wondered. She asked me to trust her and to please come—for Preston. Our graduate wore a red cap and gown. Our families came and watched. We were now the parents smiling through tears. The ceremony was beautiful, meaningful and well thought out. After the ceremony, students and parents convened to the cafeteria for food and refreshments, then Miss Steph, Preston's aides, family and friends danced the night away with him. He was joyful. And because of him so were we. The lightness we vowed never to forget was so much stronger than our weaknesses. Another realization.

Sam and I looked at two different day programs. The first was our worst nightmare come to life. All I remember is the smell of urine. I couldn't comprehend any words that were being spoken because urine occupied the entirety of my brain. In reality it didn't matter what they said. I could see by Sam's blank expression that he too wanted to run. I remember us getting in the car, closing both doors and crying. Everything we feared for Preston was here and now, scarier than we imagined.

The second program, Star Ventures Day program in Hagerstown, Maryland was wonderful. Two separate buildings, one behind the other, sat on a hill overlooking farm fields and houses that were dotted in between them. Already we had a good feeling. All I could think of when we walked in was: *it doesn't smell like urine. Thank God.* I laughed at the ridiculousness of being thankful for such a thing. Walking down the hall we saw a young man with Down syndrome sitting in a rocker. At first I thought he was all alone and pictured Pres being left alone too and thought, *oh no not again*, but he quickly started talking to a girl in a room to his left. What I noticed most was how engaged the girl was in talking with him, how happy he was, and how ordinary it seemed for them both to be talking together.

Though it was a long bus ride, Preston adapted well. The staff was wonderful and kind. They had a pool, greenhouse and a therapeutic farm. We had some transition issues, but eventually we all got to know one another.

They agreed with our plan to continue developing social and communication skills by being a part of the community and once a week, weather permitting, he was a greeter at Frantz's Produce stand and in colder weather occasionally worked as a greeter at a local nursing home.

It was three days before Thanksgiving and Pres was experiencing stomach problems again. Over the past twenty-three years his various abdominal surgeries had taken a toll on the healthy function of his stomach, at times it seemed like his baclofen pump wasn't as effective as it once was either. I worried that this would be the new constant as he grew older.

Approaching Fells Point we saw a homeless man who had been shot, lying on the sidewalk. We were stopped at the scene of the crime. Officers quickly gathered around him while police cars continued to arrive from all directions. Pres immediately yelled at the sound of loud sirens that filled every vacant space in our van. We stood beside Preston who laid on a gurney in the hallway outside the emergency room, waiting to be taken to an exam room. We knew how incredibly uncomfortable he was, the way his eyes begged us to be relieved of pain, his deep-voiced moans, and his visibly distended stomach. Shortly after we arrived the shooting victim was put in the exam room next to ours. He kept yelling obscenities from the other side of the thin curtain. He smelled of liquor and worn, stained clothes, that for weeks he had carried on his body.

Through the bottom of the curtain we could see remnants of shoes that walked him through city alleyways only homeless people know. A police officer stood outside all but attached to the thin curtain. Already on edge from the pain, Pres teared up with each successively louder outburst. This was a typical day in the ER at Hopkins, but for us, in all our forty-some hospital stays, it was a first.

And as luck would have it, we drew the short straw with the resident assigned to Pres, too. He wasn't yet skilled enough to listen to or look at the patient, or even to us—the parental advocates. Having experienced this several times before we attempted to tell him what worked best. He was insisting on putting in an NG tube, which Pres hated and fought, rather than using his G-tube to begin treatment. After Sam tried unsuccessfully one last time to reason with him, he went to the head nurse and asked to speak with the doctor in charge. I don't remember his name; I just remember him standing at the opening of the privacy curtain wearing scrubs and holding a brightly printed surgery cap in his hand. He looked tired but present and concerned. He walked in, introduced himself, then immediately stood by Pres and said, "Hi young man."

Pres almost smiled and faintly said, "Oh." Pres looked scared and pouted several times during the exam from the yelling on the other side of the curtain. The doctor excused himself, saying he'd be right back. The loud homeless man was moved away.

He brought the resident back in to meet Pres and, concurring with our treatment plan, ordered him to start it immediately, explaining why it was best.

He now wore a long white coat and had an air of authority about him mixed with an immense sense of humanity. When we spoke, his eyes studied us in a way that said *I care*. With all the doctors we'd met over the years he was up there with an elite handful of others.

We had been in the ER for five hours due to the scarcity of rooms. It had been a particularly eventful, noisy night in Baltimore's ER. Preston was exhausted; every time he heard a loud noise he startled and woke up. Around ten pm we were taken to our room. Wheeling down hallways, the directional signs we were accustomed to seeing weren't making any sense. We looked at each other confused, thinking perhaps our attendant was lost. After almost ten minutes more of walking, we were taken into another wing of the hospital we didn't know existed. Double doors, different from any we had seen in a hospital, opened. On the wall to our right was a large, gold engraved plaque honoring the person it was named after. Our benevolent doctor had seen to it that we were upgraded to a high-end luxury suite, a private room far removed from the chaos of the hospital.

We talked to Samantha several times, filling her in on her brother's condition. She was staying with her friend, Sara, and was worried that Pres wouldn't be home for Thanksgiving. So were we. Hanging up the phone, I thought about the many times he'd been sick so close to a holiday and wondered how many more were ahead.

The next morning our doctor came in to share Preston's test results, saying, "If we don't see a change by the end of the day we're going to have to operate." We thanked him for the room; he smiled quickly, not acknowledging what he heard and quietly said, "For what?" Preston gave him a huge smile. As usual, our redheaded boy listened to the doctor's proclamation and thought to himself: *we'll just see about that, now won't we?* The next morning it was determined that Pres didn't require surgery. The Preston Percentile prevailed once again.

We made it home the day before Thanksgiving. Our doctor came in to discharge us. He stood as close to Pres as he could. His whole body went still and intent; the doctor had his listening eyes. He told him, "I want to tell you what an honor it's been to meet you Preston." Pres smiled then told him a joke. We all laughed.

He then looked at us and said the same thing, adding, "It's a war zone out there. With what I see on a daily basis, meeting your family has given me hope." I believe attitude is everything and with all your challenges, you act as if you have everything."

"Well, we do. We have two great kids, and Karen and I love each other very much," Sam responded. We couldn't wait to get home to Samantha and be a whole family once again.

Over the next year Preston struggled with stomach problems and muscle spasms. Month by month we became more concerned. Yet they couldn't find anything clinically wrong. I found myself studying the look on his face. In his eyes. Wondering what we were missing.

One of the last notes that came home on Preston's communication sheet said: watched *The Grinch* and *Polar Express*. Preston was very pleasant this morning. He did great. No need to worry.

Unbeknownst to us—we were about to enter another world.

memory/mem(e)-re/ ~

the act or fact of retaining and recalling impressions, facts, etc., or the cognitive recognition of a place and time

Origin ~

Middle English: from Old French memorie, from Latin memoria, from memor 'mindful remembering.'

place/pleys ~

a particular portion of space whether of definite or indefinite extent

Origin ~

Middle English, from Anglo-French, open space, from Latin platea broad street, from Greek plateia (hodos), from feminine of platys broad.

memory place ~

dreaming fully awake.

a remembrance that conjures up smells, tastes, sights and sounds as if you were a time traveler.

a three-dimensional soul visit to the past.

Chapter 24

Green Balloons

The Prelude

Michelle's mother, Shirley, died in July. Four more would follow, one a month like a grim leaching of souls from our life. The last death was my cousin, Rosemary who felt more like an older sister.

It was Saturday morning. The house was calm and quiet with Pres and Samantha sleeping in, still recovering from our Thanksgiving festivities two days before. I sat in bed sipping my cappuccino watching *Rocky*, trying to drown out the voice in my head. I think Rosemary was trying to communicate with me. She'd been battling breast cancer for almost eleven years. From the second I awoke all I could hear was *I'm dying, I'm dying*. I attempted to rationalize it away thinking that with all the deaths lately; my mind was stuck in a bad place. I turned up the volume on the TV. The phone rang. Rosemary's oldest daughter, Romy, was on the other end. "Hi Aunt Karen." I heard her tears. "I have very bad news about my mom." Silence. More tears. "She is dying." Tears. "I'm afraid she doesn't have much time left. Do you think you can get here quickly?" she asked.

It was about a four-hour drive to their house in New Jersey. "I'm so sorry, sweetheart. We'll do our best. We have to get Pres ready, too, 'cause we don't have anyone to watch him today, so keep me posted. I love you. Give your mom a kiss for me." Tears. "And tell her how much I love her."

The phone rang. Rosemary was dead.

A feeling of discontent had attached itself to my being and no matter how hard I tried I couldn't release it. Nor did I understand it. Preston had a different look in his eyes that troubled me greatly. His laughter sounded flat, his smiles forced. This feeling sat deeply in my heart and wouldn't leave. It felt different from the ordinary worries that we'd become used to. And as hard as I tried, lately, I couldn't shake it from my soul. Still. I had no conscious idea. I assumed this would be the next stage of our life with him.

Things happen fast when you're in them. Then looking back you see a slow progression. And you know.

After Shirley's funeral we gathered at Michelle's house. She and I were sitting on the front lawn doing what people do after funerals, benignly talking about landscaping, when she stopped by. Pearl was a friend of a friend. I'd never met her before. She was tan, had long blonde hair and an extremely outgoing personality. Preston was laying in his lounge chair in the front living room listening to music with Brandon, the son of one of Michelle's friends. She knelt down beside him to say hello.

It was in that moment she seemed to have forgotten that Michelle and I were still standing there. The look of curious fascination on her face puzzled me.

She stopped looking into Preston's eyes long enough to tell me she had worked as a special ed aide. I took in a long silent breath of "ahh" and assumed that was the connection.

Pearl looked up at me again, her eyes barely leaving Prestons' and asked, "Do you mind if I hang out with this guy for a little while?" I couldn't help but notice how mesmerized Pres was with her too. It had been a long, hot, exhausting summer day helping my friend say good-bye to her mother, and he had a penchant for blondes, so I answered, "Sure, have fun. We're going to have a glass of wine and sit on the back deck. Dad's in the family room, just yell if you need something, ok mister."

He managed a quiet, "uh huh," but kept his eyes on Pearl.

After thirty minutes passed with no Pearl, Michelle and I snuck into the house to check on them. This is the moment I slipped into another realm. When I stopped fully being me, like when I had the angel visitation. We tiptoed into the kitchen then through the dark dining room adjacent to the living room. They were looking and looking and looking into each other's eyes. Preston's eyes were locked into Pearl's in a way that made me go still.

I'd never seen him look at anyone the way he looked at Pearl. My body froze looking at his that was trance-like still. I wondered just who was in control. Michelle and I looked at each other, our faces all crumpled with confusion. Just then, without taking her eyes from his, Pearl waved us away with her right hand acting as if we were interrupting a highly personal conversation.

Here's what I know: the human being, mom, woman, who is fully me wouldn't have stood for being waved away from my son. Not ever. She would have been too curious, too protective. She wouldn't hesitate for one second to see what the hell was going on.

But I wasn't there.

Instead, we went back to the deck to wait, attempting to figure out exactly what was going on between the two of them. Both of us shocked at how Pres hadn't budged his eyes from hers. Shortly afterwards, Pearl joined us, sitting on the other side of the round cast iron table across from me.

What happened next is unexplainable in the ordinary sense, but if you believe in the supernatural and psychic abilities, it is extraordinarily explainable.

She began talking fast and impatiently, like there was too much in her head and she didn't want to forget anything. "First I need to tell you that I'm a Wiccan." Then it began quickly and without control.

She looked across the table at me with tears in her eyes, in a loud emotional voice saying, "Your son is fucking amazing! I've never had this many messages from one person! Fuck!" Hands waving in the air. "I have so much to tell you. He's lived a thousand lives." Michelle and I looked at each other in astonishment.

I stopped her, asking, "Wait, why do you say that?

"Because your son told me." Then ramblings about knights and horses in medieval times and him saving someone . . .

I then explained, "I wrote a poem for his 21st birthday called Mirror of your Soul, whose first few lines are: The mirror of your soul is reflected in my eyes. I see a gentle spirit who has lived a thousand lives." Smiling at me she said, "I know."

Then continued, *He was sent here to right the wrongs done to you as a child. ~You are a different person now. ~He came so your life wouldn't be in vain. ~He wants me to tell you he's never in pain, he's frustrated. ~He came to change your perfect world. ~He chose you. ~Write his words. ~There's a bald man he pretends to like but doesn't. ~He doesn't like blue room it scares him. Fuck. I can't believe all the messages! ~ There's a pink room with sliding door— people don't think he can see them, but he can. Lots of rambling and—Fuck. Too many messages.*

Now she was fully crying the way a person cries when they're overcome with emotion. Her hands waved frantically by her head as she said, *Fuck. I can't tell you that. He doesn't want me to tell you certain things.*

"Please tell me everything he told you," I begged.

With a sorrowful, empathetic look she answered, "I'm sorry, I can't."

Some things she told us made perfect sense while others made me want to ask more questions. My mind was now thinking on an unthinkable wavelength. There was a pause in the heavy summer air. A single candle placed in the center of the table gave light to our faces against the backdrop of a starry night. I could hear a neighbor's dog, several houses away, barking in the distance. That's what I remember before the unexplainable happened.

"His time on earth is almost up, isn't it?" I heard myself ask Pearl.

I had entered another world, one where I had one foot here and the other *there.* My present state of mind existed only there, like I had been physically and mentally transported to a place of knowing beyond anything I could imagine. *Had I read her mind?* I wondered. My comprehension of Sam and Preston just on the other side of the sliding patio doors in the family room slipped away as if they were thousands of miles from me. It was getting late and at one point, seeing we were in an intense conversation he didn't understand, with a half annoyed, half bewildered look, Sam tapped on the sliding glass door motioning that we needed to leave. I barely acknowledged him and like Pearl, waved him away like a mad detective in hot pursuit of an unsolved mystery.

I had no control of the questions and thoughts coming from some mysterious place inside me. I was a transmitter—a puppet whose words were sitting on a string that was being pulled out of my mouth by some other force larger than any of us. I felt like I was in a trance yet fully present, but in what realm I wasn't sure. And in that moment I didn't care. If Michelle hadn't been with me I don't know if I would have truly believed everything that was said.

The raw emotion exchanged between Pearl and I was unexplainable. I could see heartbreak in her eyes and it scared the hell out of me. It was like one of those scary movies where you wonder why someone is walking around in their dark house after hearing a strange noise.

That's where I was, scared as hell, but instead of darkness I pursued a mysterious tunnel where Pearl sat at the other end holding answers to unlocking the mystery of our son we'd been trying to unlock for years. Mentally, I kept walking towards Pearl. Looking intently into her eyes, pleading with mine, I asked once more, "His time on earth is almost up isn't it?" There it was again, the heartbreak in her eyes.

It was clear that as a mom she wanted to tell me so much more, but she'd promised Pres she wouldn't. Instead, she extended her hand across the table to mine, telling me with her eyes what her mouth couldn't say, and with a tight hold said, "Tell his story Karen. Write his words." I fell back into my chair, mouth open, fully believing what I couldn't believe. And I knew. There was no way she could have known that for the past several years I'd been toying with a book. Except for Preston telling her. Another realization.

It was the end of Samantha's first semester at University of Maryland. I remember Sam and I watching her car pull away, wondering how we would recover from the sadness we felt walking back into the house—floored by its quiet, empty feeling. But I'm sure it's what most parents' experience. As the initial months of college passed, our family slipped into a comfortable new routine once again. Preston continued to participate in his day program and loved being a greeter at various places in the community. Now the Christmas break was almost here.

We were so excited to have everyone home for more than a fleeting weekend. I'd decked the halls with more than my usual ridiculous adornment of fresh greenery and multiple trees. It was Saturday night; Sam had another business Christmas party to attend. The three of us had attended one the night before, but Pres was worn out and cranky, so he and I stayed home. It seemed that nothing I did made him happy for any length of time. I snuggled in the huge lovesac beanbag chair with him, massaging his cold legs, put several holiday movies on, but nothing worked. The only time he perked up and smiled was when I told him Samantha would be home next

Friday. Then after a few minutes of happiness, out of the blue, he just looked at me and yelled like I had done something horrible to piss him off.

It was nine-thirty. I asked him if he wanted to go to bed. He answered, "uh huh," in a flat, dull tone. I carried him up the basement stairs and put him in his wheelchair waiting at the top of the stairs, then took him back to his room.

What happened next is unexplainable in the ordinary sense, but if you believe in God, the Divine, Angels, or otherworldly beings, then it is extraordinarily explainable.

The one precious thing Preston didn't have, the thing he would never have no matter how hard we tried; was freedom. Unencumbered freedom to do with what and how he wanted—without anyone translating it for him. That I could never give him. Until now.

His body flattened into the foam like it didn't want to leave, the undefinable look on his face startlingly different from the thousands of nights we had laid him in bed. So removed from this world. So knowingly mysterious it caused me to speak words that would become silenced in my soul as soon as I left the room. To this day my mind has conjectured all possible scenarios. Had he communicated to Pearl so easily because he knew instantly of her special powers? Did he have special powers? Did he want her to tell me so I would ask her my unbelievable question? So my subconscious mind could begin to process what the universe had been hinting at so that ultimately I would have slipped away from myself enough to ask the unthinkable question to our son. I don't remember thinking whether to say it or not, beforehand. It was as if the look on his face hypnotized me into an altered knowing, and with the snap of a finger out came my question.

"Do you need permission to go? If you need to go don't worry, we will be okay. I promise."

Preston turned toward me with a slow purposefulness completely uncharacteristic for him. We locked eyes. His eyes glowed with certainty and knowing: incomparable to anything familiar. Then he said slowly, yet so intently as he held his gaze, "Uh HUH, uh HUH." His emphasis on "HUH" wasn't his usual excited tone. It was lower. It was almost like he was telling me how tired he was, like the tone itself was letting me know he was ready to leave. And the smile that followed: fully formed, but purposely softened around its edges, though inadequately described, was one of transcendent peace.

That mystical night his face wore the sleep of the Angels. Like a beacon of light had called me to see what I had never before seen, to say what I'd never thought of saying. I had been whispered into an ethereal world. When I left his room my conscious mind had no afterthought. No panic. No freak out moment. Not one, "Oh my God, what did I just say" moment. No motherly remorse. Only the peace of gently slipping back into the real world the way a leaf slips into water, gliding onward as if it had been there all along. God, the angels, the universe, and my Mothers Being had administered another layer, soft and mysterious as heaven itself.

Samantha arrived home to a completely decorated house brimming with holiday glee and a Friday night feast of lasagna, Caesar salad and chocolate fudge. Meanwhile, invisible flu bugs mutated in the air around us. On Saturday she and I went shopping for stocking stuffers and found a silly push button toy that when pressed said, "What's up?" We laughed, knowing Preston would love it. On Monday Miss Steph came to watch Pres while we took Samantha on our annual Christmas shopping day and dinner. Luckily I was just about done and she had only a few things to buy. Halfway through the day my ear began hurting and Samantha's throat became sore. We were a sorry sight drudging through Tysons Corner Center. We made a futile attempt at dinner then exited early for home.

Miss Steph met us at the back door, "Our boy isn't feeling well; he's got a sore throat, he wouldn't eat anything but applesauce and he feels a little warm. I put him to bed early and hung out with him for a while till he dozed off. I just checked on him a minute ago; he was sound asleep but didn't feel any warmer."

"Okay. Well. Our family Christmas is off to a great start, isn't it?" I groaned.

On Tuesday morning I was diagnosed with a sore throat and ear infection. My doctor warned, "Stay away from everyone for twenty-four hours." When I got home Samantha was feeling a little better, and Sam was getting Pres ready for his doctor's appointment. Not wanting to make anyone sicker, I didn't walk in either of their bedrooms. Instead, with my red flannel polka-dot pajamas on, I went down to the theatre room, grabbed a pillow and blanket from the chest and plopped into our Lovesac chair;

ready to watch Hallmark Christmas movies. My doctor gave me painkillers and instructed me to take one as soon as I got home, but I didn't.

Sam yelled from the top of the stairs, "We're going, Mom. Hope you feel better. And don't be a hardhead—take your painkillers. Okay?"

I wanted to go give Pres a kiss good-bye, but I heard my doctor's voice telling me to stay away. I yelled up the stairs, "Mom doesn't want to make you any sicker, pumpkin. I'll see you later. Be good for the doctor. Love you guys. Bye."

If only . . .

I knew we were in the midst of this prelude to death.

I would have kissed every inch of his face.

I would have gone with them no matter what.

But we never know.

That's precisely the point.

Sometimes things happen for a reason for which reason doesn't exist.

Sam and Pres called from the emergency room. He sounded happy and verbalized back to me, "I uv ou, um mum mum," and other gibberish I couldn't understand. We'd requested an abdominal ultrasound just to be certain. Sure enough, he had the beginnings of an impacted bowel, but everyone was confident it was caught early enough and that possibly, he could go home tomorrow.

This evening wasn't typical in that Preston was in the hospital, but in the scope of our life it was. Sam and his friend and associate Mike going over a file in the emergency room said so. Samantha stopping by the emergency room to drop off his boom box, CDs and clothes to go home in, on her way out for the evening said so. Sam and I thinking it was a minor holiday inconvenience said so. Me going to bed early with a painkiller said so. My festive red flannel pajamas with big pink and white polka dots said so.

I wasn't worried in the least. What's that saying? Ninety-nine percent of the things you worry about never happen. I never once worried that Preston wasn't coming home. Not once. I never considered the Preston Percentile. Not once.

The next morning, still in a post pain-killer haze. I was awakened by the sound of the driveway sensor beeping. Sam said he would call Preston's day program since I wasn't feeling well, but he and Preston didn't get to their room until two am. At eight am he was still sound asleep. Not knowing,

I reached for the phone to call Sam. Sleepily he said he would call them. I asked, "How's Pres?"

With the room still dark, Sam looked over at him and answered, "He's sleeping like an angel."

"Good. I'll talk to you in half an hour then."

I fixed a cappuccino and bagel. Sitting in bed waiting for Sam to call back I highlighted what was left on my holiday to do list. No phone ring. Silence. I waited a little longer, then reached for the phone. It's ironic when I think about it. I didn't find out Preston died like most people do. No police officer knocked on the front door. The phone didn't ring like in the past, bearing bad news. We didn't take him to the hospital together and wait anxiously for him to come out of surgery. I called to hear of death, unknowingly, on my own. So many things had already whispered death to me, but my conscious mind hadn't dealt with any one of them. They were for afterwards. Like my Mothers Being had saved them in a diary for me to read when I understood enough to look again.

"Hey hon, why haven't you called me back?" Silence. He answered, "Uh, we've been busy. Can I call you back in a little bit?"

"Ok, but first put Pres on the phone, I just want to say good morning." Sam started talking nervously, like he was trying to fill a void in the air. I listened to his voice vibrate words that didn't make sense. "Are you watching TV, cause you really don't seem to be paying attention? Please. Put Pres on; I want to talk to him before I jump in the shower." Through the phone I heard another male voice, familiar, but at the moment, anonymous. There was chaos in the air. That's what I heard without knowing.

Chaos—the prelude to hearing of our son's death. What I'd been feeling the last five months, like a bad dream you can't remember enough to explain, yet you feel its eeriness in your soul. Chaos in my husband's voice, chaos in my heart.

The Chaos

All of life is filled with life altering moments—declarations of joy and tragedy, love and loss, success and failure. All of which beg that we respond from the truest part of us.

"SAM! Are you there? I'm starting to get annoyed . . . why won't you let me talk to Pres?

And who is talking to you?
What is going on?"
"I want to talk to Pres!"
He answered slowly and chaotically, "It's Mike."
"Mike? Why is Mike at the hospital this early? How many files do you need to look over? Ok, whatever, just put Preston on. Please."
The substance had left his voice, like a harsh, bitter wind had taken over the strength in his vocal chords. All of a sudden I didn't know his voice. This was my skewed perception of what Sam was saying because there can be no real perception when someone you love is shooting bullets through the phone into your heart.
"I can't put him on the phone." Silence. Tears. Chaos. "Preston died, Karen." Silence. Tears. Chaos. "He's dead."
"Dead? What do you mean . . . dead? No. He can't be dead. Noooooo. NOOOOOO."
At that moment I felt but didn't, as though I was outside my body, yet tightly held in a bizarre, incomprehensible pain. His words sounded garbled like they had been sifted through a slow-motion time machine. My thoughts muddied under complicated layers of shock. The first round of tears felt as if they were the worst of the worst. They were not. Grief would come later I discovered. These initial tears were just warming up for the real marathon ahead.
Then it hit me all at once and not at all. This was really happening. I heard, "I'll be home soon, hon," and thought back to coming home without him twenty-three years ago; and I thought again: what is home now? I sat loosely anchored to the world, teetering precariously on the edge of our bed that felt like concrete beneath me; looking numbly at my half-finished cappuccino on the nightstand, my prioritized to do list beside it. As if choreographed, my hand loosened its grip on the phone and my known world. I remember my eyes readjusting to an unfamiliar downcast setting like it was their only mode; staring blankly at my phone lying upside down on the carpet by my feet. Feeling disconnected from reflexively bending down to retrieve it.
Our son is dead? He can't be dead. My festive red and white polka dot pajamas say otherwise. My lists of things to do, like bring him home from hospital, finish wrapping presents like the silly, noisy toy. *I can already hear*

him belly laughing, I thought to myself. That's what's supposed to happen. Everything around me was telling me to prepare for a big celebration. Outside the weather was fair and calm for five days before Christmas in the northeast, the cloudless sky a vibrant blue, yet an unforgiving darkness pierced my eyes.

Then it came. The rushing in of a pain, like an angry torrent of everything caustic had found me at once. My brain felt strangely, delicately tethered to my body. I heard, without hearing, the harsh, loud sound of grief sweeping throughout my body. Attached only by the recognition of unimaginable heartache.

The mad rushing sound of death had overtaken the entirety of me, drowning out all I recognized before. He had slipped into the light. He is indeed dead.

That's how it happens:

In between your cappuccino and to do notes.

In the middle of everything.

In your festive pajamas.

We held tight to some form of worry Preston's entire life. Then came the miraculous moment when we didn't worry, not even one bit—he peacefully slipped away. Without my conscious knowing. With my unconscious permission.

I was supposed to know. I was his mother. And while I did unknowingly know; I didn't know. Not at all. I rose heavy bodied and stood still for what seemed like a minute or second stretched into the emptiest of hours. Preston's death had instantaneously set rock hard and heavy in my heart. I didn't know how my body would carry it around anymore. I looked unknowingly through the window at the world outside. Maybe if I moved, something inside me would shift. What the hell do I do without my son? I wondered. I had no guidance. No nothing. My head was as empty as a hollowed eggshell. Not even my Rapid Shock Process could help me now. Then I remembered hearing Sam's voice telling me to wake Samantha. I paced back and forth between Sam's mahogany highboy and the striped wingback.

I automatically walked into Samantha's room with a recklessness that shock brings. As if on some anesthetic autopilot blurted, "Hurry. Wake up Samantha. Preston is dead." In one fell swoop, without a breath, I'd uttered the single most unthinkable sentence to my half-asleep daughter.

She startled awake, looking at me like I'd lost my mind, saying, "What? What are you talking about, Mom?" But she saw my hollowed-out eyes against my pale, dazed face and it scared her. She told me to stay put, and grabbing her phone, she jumped out of bed, ran to the pool building and shut the door.

Her dad confirmed the news: "Yes sweetheart, Preston is really dead." Now she wore the same expression.

Samantha and I stood in the bathroom hugging and crying. Holding my hands, she looked at me and said, "Please don't misunderstand what I mean, Mom. But I think this is Preston's Christmas gift to you and Dad. One he could never give you—the gift of never having to worry about him. He's taken away your worry, mom. You never have to worry about all the things you and Dad worried about ever again. He's safe and happy; he's free from pain, no more doctors or surgeries, and I bet he's with Pop."

Little did she know that my first conscious recollection of giving him permission to go flashed in front of me like a neon ghost as soon as she spoke. "I love you. So much. I understand exactly what you're saying, and that would be just like your brother, wouldn't it?"

"Yes, it would," she answered.

My friend, Caryn, found me sitting on the vanity bench in our bathroom with a pile of tissues beside me. At one point she looked at my pajamas and said, "I really like your pjs, they're cute." We both looked at each other and automatically started laughing. The death laughter that reminds you to breathe when you don't remember how, had begun.

I don't remember calling anyone. I can only think I did so reflexively according to the few people I called in an odd, get to the point fashion saying matter-of-factly, "Preston died. He is dead," I told them. Maybe I was reciting what I heard through the phone from Sam, "Preston died, Karen. He is dead," so somehow I would comprehend it. I was too in shock to mold any more words together.

Our neighbor, John, came over to check on Samantha and me until Sam arrived. I remember seeing the shocked look on his face, like he had just lost someone dear, too. He had. Our families were close. His daughter, Rachael, liked to hang out with Preston. She had a way of making him laugh. And he had a way of making her smile.

Sam walked in the back door, and at the exact moment I saw him the energy in our house shifted. Our home: the place where we lived and loved as a family of four. Where, upon returning, its scent always greeted us as if to remind us. Welcome back to your home, the only one of its kind. We exist here in the air of the known and familiar to gladden your heart. And to greet you where you are. The three of us hugged and sobbed together. The moment that Samantha had worried about her whole life was here. The three of us. That's who we were now—a family of three—in our unfamiliar home.

The Descent

Grief is fear brought to life in three-dimensional form. It's a searing numbness of pain, a misery held tight in every orifice. It's utter blindness in the barbarous blackness. It's your worst enemy and your best friend. And we are the human beings caught between this tug of war.

When all gravity that supports you, when all that keeps you buoyant and breathing is yanked away, you fall the way a person plummets from a plane without a parachute. This time our souls could not catch each other. No trapeze, no net. We fell together, separately, and at once. A father lost his son. A mother lost her son. And a sister lost her brother. A family lost a member.

The brevity of time and words it took to unravel our world seemed to mock our very existence.

Leaving for the hospital it was unusually warm for a late December day. There was such blueness to the sky, like heaven had already started to celebrate its newest arrival—not a cloud—just a bright blue dome of heavenliness. My friend, Lisa, stood by her car pulled in the grass alongside the driveway with a meal in her hands. She held me tight and we cried together. She spoke of imagining him in heaven running and leaping and playing.

Our friend, Craig who worked at the hospital, met us in the lobby. Seeing him made me cry even more into a deeper, unexplored place. Another layer of reality was beginning to sink in. He put his arm around me and led me to Preston's room while I held fast onto Sam's hand. Family and friends were lined up in the hallway just outside the room. Samantha was standing with her close friends by her side. Gasped whispers of what a shock his death was poured from various mouths, like water from a fountain as Sam led me into his room. That was it. Death's energy felt like electricity in water, or at least what I imagine it to feel like—sudden and larger than a body can bear. My pain was so strangely intense I couldn't acknowledge it all at once, or I too would have died.

I suppose there's an obscure grace in grief's stages.

Sam's sister Sarah and her husband Gregg stayed with Preston's body while Sam came to get us. Walking into the hospital room, my eyes blankly looked at them sitting side by side next to Preston's bed, but my wrecked heart saw him. I knew in that moment seeing my son's dead body would be the bravest thing I've ever done. There would be no privilege of rocking him into heaven. Sarah began talking to me, telling me how she'd been rubbing his feet the way he liked to have them rubbed. I stared numbly at her for a quick second while our son's body loomed largely in my peripheral vision. Her words sounded jumbled as if they'd been thrown across the room without vowels or punctuation. I had lost my capability to comprehend them.

Shock had immediately set in, like concrete being poured into my soul, the minute I heard Sam's hollowed out voice. But seeing Preston threw me hard into the next stage of shock. There were no words of comfort, no amount of hugs or prayers that could have prepared me for seeing our son as a corpse. My brain couldn't process the fact that he wasn't moving. Breathless. I kept waiting for him to turn his head, smile his crooked smile at me and utter, "um mum, or "uv ou" in his gravelly, hospital-tired voice. "Dammit, just say hi or move, pumpkin," I pleaded through sobful breaths. But his body remained rock still, the silence unbearable, like the day he was born, only worse. My motherly instinct automatically fixed his blankets so he wouldn't get cold, while mournful-size tears dropped hard and fast onto the sheets that covered his sterile white skin.

His head wasn't slightly turned to the right like usual. *Who straightened his head?* I wondered. His arms and hands were fully outstretched by his side, no longer bent. *Who straightened his hands?* I wondered. He wasn't smiling his uneven smile. *Who took the life out of his smile?* I wondered. *Who took our handsome boy, the one with a crooked tilt to his head, the one with turned in crooked hands, the one with a beautiful crooked smile?*

I stared unknowingly at the perfectly straight body of our son. The quiet, unnerving, like the day he was born. His red hair: still bright against the pallor of his skin. He was returning the same way he arrived.

I wanted so badly to touch him, but I wanted more for his warm skin to touch me back.

Just yesterday this once warm place inside of him, where a ceaseless flow of breath and energy automatically stirred within him, now, had irrevocably gone cold. How careless I'd been to assume I would see him again. How many times did I think he could cheat death anyway? My Mothers Being had tried to prepare me as gently as she could. After all, I gave him the permission he'd been waiting for. My subconscious had known what my conscious being couldn't bear. I leaned down to kiss his cheek, the first of a million more last kisses, "I suppose you taught us enough of what we needed to know. It's why you let me know you were ready to leave. Your lessons here on earth were done, weren't they, pumpkin?" I whispered to him, hoping his spirit was still floating above the bed like in the movies. How would I tell Sam that I'd given our son permission to go when I hadn't yet begun to process it myself?

Now the second devastation of tears was upon me. I was no longer crying as I know crying. It's as if someone opened a spigot—my face perpetually moist and swollen. Red blotches appear across the landscape of my Irish skin. My lips, a quivering jello-like blob unable to form words that make sense. Only whys and nos, then quivering back open in disbelief. I knelt beside his bed laying my head on his child size chest, wrapping my entire being around his lifeless body. The warmth of my skin lie against the coldness of death. My heart listened for a beat to match mine as I willed his chest to rise and fall. Nothing.

Then came the silent weeping that grief brings, my heart screaming inwardly to my soul as my body shook uncontrollably, grief's heavy hand squelching any sounds too primal to be heard as I lay across the remnant of our son's lifeless body.

Our beloved boy—the warm vibrant energy gone from around his being.

I wondered if all his energy left at once, immediately with his last breath. Dramatically, in a vacuous void that could be seen and heard, like a faint light beam on a rocket ship to heaven. Or was it silently invisible so to spare us from an already torturous departure, so mourners wouldn't try to reach out and touch it once more?

I slipped deeper into another dimension, black and vague. I tried desperately to keep it together on the outside, trying not to beat myself up for not kissing him good-bye. But everything inside me was disintegrating—cracks appearing then breaking, then shattering. Blackness, then bright sharp pain, then blackness.

I would come to realize that while not fully aware; I *had* said goodbye. I'd been blessed with a most profound, peaceful goodbye. My Mothers Being had gone before me. My remembrance was of an ethereal goodbye with no tears, only drenched in unconditional love under the guise of an ordinary good night kiss. After all the powerlessness in his life, he was allowed, through the grace of God, the ultimate power. The choice of moving on. The gift of my promise that we would be all right.

One day when I could see past the guilt. When I'd recovered enough, I would open what Samantha called Preston's Gift. Looking around his hospital room, hearing all the familiar hospital noises around me, I started thinking about what my sweet husband had witnessed, realizing I'd been given another gift.

Sam had spared me the horrific hospital sights and sounds. I didn't hear "Code blue!" called as a rush of doctors and nurses swarmed around his body. I didn't hear the accelerated clatter of wheels on the crash cart against the cold linoleum floor. I didn't see his skinny, pale chest arch against the paddles after which his ragdoll body would drop hard and flat onto the hospital bed. Only Sam heard the anguished sound of a failed resuscitation over and over again. I didn't hear time of death being called by a stranger's voice. I didn't hear the eerie silence seconds after. Where his gasps of empty breath scooped up death. Though I saw Sam cry enough; I didn't see that cry. Sam carried all of them for me in his memory place. I would never hear what he heard. I would never see what he saw. For whatever reason, that was meant to be his and his alone with Pres. It made sense in the most nonsensical Preston Percentile way. Preston died with his father, his best buddy, by his side. I had given him permission like mothers often do and Sam sat a mere inches from his son while God carried through with his wishes so he wouldn't be alone. And I can think of no better human being in the entire world to usher our son into heaven. That's what was meant to be. I said, "Go," and Sam sat by his side while he passed across the way.

I always had a feeling that Preston wouldn't live a long life. I really can't explain other than the whispers I heard in my sleep. The ones that lay dormant in my mind until they were ready for the light. I kept this thought folded neatly in a tidy square. Pulling it out once in a while to examine it, but never brave enough to unfold it. Though I always supposed his death would be a dramatic one given the litany of illnesses and surgeries. The rhythm of his life said so. I supposed we'd be keeping vigil in a hospital room, or, like after his birth, preparing to bring him home to die. But what I never supposed. Not ever. Was that I wouldn't have a conscious clue. I never supposed that I would know in some secret, deep compartment in my soul—where my Mothers Being lived. I hadn't a scarcity of a clue that my unconscious being would take me there along with angels, softly and secretly, so my conscious self wouldn't hurt before the unknowable hurt arrived. Just like when Emory died, the angels had conspired once again.

The Goodbye
"The cure for the pain is in the pain."   Rumi

After we left his body, all my stunned brain could think was, *I must write a poem for his funeral.* That was our thing. My caregiver brain needed something specific to do for him. In the car I began chanting poetic lines in my head. What Lisa said about him playing in heaven stuck with me: I would use that in my poem. My writing brain could soothe my caregiver brain. That was the plan.

Pulling up into our driveway, we saw Helen standing at the top of the hill on the sidewalk by the garage. The entire car erupted into a low-pitched chorus of, "oh shit." We hadn't spoken in years. After our last debacle I declared that if she couldn't honor Pres while he was alive, she sure as hell wouldn't be allowed to pretend to honor his memory. But sudden death's Novocain had numbed any sense of righteousness. She stood without movement. I think she was waiting to see if I was going to throw her out once more. I glanced in her direction, blankly acknowledging her presence and without inviting her in, did so with one nod of my head.

My sister-in-law, Sue, walked beside me through the garage. I saw before me the dark blue door leading into our house. I stopped. Sue looked, asking if I was all right. The symbolization of a simple door we had walked in and out of never thinking of what we were walking away from or to threw me. When Preston left through that same door he was leaving us forever. We didn't know. Perhaps he knew. We didn't know. Now what I knew devastated me to the point of not moving. Maybe if I didn't go through the door I would find him in another dimension. Somewhere. Anywhere. Just please God don't make me face all the Preston things on the other side of that damn door. I looked at Sue and said, "He's never going to be on the other side of the door when I come home. Not ever again." Another realization.

Sensing my weakness, Helen swooped in through grief's portal, like a bird of prey disguised in the form of a white dove. Posing as the thoughtful sister perched in the kitchen cooking feverishly away—attentive to my every need.

If I mentioned to someone that I needed a picture frame, by days end it appeared, compliments of my oldest sister. I'd never seen her so attentive, particularly to me. In reality she watched as she took notes, listening to my conversations with Julie, watching me with her daughter, Vicky, who no longer spoke to her; thinking no one the wiser. Part of her wanted to be that sister, a person of kindness and understanding. But letting go of past pain and perceiving things from only her point of view was her Achilles heel. She never learned how to love unconditionally, and that was her undoing.

While I attempted to write a poem, Sam and his friend, Todd, installed a railing on the wall down to the basement. Caryn's then husband, Spyro, came by to help set up tables and chairs for after the funeral. That's what his big caregiver hands needed to do as they came to grips with no longer busying themselves with caring for our son. Michelle and I worked on a list of everything we needed for the funeral. That's what you do before a funeral, what saves your heart and your brain from dying too.

People arrived in clumps. First, Sam's sisters, then various groups of family. Mom, then Julie. Then more clumps of friends. Everyone talked in clumps too. Sam and I spoke in disorderly questions, lists of things to be done, and people to be called. A condensed loop tape of how he died was recited through the phone. Preston's death had cut through our hearts and minds, leaving them vulnerable to everything around us. They no longer functioned as a pair, one listening to the other. It was a paradox to be in such pain and feel nothing at all. I felt incapable of putting anything in order. Everything was one big clump of death that I couldn't see past.

Julie and Michelle helped me struggle through my new list of to dos, Michelle remarked that it was breaking her heart at how weird it was to not see me planning or in charge. In charge. That was a bizarre concept to me now.

Returning from the funeral home the next day, Sam and I walked through the back door to find Michelle and Caryn standing by the buffet with Swiffer dusters in their hand, smiling sympathetically, claiming in unison, "We tried, but we couldn't find any dirt." They surprised me by cleaning the house. I remember thinking what treasures they were. I remember the hint of a smile appearing on my face, and then quickly receding like a seedling not yet strong enough to push through the force of the fertile earth. That was it. The oppressive force of death, of grief, of shock had pushed everything inside our beings down under the earth of us where pain is captured and held until you can grow toward the lightness again. Grief in all its variant forms was settling into our souls. Establishing itself by pushing our senses, our thinking, everything we knew before, down to an undetectable level. Until we hurt in places we didn't know how to hurt. A hurt beyond any reasonable hurt. An unknowable hurt.

That's what the death of a child does to you: first it fills you quickly, violently, like a gun blast. Then slithers it way up from under the earth of you, encroaching on all of your senses. I had carried him inside of me. Grew him the way a flower sprouts from a bulb stuck naked into the earth. How would I go on after losing what I grew way down in the earth of me?

Helen and Vicky were cooking away in the kitchen. Two human beings once connected, now strangers. It seemed out of place and time to see them in the same room together. Everything in our world had been strangely rearranged, like smelling the food they were separately preparing without really smelling.

Our house sat at the top of a cul-de-sac on a large lot with three other houses. Arriving back home from the viewing, in the darkness of night and soul, attempting to come to grips with the finality of tomorrow felt heavy. Suddenly Sam stopped the car at the bottom of our driveway. Along both sides of our one hundred and forty-foot-long driveway were bags placed a foot apart, lit with luminaries. Our mouths flew open in wonderment. Tears flowed. "Oh my God. It's beautiful. Who did this?" I asked. The symbolization of lighting our way home through our darkness was such a profound act of love and kindness. Sam drove slowly so we wouldn't miss a one. Our battered hearts and souls had been attended to in the most delicate manner.

Through the kitchen window I could see the candle that John's then wife, Susan, brought in honor of Pres, still glowing. We got out of the car. With the backdrop of a black canvas of night; we stood, all of us, looking down our majestic lane of flickering lights; awestruck at such a sublime sight, and for a twinkling our hearts found the lightness we vowed never to forget. Even though I didn't know what our house now represented. We were indeed home. We find out later that it was our dear friend, John and his family who placed the luminaries that filled our hearts with light.

The funeral was blurry the way funerals usually are. We were half present as our other selves raced to claim remembrances of the past and lock them safely away in our memory place forever, while still trying to fit the mismatched pieces of the last forty-eight hours together. I remember my black wool funeral suit, the one that hung in the closet never wanting to be worn. And smooth pearls against my chest. I can still see Sam in his black suit, white shirt and black tie; and Samantha in her black dress, sitting in between us, her long brunette hair falling softly against big pearl earrings. I remember Miss Steph in the front row beside Sam looking as shell shocked as the rest of us. My mom and Julie sat beside her. We'd invited her to sit with the family, because she was. There was a reason she was lovingly known as Preston's other mother. I remember seeing everything in black and white like old photos through Preston's eyes. Black clothing and white tissues. Pale faces and dark eyes. Death had taken the energy and color, all of it.

I remember hearing the sound of hearts breaking around me, of tear droplets avowing the fabric of a life. I remember dear family and friends standing to speak. How exhausting it felt trying to capture all the love. I remember feeling overwhelmingly moved by music when your heart is raw. It was a constant source of such joy in Preston's life. Through it, faint colors began to emerge. I can still see our brother-in-law, Gale's kind eyes as he sang: "His Eye is on the Sparrow" so beautifully, which still wrecks me to this day. A friend sang "Danny Boy," like at my dad's funeral. Then finally, Michael Crawford's rendition of, "On Eagles Wings" pierced through every corner of the room. I sat thinking of how Pres would have enjoyed all the music.

At the cemetery everyone was given a green balloon. Preston's favorite color.

On the day before Christmas Eve, while bagpipes played "Amazing Grace"; a sea of green balloons drifted into the heavens so the angels could throw a party. One lone balloon hung insistently in the bright December sky like something was holding it in place. Overcome by the solitary balloon, I walked over to Preston's coffin touching the cold wood that contained his ice-cold body, wanting to open it and scoop him up. Wanting even more to kiss his face, just one more time. My angry tears ricocheted off his coffin like bullets. I watched the last balloon soar out of sight. Spyro came to stand beside me. Wrapping his arm around me, he pointed up to the balloon and through the most compassionate smile said, "It's heading straight for Ireland."

My Mothers Being smiled at the imagery. The balloons. Angels in waiting. The Party. And Preston, standing boldly in the center of it all, encircled in joy and love.

I remember sitting in the white pool building where all the food and tables were set up watching everyone eat. I had no desire to eat and when I did all food tasted like cardboard.

Helen walked over to me and said, "Wow, I'm impressed. You have quite a community of friends. People really knew Preston, didn't they?"

I saw bewilderment on her face as she attempted to input all that was opposite from what she'd convinced herself to believe, and replied, "You seem surprised."

"Yes."

"We're very lucky to have such good friends. Welcome to our real life."

Considering all that had happened, these days it didn't feel like there was much to be thankful for. But I was thankful that Preston's search for the lightness his home of a body never knew was fulfilled. Now he was lightness forever and always, and from our darkness we could see it well.

Above all:

I'm thankful he wasn't asked to die bravely; he had lived bravely, after all.

Chapter 25

The Other End of the Rainbow

Darkness

As if by declaration all things from this moment on will be known in terms of *before* and *after*.

The world is full of names and labels, titles and groupings. There's a name and identity for every loss. A child who loses both parents is referred to as an orphan. A bereaved spouse is called a widower. But there's no name for a person who loses a child. That one specific grief is an undefinable pain. It is unnamable. What or who or how is a person who loses a child? There's no other sorrow that comes close. Grief's initial unbearableness, like that of childbirth, is meant to be vaguely remembered so one can carry on with living in some fashion.

Looking through Preston's baby book, recalling the details of his birth, I remember how my body convulsed with the rhythm of a new life fighting hard to enter this world. I had to remember how to breathe through it in order to cope with the pain. A pain so unfathomable, describing it is utter nonsense. A pain that lasts longer than what one should be able to endure—one that ebbs and flows—that needs to be monitored for a healthy outcome. A pain that is unbearable without yelling out to the universe or grabbing someone's hand so tight it could break.

Then just when you thought you had nothing left; the last push as you scream with the force of your entire being. Your body—limp from exhaustion, then overpowering tears like you've never known. This is childbirth. This is grief.

While mere words can't sufficiently describe grieving the loss of a child, this is purely my portrayal of how we survived unbirthing a life.

Walking backwards through his life, I wondered how long he'd been waiting for permission to go. I don't know which tormented me more at times. What had he told Pearl? Did he know? I think he did. Or was it just his time, and the look on his face that night told my Mothers Being so. Was it my Mothers Being that spoke to him that night?

I have vivid, three-dimensional memories of certain moments, then hours of nothingness. Initially, waking up was the cruelest part of the day. In the minute dot of a second between waking and being awake, morning after morning, I relived the horror of discovering Preston was dead. Sam too. Without a word our bodies rolled into each other and we wept ourselves awake. In that vulgar smidgen of time I felt like a coma patient awakening after years, attempting to piece together what was real, what was gone, and how I fit into this strange new life. My recurring nightmare of piecing Preston and Samantha's bodies together was a certainty that my brain was still trying to keep everything from my previous life intact.

Grief was the sound of nothing and everything colliding together at once. Whether in the darkness of evening or the wee morning hours, we felt as though we were crawling through to nowhere; too many sensations, then back to dark black nothingness.

So much of what I remember after his death happened in the hearth room; a room styled after an old colonial house where everyone gathered because of the utilitarian necessity of the hearth. Now it seemed only fitting as the intense heat and extreme cold of shock and grief inhabited the entirety of its space. The room contained, naturally, a large fireplace with a seven-foot long mantle. A navy blue and cream checked wingback chair sat in the corner to the left; next to it stood a small curly maple side table. A rack containing a collection of redware plates hung on the wall over it. Our old pine table held center court while a custom-made tin chandelier floated above. A cream-patterned settee sat at an angle to the right of the fireplace and a buffet I'd admired at an antique shop occupied the wall opposite the fireplace. It was a big, open, welcoming room. Open to the kitchen, family and tavern room. Apparently even open to death and all the friendly mourners it brings.

It's where I sat at the table, struggling to read my poem as Sam, Samantha, Mom, Julie and Miss Steph listened, where we all cried together, deciding it was acceptable for the funeral. It's where Spyro sat comforting Sam, asking what chores needed to be done. Where we sprawled pictures across the table and shook our heads in disbelief at how precious an ordinary day now looked. It's where Julie sat with me for hours talking, or making sure I had eaten, or fixed me a drink whenever she thought I needed one.

Where Julie and Michelle helped me go over the list of to dos. It's where I watched Helen and Vicky cooking in the kitchen alongside each other as separate entities. Where I watched Sam walk by time after time as he tried to tamp down his grief with chores. Where he stopped to hug me and make sure I was all right. It's where we sat gazing at the fire, burning grief. Where we stared at Preston's pictures of a life displayed across the length of the buffet.

Maybe this room with the big hearth and the roaring fire we loved so much, where sunset colors emerged from flaming logs popping and crackling as they fell into their new place on the grate. Where the fire's toasty heat felt like a warm poultice for our pain. Log after log burned to ashes only to be replaced by another hefty log that looked to defy the fire's heat. And the process began again.

Maybe in this place of receiving pain and letting go of pain is where we would find a way to begin again. In that ethereal, mystical place in the middle, that is really beyond, to a place of unlearning the knowing in the center of our souls.

Certain things became familiar after his death, like the ringing of the doorbell at dinner time every evening as friends dropped meals off, the crinkling of aluminum foil and soft voices telling Sam what they brought and how to reheat it. The flat sound of a stack of sympathy cards hitting the butcher block countertop followed by the releasing of paper from glue as we opened them, then sniffles and blowing of noses at the kind words of so many. I began to look forward to the mail.

I knew no matter what kind of day we had—whether we steeled ourselves from grieving or not—the personal written notes would release whatever we had attempted to hold in.

Losing a child is a devastation to a soul. That's the first layer. Losing a child without warning. No preparation to our delicate parental being was the second layer. Losing a child without the privilege of goodbye felt wicked and evil, its pain entwined with barbwire, tangled throughout our hearts. Leaving messy appendages dangle, turning our insides out, open to the bitter wind and scorching sun of grief. The ever-changing conditions of the soul to which a body cannot acclimate itself.

Now that the impossible thing has happened I cannot see my way to any form of possibility as of yet. I wait for the day when my heart will flutter with genuine excitement, when a smile will be more than a façade. I imagine it will not happen all at once, but rather like most of our realizations. In the slow blink of an eye. What do I do now with this most specific love, the momness designed just for Preston? Where will it go? I frantically wondered what would happen to my love for him without any further input or output. I'm still his mom, but not in a useful way like before. Part of my heart's footprint had been abstrusely erased. The thought of no more daily love exercises to exchange with him overwhelmed my heart. Maybe that's why we're referred to as heartbroken. Suddenly there's nowhere to put your love. So your specific pent-up love expands and expands and expands your heart until it can't hold it any longer. And it breaks from all the weight. The weight of grief. The weight of love.

Sam's family came over for our annual Draper Christmas. If it weren't for Samantha we would have skipped it without a thought. Watching his sisters fix dinner was like watching an out of focus movie. Dull silhouettes moved around our kitchen appearing to be talking out of focus, as well. Vague shadows of pots and pans seemed to drift from counter to counter. I was uninterested in trying to relate to anything I saw or heard. I saw no point. For whatever reason I remember green beans. I don't remember who made them or what else was served. I just remember everyone dancing around me in a haze. And green beans. I think the mundane things linger in our minds to blur the absurd. To keep us from going insane when our world doesn't make sense. For when an explanation of how he died doesn't really matter, for when tears begin and end the day. That's what the green beans were for. Sam reached down and gave me a soft kiss on my lips along with a glass of red wine. I remember his salty lips. I sat on the settee staring at the fireplace crying more of the hurt out, thinking, okay, I can't possibly cry any more today. I cried some more. Then back to the roaring fire. Then to the confusion of our obscure reality.

Four red and green plaid stockings that made up our family anchored the fireplace. Sam and Karen hung to the left, Samantha and Preston to the right. My mother sewed them and I'd stenciled our names in hunter green on the off white cuffs. That was our truth just days ago—what I assumed was promised to us. A merry Christmas morning where Samantha would sit where I now sat, opening her stocking before going downstairs while Sam made cappuccinos and Preston slept in until breakfast.

Samantha would be alone now without a stocking beside hers, without her brother. My heart broke for her. I cried some more. Preston's stocking, still filled to the top, hung just out of my reach. A full stocking of a life I could no longer touch. I wondered how I would possibly hang just three stockings next year. I cried some more. We were a four stocking family, dammit. Not being able to tame the sting of Sam's salty kiss, still lingering on my lips, made me hurt deeply for him. I cried some more. Grief's sting was what I felt. Then I went numb and came back, then numbness and back to the out of focus movie. Like when your legs go numb, then it starts to come back and the more you move the more it hurts. So I sat paralyzed, staring into the roaring fire. And I cried some more.

My Mothers Being rusted over the way a metal chair unprotected from the elements rusts outside. I saw grief like the chair, opposite of any form of protection. My heart felt vulnerable to all elements of life. I bruised at the slightest of touch, every word sounded shrill to my ears—everything felt in gross exaggerations. Eyes felt too close, like they could see into the pit of me. I thought, without thinking, that if I let everyone see my tears in their exaggerated form of utter hopelessness they would never cease.

I remember our first outing. Caryn and Spyro invited us over for New Years Eve. At first, the thought of going to the home of our good friends felt safe. This I could handle. As we stood at their front door, all the protection I felt fell swiftly away like it never existed.

My memory place took me sharply back to the last time I was at their house. Before. Caryn and Spyro greeted us in the foyer with warm hugs that lasted longer than usual. Caryn hugged me and whispered, "You'll be all right, we're here."

The rusting over began the minute I saw the look on their faces. I had no control, no shelter from an emotional storm. Another piece of me proceeded to disintegrate without my permission. I remember Spyro's parents talking about their recent trip to Greece. I remember the effort it took to force a faint smile, feeling like I was going to scream if I heard one more happy voice. Spyro's mom watched me—she knew. The harder I tried to outwit grief, even for a couple of hours the more I rusted over. I surmised from all this that grieving does require shelter. Shelter from good, well-meaning friends, and family. Even, at times, shelter from your spouse. It's human nature to protect someone you love from disintegrating completely. Grief is ugly and raw, begging you to rust and disintegrate.

We felt bad for leaving. Still, we excused ourselves early realizing how foolish we'd been to think we could welcome in the New Year without falling completely apart. Without disintegrating. Arriving home, we made a beeline for our bedroom. I quickly changed from my winter white sweater and black jeans. Then the obvious happened. What always happens when you try to hold back a mighty force. Slipping off my black flats made me weep uncontrollably, realizing I had worn them at my doctor's appointment on Tuesday. Which meant I was wearing them the last time I saw Preston. Before.

I sat on the closet floor crying, surrounded by all of my before clothing and shoes. I heard Sam sniffling as he changed in his closet across from mine. No words, just a private moment in our separate, closeted state of after.

We sat on the family room sofa in our Christmas pajamas crying in each other's arms, our bodies shaking with each tear. Tears bled through our clothing, seeped into the walls, escaped out every door and window, howling out into the universe. Our grief was uncontainable. Out of habit we lit the Christmas tree lights, the room still silenced by the absence of TV. The thought of watching throngs of people cheering as if there was something to celebrate was incomprehensible. We didn't need to know if the New Year had arrived—we weren't there yet. We wouldn't be for a while. We were stuck in the obscure, nameless place in between the *after* of the *before*. In the process of disintegrating.

The rusting away of our old selves, contrary to what felt good or sane, was upon us. In the exhaustive disintegrating that was inevitable for a healthy outcome, without knowing it at the time, we came alive again—piece by rusty piece—ready to be reclaimed by a different knowing. Another realization.

Samantha left to go back to college. She no longer had to worry about something bad happening to Pres while she was away. She no longer had to worry about us worrying about her brother. So much worry for one human being in the form of a sweet daughter and sister.

Even though we talked and cried together plenty during the last month, the three of us did Oscar worthy performances of pretending to be all right so no one would worry. We were a worry-free family.

When life tries to break you; the funny thing is you want to break. All over the place in messy, ugly little pieces so everyone will understand. So they will gasp at what they see. And you can then say, "Now do you understand how broken I am?" But you can't, you're a wife and mother, a husband and father, a daughter and lone sibling. And you know they don't want to see you break. Not in that way.

Once Samantha left to go back, I no longer liked the quiet; it unnerved me. The idleness of our hands, the physicality lost due to his care screamed and hissed at us in such vulgar tones I was afraid of how totally it consumed us. Never had we imagined so many hours in a day.

Two months after he died with my forty-ninth birthday five days away, I was filling my listless hands with projects in hopes of passing the hurt onto something else. *Maybe this project would be willing to receive some of my pain*, I thought flatly to myself. The fire popped and crackled with heat and life. I stared into it thinking if only I could feel like I once did, like the fire. I sat on the blue and burgundy braided rug in my painting pants, the ones that wear remnants of past projects. I was a disheveled painter, an unshowered mess sitting beneath the table with a paintbrush in my hand, hoping to transform the legs of the hearth room table. It seemed fitting to me that they should be dark black.

My world is dark black. I don't think I'd ever heard anyone say dark black. I wondered why and dryly snickered to myself. There are shades of black, after all. I would think that the darkest black is the color of nothingness. So I painted nothingness onto the table legs and I wept dark black tears. They repeated down my face, one then one hundred more, like ants at a picnic.

Wisdom

Grief will quickly kill you if you don't first suffocate it with tears. We had already cried an uncivilized number of tears, it seemed. But wisdom now told us that tears were meant to escape, that they were no longer a sign of anything but love and healing.

During the course of our grieving, Sam and I experienced wisdom, we heard wisdom, saw wisdom, felt wisdom and had wisdom imparted on us. Murmurs of *Thank Gods, he's better off this way* came from the mouths of those who couldn't understand the brilliance of loving a child with disabilities. There were people who actually asked us if we missed him. Then, there were people who were more than eager to tell us how good we were doing. *What exactly was it they thought we were doing beyond breathing and walking*, we wondered. We heard: *You two are amazing! You were such good parents to him. You know not everyone would have done what you did.* Or. *Wow, you two look so good. If I lost one of my children I wouldn't be standing upright like you guys right now.* It seemed crazy to us this notion of being superheroes, not once but twice: once for loving our son and again for being in this world after he died.

Albums and boxes of photographs remained spread across the pine hearth room table for a gallery wall project; that they became the tabletop: pictures of Sam and Pres in the ocean, kicking his legs and laughing in his dad's arms after being overtaken by a wave. Photos of the kids at Disney World with Mickey Mouse, laughing on the raft ride that soaked them, Pres grinning at Snow White's beauty as she autographed his book. A myriad of Christmas photos strewn across the years, him reaching out to play with an adapted toy. Photos from hospital stays, or of him in a leg cast of some sort as Sam wheeled him around the yard in a wagon, looking like he could have cared less about the cast. Photos of Pres and his beloved Miss Steph, and his Grammy and Pop, all beaming brilliantly happy smiles. The last photo of Emory, staring into Preston's soul. Looking at the posed Christmas card photos where Samantha had to endure smiling constantly so we could capture one picture of Pres when he's not anticipating the flash with a frozen look on his face makes us smile at her compassion. School pictures, Halloween costumes, Samantha helping him play with a toy or open a present, photos of Laura and Angie coming over to play. The classic picture of Sam and him at Hooters on his twenty-first birthday surrounded by the girls, Pres staring right at them makes us laugh uncontrollably.

These photographs of an inclusive life, of a happy child make us weep with joy for what we did have, realizing, like our funeral card said, sometimes we were impatient and frustrated students.

But of all the photos there is one that stands above the rest. It's the photograph of Preston under a banyan tree in Florida. In our unknowing we thought it odd how uncharacteristically still and welcoming he was to have his picture taken, no bug eyes anticipating the camera's flash. Instead he is looking up with a peaceful enlightenment in his eyes, as if seeing into the heavens a glimpse of his future home made him happier than ever. He didn't flinch when we took his picture, but instead appeared to be inviting our future selves to take as many as we would need. I remember thinking—*his eyes look as if he's seeing something we can't.* A knowing that offered a calm, peaceful net over his tight body.

All of the photos on the table happily overlapped one another, some benignly intersect others, almost contradicting the reality of his life—the struggles, the fight to be seen or heard, the pain, illnesses, the isolation, the tears and worry. Or do they? All of those things were indeed the constant underlying current of his life, but these untouched photos of a life are the victorious moments in the life of an uncommonly typical family. And while they don't show all the toys we couldn't buy for him at Toys R Us because his hands didn't work well enough to use them and the one adapted toy from a special catalog costing four times what it should or the three million trips to set him up on the beach for a few scant hours of pleasure.

They don't show the public places we couldn't use because they weren't handicapped accessible. Or the trips he couldn't take as he got older because it was too physically difficult for us. They don't show us begging Samantha to remain smiling even longer when she had already been smiling non-stop for an absurd amount of time. Or Preston's frustrations or yelling. They're not supposed to, though they lie underneath each and every photograph.

Some remain in our memory place where all the other life pictures are stored, and the rest vaporize because they're too heavy to hold.

Sam and I sit side by side with both elbows propped on the table as if holding our heads on straight. Tears slide hastily down our cheeks like they're racing each other. We smile, knowing Preston is where he wanted to be. We're appreciative to have been chosen as the host and hostess of his life, feeling blessed at how many people showed up to help. Grateful for the beauty of it all. Another realization.

Though ours was a complicated sisterhood of dazzling proportion, an incongruous mixture of tales steeped in variegated family histories—still, I wanted to believe Helen had changed. She'd been visiting frequently since Preston's death, saying repeatedly how sorry she was for everything. Even the little Irish redhead in my brain stood at full alert. Hands on hips, legs firmly in warrior pose.

She insisted on taking us to dinner at the Melting Pot. Samantha was home for the weekend, though we were leery; we thought it might be fun. Her face changed from carefree to seriously on a mission the minute we settled into our cushioned booth. I felt annoyed at the thought of her coming once again with a hidden agenda. I worried for her safety if she dare ask me a disrespectful question about Preston. Not even the little Irish redhead in my brain would be able to save me. Or her.

Her pensive look told me one of her questions was coming. Funny how they never felt like a genuine question but more like a test. How well I answered was always revealed by one of her characteristic expressions. I hoped I'd read her wrong this time but I had a strong feeling I hadn't. I suspected her visit was for a reason—they always were. Lately her behavior made no sense, not even for her. She'd begun asking endless questions about Preston. The same someone whose existence she had denounced for the past twenty-three years. *Please don't ask me about Pres, not tonight,* I thought. I wasn't in the mood to talk about him. All I wanted was to dip outrageous amounts of food into hot bubbling pots of cheese, oil and dark chocolate. And to laugh—really laugh.

She watched me, waiting for just the right opportunity when my mouth wasn't full. The calculated look in her eyes gave her away. Halfway through our meal, looking across the table as I reached for my glass of wine she finally revealed herself.

Looking intently at me she asked, "So. What exactly was it that Preston did to have so many people enamored with him?"

Before Sam or I could draw a breath, Samantha turned toward her and said: "*Don't you get it, Aunt Helen? It's not what Preston did; it's what he caused other people to do, because of who he was.*"

A symphony began playing in our hearts. This was one of those tender moments that as parents would brilliantly fill an entire page in our storybook of life. Our insightful daughter had so eloquently encapsulated Preston's life in one profound sentence. Tears instantaneously formed from beholding the sheer beauty of her soul, wise beyond her years from everything she'd experienced. Sam and I tightly gripped hands under the table, creating a dam to hold back the ugly cry. Samantha looked up surprised to see us wiping away tears.

For her, the ordinary words that poured from her beautiful soul had been there all along, in acknowledgement of the many people drawn to her brother and his energy. All the relationships she watched and was a part of since she was little were right where they belonged—stored securely in her memory place, ready and waiting for a moment like this.

Her niece's answer confused Helen even more, she stared at Samantha like she was searching for a translation in her face, squinting her eyes so severely she looked like she was trying to squeeze understanding into her brain.

I know she was shocked that her niece had answered at all, but the gravitas in her voice and the ease by which she answered puzzled my sister greatly. Always one to have a follow-up, debate-stirring question, this time she sat silently, attempting to think it into her brain. Stunned by the profoundness of it, even more stunned she didn't remotely comprehend what Samantha clearly saw.

This moment, when an extraordinary sentence filled the wholeness of our hearts due to the enormity of its message, made us feel blessed beyond reason. Because of who *she* was—we could check the miracle box tonight.

Without realizing it, Samantha had all but spit Carl Jung's ideology out of her mouth. Which led us right back to Preston's *mana*. Carl Jung defines it as the unconscious influence of one being on another. The energy of being real has more power than outright persuasion, debate, or force of will. Being who we are releases an extraordinary power that, without intent or design, affects the people who come in contact with such realness.

It made perfect sense that Preston and Miss Steph immediately connected on such a spiritual level. When she met him she was on the verge of becoming real herself. And when she saw his realness being celebrated, their souls drew together. Her realness attached onto his and never let go.

There's a saying: "If you don't remember someone out loud they die twice." Grief is such a confusion of the heart that, at times, I didn't know how to speak or react. This Grief Anthem about how it feels to be in the world without a beloved child is what I wish I could have written on a note pad and handed to everyone I came in contact with after Preston's death:

Do you know that while I sit quietly listening to you, that as I faintly smile back at you; my heart bellows and whimpers at the thought of being in this world without my son?

It speaks his name over and over as I mouth words that mimic conversation.

My eyes weep invisible tears of grief as my heart bleeds out.

I am an actor portraying the role of a human being participating in life.

That is who I am in this world. It is all I can be right now.

There is no cheering me up. Just allow me to be.

Sit by my side in this tomb of grief where I reside.

I am not who I was Before.

I am yet to be who I'll become After.

For now I am but a pause.

A breath held.

Letting Go

With the passage of time came a soft, unexplainable letting go: not of love, but of the firm, encircling pain of grief.

It was Thursday evening. Yesterday was a long day for Sam. He had surgery to repair a torn rotator cuff. Today would have been Preston's twenty-fourth birthday. A bottle of Cabernet sat breathing on the hearth room table. I was a lightweight, but tonight I had every intention of finishing the entire bottle myself. Sam sat to my left. I don't know why but I sat at the head of the table. His boozy eyes looked at the pizza like it was an ordinary pizza night, grabbing a slice before I could help him. He held it in the air pointy end facing down, almost childlike in his mannerism, then sent it nose-diving like a toy plane into the extra sauce. Up it went again, this time pointy end facing up while sauce dripped onto his hand, his face still looking similar to when he came out of surgery. As the pizza saluted our son in midair, with a groggy voice and far away eyes he said, "Happy Birthday bud."

He looked directly through me with an almost smile, then up at the ceiling like I wasn't there. With that I started to sob uncontrollably from some newly torn perforation in my gut while he ate a few more bites of pizza and stared numbly into the dark opening of the fireplace. I didn't care about wiping the wetness from my face; it seemed like a futile effort when it would soon be drenched again. Happy Birthday sounded so cruel now. Two simple words were forever rearranged—displaced into some dark part of me. Sitting at the table I thought: *I'll never be able to hear those words again without counting backwards.* Initially I thought it would be a good idea for Sam to come to the table with me, to share in our pain the way we had for the past seven months, to declare some sort of morbid victory for having made it this far.

I had supposed we would reminisce about him: recall happy moments then share a few tear-filled smiles, but Sam was in a world of painkillers all to himself. And I couldn't have been more off base about how this birthday that wasn't really a birthday would actually feel. Never did I suppose hearing happy birthday would ignite such fresh, new pain.

I helped Sam, who was basically sleep walking, back into bed and put the ice pack on his shoulder as scheduled. Then I heard our westie, Cooper, ring his bell to go out that hung from the knob of the French doors in the hearth room. Outside he pulled me across the brick patio to the edge where the bricks stopped and the grass began. The backyard sloped off the patio giving it a terrace-like feeling. My downcast eyes stared numbly at Cooper and the green grass he was watering underneath his white furry paws until he started to bark. Then my eyes looked up and there it was. Lit up against a dome of blue sky like its very own stage, as big and bright as a rainbow could be—almost neon—was a rainbow. Being Irish rainbows hold a tender and specific meaning for me. For the last ten years, 'The Other End of the Rainbow' was the working title for my book. *What are the odds? I wondered. Don't analyze, just take in this gift in the same precious manner it was given to you. Open everything. Question nothing.* For once in my life I would question nothing.

The birthday boy had sent me a message. It was in our backyard that evening when time stood still, when the universe curtained off everything around me so I could lose myself in this coincidence or synchronicity or dream or visitation, and I could hear our beloved boy say *I'm here, it's amazing! Go on mom; go on with your life. Are you paying attention to this rainbow of mine? You see what it's telling you, don't you? How cool and convenient this rainbow thing was! I really couldn't have spelled it out anymore clearly you know. You get it, right? Write the words you've been speaking for years. Speak the words I could never say onto paper. You've been forming them in your head for so long. They're right there waiting for you to sit down with them and claim them. If you don't hurry up they will soon travel to someone else. Now it's time to really begin. Don't be afraid; it won't break you. Just begin, mom. The rest will follow. I promise.*

I stood motionless, oblivious to Cooper tugging at his leash. Still in a trance, I stepped off the brick patio as if the rainbow was pulling me closer. I walked past the stone fire pit, stopping in front of the fuchsia rose-covered archway marveling at the rainbow; my face watered down by droplets of fresh grief and wonderment.

I opened my arms, barely able to speak and said, "Hi pumpkin, I see you. Can you see me? I'm trying. It's still so hard, but mom is really trying; I promise you I will tell your story. I love you to the other end of that big, beautiful rainbow and beyond."

Suddenly I was overcome with guilt for not sharing it with Sam. I ran into the house with Cooper excitedly prancing beside me thinking it was a fun new game, then down the long hallway into our bedroom. "Hon, guess what! I just saw the most beautiful rainbow in the backyard. I think Pres is trying to tell me something."

Sam slurred in drawn out letters, "Huh? What did you say?"

I wasn't talking to my husband, just a sleepy, souped up on painkillers, sweet man of mine. "Never mind. Just rest." I removed the ice pack from his shoulder. I felt comforted standing by his bed watching him sleep, knowing he wasn't in any pain whatsoever.

I looked out the bedroom window but the rainbow was gone. I couldn't fault the rainbow; it was just being itself. It never intended to stay here long. The rainbow, Preston, it all fell on my heart the way a tiny snowflake becomes an avalanche: delicate and pretty, then crushing.

Cooper jumped up on the sofa and laid a fuzzy yellow ball by my leg, giving me one sloppy kiss after another. Through sniffles, I petted him saying, "You're a good boy. It's okay." Which made me cry even more 'cause I felt the lie stick in my throat as I spoke it, even to a dog. He jumped off the sofa and returned with another toy as if to say, "The yellow ball didn't make you happy? Here, how about my Tigger toy? Would that make you feel better?"

The portrait painted across my piece of the sky wasn't accidental. I know that. One thing I've learned is not to question a choreographed coincidence.

A story from the universe doesn't require an explanation any more than the rising of the sun. It's there to bless our day with light. And it's exactly the wonderment I saw and felt in that precise moment.

I lived on the sofa for the rest of the evening, writing a poem through gasps and torrential downpours of tears from somewhere deep within I hadn't yet reached. I thought I had tapped into all the broken places, but I had not. Another realization.

Initially grief was a monster that swallowed us whole and spit us out piece by piece. That's the way you come back to life, too—piece by piece, breath by breath, step by step, until you can be real and messy again, until that day when you glance in the mirror and see not grief, but love.

My hands shook as I poured myself a cup of green tea. Maybe sadness is literally shaking its way out of me, or reality is shaking its way in. I suppose they're one in the same—the implicit act of releasing and receiving had become a means to reconcile my new life. In the kitchen pantry I reach for walnuts and almonds. My ritual of afternoon tea feels different, like I sat down with an awkward acquaintance instead of a comfortable friend. It's absurd how the sameness of my daily routine is so unknown to me right now. A book sits unopened on my lap. I stare at it, begging it to open and enlighten me. Nothing. I turn on the television realizing a book would be wasted on me today. This is one of those days where I can do nothing but exist, like when I was waiting for my sonogram. This time I will accept it for what it is. I'll put my book aside and open myself up to receiving the pain and let go of another morsel of grief.

I look down at my cup and wonder how many cups my tears would have filled so far. I laugh out loud at myself for being so ridiculous. An honest to goodness hearty laugh. I am healing.

Now I was strong enough to cry. And in that life altering moment I became the new me. Not the better, improved version. Just new. Different. Reformed and remade. I still had ten fingers and toes, yet the way they touched the ordinary things in my world like the pine flooring and brass doorknob of our home felt altered. Maybe I did need to be flattened, as if by a bulldozer, so I could be reformed and remade into a different knowing. One that declared out loud so it couldn't be denied: *you will never again get to act as Preston's mom. You will never get to hug or kiss him. Nor care for him. You have given all of that up to God now.*

At the loss of a child you stop knowing yourself. Until one day you meet the new you. It was like I woke up one morning and caught a glimpse of myself in the mirror. The mysterious, knowing eyes looking back at me saw everything from a new perspective. They had seen and felt an unknowable hurt, but for the first time I could see specks of daylight flickering in their blueness. Curious and somewhat skeptical, I went back, looked again and asked, "Wait. Who are you? I've never met you before. Hello. And welcome. I'd like to get to know you. It will take some time I'm sure, getting to know you, that is. Please be patient with me, I'm still adjusting. I've seen and felt a lot of things I never thought I would. You should probably know I ask a lot of questions. Some things can't be changed. But I have a big heart and you seem like a nice lady.

"You're aware, of course, that I've seen my darkest shadow, the one birthed in some strange Petri dish of death. Even though you come from a dark place deep within there's something interesting about you. I can see fierceness in your eyes. I like that. Maybe together we could begin again. One more thing you should know—I'm pretty good at beginning again."

I had to be careful in my knowing though; depending on the day, the mirror that I attempted to glean a new life from either reflected or retracted the light. In my new knowing, when in it I saw the lightness, I could see the wise mountain. I could see Sam and Samantha smiling back at me. Still, there remained days I looked, not knowing who in the mirror I would see. But I was beginning to feel her heartbeat as if it really belonged to me. I could hear the hearty sound of my future heartbeat cracking through the veneer of past pain.

What had this new lady in the mirror done for me? Had she reached through me with her light, flickering blueness of eyes, with her lightness of spirit, and extracted the crushing sadness out of me? She had. In the life saving place where beginning again crushed what was crushing me.

Through the years time thoughtfully rewound itself, putting a soft cushion between the pain and us, enabling us to live past the dying to a remembrance our hearts could bear.

There are some things, though, that no matter how many years pass, time can never change. Every December as I get the Christmas decorations out, at the bottom of the last box that I've been avoiding, I reach down to the bottom of it and I pull out Preston's old stocking. My fingers graze over his name stenciled in green on the cuff, each letter holding a different remembrance brought back to life. I hold it tightly to my chest. For a moment I forget to breathe. Then my memory place will take me back to the last time I hung it on our mantel. I see my past self smiling, thinking of the silly, noisy toy I put in it, and I weep for him once again like I just lost him again. I weep as if I can't be repaired, knowing I have no choice. I imagine every parent who's lost a child has that one thing that disassembles him or her. This is mine. And when I'm 100 years old it will still be mine.

Love
In the darkest hours of grieving, I learned how hard we had fought for love.

We are broken. And whole. We are human and unexplainable, with spirit guides who tiptoe beside us through life.

If we're lucky, we become more aware each time life breaks us open revealing another layer of might. Even though, as a family, we've experienced both extremes of the rich plump skin and the hard, brittle bones of life, we continue to be more of who we are meant to be. For we are defined not by our losses, but how much love we carry in our hearts. Life is hard. Grief is harder still.

But love is the mender of all things broken, the hope for a happy tomorrow. It reigns above everything hard and sad and gorgeous and profound. It's what lets in the light to heal a receptive heart.

When a day was stripped bare, when hope had all but been bleached from our DNA, one entity seemingly immune to bad news—love. The one supposed thing that never failed us, not once, but rather grew stronger like the sun, even as a wretched day insisted on.

Love *is* a many splendored thing. It can be a villain or superhero. In its mystery or gift it can either be magic or myth. We didn't know what Preston's favorite time of year was, or his most favorite song, or his biggest pet peeve. But the love that was emitted through his soul and energy never left us guessing. No disability existed in his ability to love.

Love is one hundred million feelings that are things, one hundred million things that are feelings.

Love encompasses all feelings, places, times and conditions. The truest love lies in the messy parts, coerced and configured by life's demands. Our family's unconditional love was the constant in between the highs and lows of life that sustained us. The way we used love and moved love from one person to another is what defined our humanity.

The greatest love, partnered with courage, is what takes us outside of our own boundaries and returns us enlightened for having taken the journey. A boy who couldn't walk or talk caused us to do just that. Love doesn't need a voice. Love is the voice. And every day of his life, Preston's voice was heard loud and clear.

Maybe it was simply that when people looked at Preston there existed a subliminal exchange of love and courage. Beyond that, what more do we as human beings need? I wonder how much love we have stored up inside of us that never gets handed out or offered because we're too afraid or stubborn.

Every time Sam and I began again, without conscientiously knowing it, we quickly harvested our courage before it went dormant. We gathered up everything we saw in Preston and Samantha, everything we felt within us, and began again as if it were the first time.

That was the alchemy of each new beginning.

Being mostly nonverbal, there were stories, songs, questions and answers we never heard from Preston. He had just a few words at his disposal. Of all the words in the English language, the greatest words we ever heard; the only ones that really mattered at all were "I uv ou"—spoken by an uncommon boy in an uncommon way. How poetic that our non-verbal boy found a way to consistently say the three most beautiful words in the whole wide world.

I wonder what Preston saw when he looked at all the people in his life? The ones who looked back at him. Did he see beyond our skin and bone, straight into our soul? I think he did. I think that's why he was here. Did he see a specific lesson in each of us, a transformation from who we were to who we were meant to be, because of knowing him, as Samantha said? There are certain people whose mission in life is not theirs alone to live, but moreover to find the invincible in each and every one of us. We hear about them all the time on the news—our kiddos, the too-soon angels who left their immense heart prints behind.

They are the ones who carry a peace of heaven with them here on earth, profoundly touching another's heart.

Here's to all the spirited children who possess a different energy, the ones on loan to us for but a tender sojourn on this wonderful earth. Thank you for the gifts you gave so heroically.

When we encountered people like Dr. Rolex who didn't care to look at Preston, or the grocery store mom who was afraid for her son to go near him, I wanted so badly to say to them: *let's trade hearts for just one day. I'll wear yours and you'll wear mine. We will see and hear and feel the world through each other's heart, and through the various chambers we'll visit each other's memory place. Then we will weep together at what we feel. Afterward, I will ask of you one more thing. I want you to wear Preston's heart, but only for an hour. Trust me, I'm doing you a favor. That's all you'll be able to bear. For your heart has been built on judgment, indifference and an all-knowing sense of right or wrong, of worthy or unworthy. It's simply not that strong. And yes, you will weep again at how much more alike you and Preston are than different. Then you will understand.*

Looking back through my memory place, it was at times, many times actually, like moving against the common grain of life. As if we were constantly traveling in the opposite direction, to the other end of the rainbow. I see the old me and my metamorphosis from a benign being to two conjoined—human and Mothers Being. I learned over and over that I was more than capable of doing what scared me, even the scariest of all: surviving the death of a child.

Preston's challenges and energy, Samantha's spirit and humor were the silent messages stirring within me for years like a voice spoken to me in another language until time translated what I needed to hear. Writing this book has been much like coming home to myself. Coming into my own skin and properly filling it out.

Grief is like an illness: you either recover or you don't. I lived and found myself again amongst all the lost words.

I daresay we survived it all. I used to think strong meant putting on a brave face and pretending because I didn't know any other way to be. Strong always felt like shrinking into a shape I didn't fit into. But in the quiet, naked moments I knew my truth. Inevitably that is where I found my strength. In those moments there was no denying my mistakes and imperfections, not if I really looked. Sometimes in the looking it hurt like hell; it's supposed to. But what I saw in the reflection was my soul. My truth was where there existed beauty and flaws, and I learned to accept them both.

I've come to understand that strong is the mysterious root that grows underground only allowing us to see its beautiful flower bursting from the earth as if it got there standing tall and colorful all by itself. But the hard, dirty work was done in the darkness, the stretching and bending of ones soul to eventually reach the light. I was strong because I'd been bent and stretched, sometimes to the point of snapping; but, just as I was ready to break in the darkness, someone or something turned me toward the light again.

Strong is that word that's indefinable or at least it should be, because how do you define a twisted root growing underground that no one can see? No one asks how hard the twisted root had to work to unearth such a flower.

Preston was a unique, old soul who came to us to teach us what heavy metal we carried in our bones, and because of that our hearts were stirred and disrupted in all manner of ways. Grieving the loss of a child is as boundless as loving a child. So for us, in accordance with our hearts decree, we grieved properly—in our own time, in our own way. Losing a child is much like being a recovering alcoholic or drug addict, I suppose. If you visit with it too long you feel the edge of your heart fold inward and your toes, without meaning to, curl under, and everything within you starts to crave something it can never have. And in that moment, you know that forever and ever you will be in recovery.

Being in recovery helps me remember that life altering moment years ago, when the fuel we needed to breathe, to walk, to think, and to live was emptied from us in such a sudden, violent manner; leaving our soul vacuous of all life forms. But from which there remained a single cell composed of all our life's melodies with Preston—that when given the right moment sent our hearts singing back to life to a place where one cell of love grew another cell of courage, which then grew another cell of hope, which grew yet another cell of light. Now, most days, that's where we live: where a sliver of lightness begins again.

Our life story began with a question, the one first in line in front of a plentitude of twenty-three years' worth of questions: *is he going to die?* And it ended with another question: *do you need permission to go?* We'd traveled a concentric circle back to the question of death. His life, though, was about the right to live, and to live however we saw fit. It was about the right to choose—however limited our choices—the right to learn—wherever and however—no matter your ability. And most importantly it was about the right to love and be loved in return.

In dance you get dizzy if you don't spot something and come back to that same point. In life you can rarely come back to that same point. The hands of time carry you swiftly along, each moment as fleeting as a feather carried on a swift breeze: one moment floating lazily in front of you, the next quickly scattering in the wind to a destination unknown. It's what calls out to us to name each moment as wasted or precious.

We couldn't go back to our old life. It exists in the slippery before of time where Preston remains, through the looking glass of our memory place. But we could come back—back to living a joyful life in a new uncommon way.

Sometimes you need to lose your place in the world in order to find your place. We lost ourselves to begin again.

We would never be the same, but we would be happy. Happy with our new family of three: Sam, Samantha and I. Happy to begin again in a new place.

A fresh day sits in between the restlessness of the past and the whispered promise of tomorrow that breathes hope into us each time we arise and open our eyes to the possibility in the impossible. And a renewed knowing stirs within us, never to be forgotten or taken for granted.

As I see it, and as our human family has experienced—for all our countless beginnings and endings, our infinite similarities and differences; there is only one way to go through this transcendent opening called life.

Only one way to reach *the place of us.*

Heart to heart, hand to hand, bandana to bandana.

We survive because we are all connected.

space/spas/ ~

the unlimited or incalculably great three-dimensional realm or expanse in which all material objects are located and all events occur

a place available for a particular purpose

Origin ~

Middle English, from Anglo-French espace, space, from Latin spatium area, Room, interval of space or time

space ~

a place to think and to grow and to breathe and to love

Chapter 26

Lightness

"*The soul would have no rainbow, had the eyes no tears*"

John Vance Cheney

THE RAINBOW ON PRESTON'S FIRST HEAVENLY BIRTHDAY, and in all of life's choreographed coincidences, were layers presented to me one at a time so I wouldn't miss any one of them, graciously allowing my Mothers Being to tune in to what I needed to see. They were life's gray areas that I'd been drawn to for twenty-three years, each surreptitiously building up to this moment.

We were given an uncommon vantage point from a redheaded boy in a wheelchair that we wouldn't trade for anything. I think the saddest life story is one that doesn't recognize the truth. Mark Nepo tells us, "*The heart is much like a miraculous balloon. Its lightness comes from staying full.*" We not only recognized Preston's truth, we celebrated it. And in doing so, it filled our hearts with what we did still have.

His life had been black or white, a good day or bad day. But the negative spaces in between the finite of the black and white of his life are where the astounding beauty gets in—where we think and grow and breathe and love.

The visceral gray spaces in between the rainbow's colors were his silent lessons reaching the people that were meant to receive them. No matter your story, life is a series of realizations if you allow yourself to be open to them. Our life's realizations with Preston taught us that the thing you didn't think you were meant to do is the very thing that makes you who you are. Our realizations began slowly as unconscious awakenings eventually helping us unlearn what our past taught us. Our days were often heavy with worry, lack of sleep, and imbalance, as we struggled not to appear over-wrought, and it took some time before the realizations restored within us the lightness to see what couldn't be seen. We learned as we went along that some days have to get ugly before you can see their beauty.

Looking back, it makes perfect sense that the gray spaces in between were the learning moments. Preston lived in between two worlds his entire life: in the stillness where everything quivers gray and whispers can be heard as easily as thunder. And now he abides in the everlasting lightness of being continuous and whole. We too bounced from typical with Samantha to disability with Preston. Other than the black and white of sick or well, everything existed for us in shades of gray. Within the subtle shadows we learned a depth of perception we would have never otherwise known, and it was life giving.

The sinewy gray areas were in everyone Preston found with his listening eyes. By exercising his human right to choose he taught us that sometimes the lessons lie in the deepest shadow waiting for the light to find them—reminding us to look for the possibility in the impossible.

Preston was one singular human being who poetically affected others in their storybook of life. It was all the small stories emitting an energy force that floated around him like fireflies in the night, which lit an uncommon knowingness in those who loved him. We were the lucky ones, the ones that despite all the challenges and uncertainty saw the rainbows and fireflies because we knew him.

Preston didn't do any one great thing, depending on what you consider to be a great thing. He never learned to walk or talk. He never stopped get-ting sick. He couldn't escape his recurring physical pain. He often lost his temper at being trapped inside a body that didn't work. He got frustrated at not being able to communicate clearly and consistently, but to us he did a million and one miraculous things: like speaking without words, loving greatly, smiling an unending smile in the face of doubt, laughing and mak-ing others laugh even more, reaching across borders, teaching those who stopped long enough to put the Preston puzzle together, and being utterly resilient to whatever life threw his way.

Though he couldn't reach his arms around those he loved, he hugged everyone with his humongous heart.

His ineffable energy everyone spoke of was both tiny and grand, the way tiny light clusters together to form a grand illumination. That's what we are—tiny light clusters with the potential to be big by living the life we're meant to live. And when we do, the heart swells past our internal borders to reach those who need it most. Sometimes the far-reaching light touches those we can't even see, those we will never know.

A tiny cluster of light named Preston showed everyone that the light that shines the brightest is the light from within.

Somehow or other, with the glint in his expressive eyes, the ornery slant of his smile, or his unique utterances and scant words—from his wheelchair he commanded those around him and taught them to think uncommon thoughts.

Preston taught us all that love is courageous when offered with a pureness of heart.

He enabled everyone who knew him to give color to his black and white renderings so others could understand, and remind us, that messy parts and all, life is to be lived with gratitude, love and humor.

His silent lessons live on so that we can remember how a singular small being, a life lived in unison with the heart of another heart, had the immense capacity to change the trajectory of another human being's life.

Through it all, a force called love never surrendered—not once—through all the good days and bad days, the horrid days, the miraculous, joyful days, even the days that made us ask why.

Through all the gray spaces in between there was an enigmatic, redheaded boy who smiled an uncommon smile. We smiled back. And that was enough.

Whether Preston was sick or well, his *mana* remained with him and the power of love and courage transcended all manner of reason. Because of who he was.

Dear Preston,

Here I am once again writing a note to you, like I did not long after you arrived on this wonderful earth. When I finished the last chapter I had an epiphany that gave me chills. It reminded me of the many times when we thought it was the end and it wasn't. It was as though your uncooperative, taut body that long ago softened into the universe had fluently reached out to me for one last lesson, and I knew I had to end with one last note.

How are you today, my handsome guy? As I recite these words they seem to rise off the page almost taking human form, with eyes and ears and a mouth that speaks them distinctly. It startles me that I had almost forgotten what I used to say to you every morning. But I don't live there anymore, the same way you don't live here anymore. This reinforces in my heart how healing's genius grows wiser and softer with each year. Of course you know I could never truly forget those words, they sing to my soul from the belly of my being.

That's what true healing is; what I know to be your intention for our life, what I promised you that night. It waits there in the midst the way all long-ago remembrances wait, deep in my memory place for the days I summon it up, the days when I miss you the most. And the other days are for living.

I know you are well and whole and filled with light. I dream you awake, from the darkness of night into the daylight of love. In my dreams you're always small so you can fit precisely on my lap, allowing me to hug every inch of you. If that isn't God's grace then I don't know what is.

I've written your voice in black and white, filling in the gray areas as we discovered them. I know you've been with me through it all, from the first uncertain moment long ago when I scribbled that note with shaky hands, and later through the years as I wrote scraps of thoughts and tucked them away because I wasn't yet ready to write about you, about us. Most of all, I know you are there in the stillness between the words. Once, when I first starting writing your story, when I doubted that I could make my words dance and swirl off the page into visionary beings, the blinds in front of my desk started to move like a warm wind was blowing them. That was the day I found my unfeigned writing voice.

How do I forget the gaping silence that followed your birth as if it were an omen? How do I forget the day you died without good-bye? I won't.

I can't. Your life and death are aggrandized in my heart so all my brokenness can shine outwardly to the precious ones still in my life.

Losing you hasn't been easy, but time has been kind the way a beautiful day feels kind, for it followed a bleak day.

There is no real logic to your story, nor should there be. How can there be logic in disabilities, illness and death? But that's what we're wired to do: to logically try to give everything some kind of sense. Logic tells us to look for specific things we know, never regarding what at first can't be seen. Logic doesn't tell us to look inward.

Beyond everything knowable and unknowable, your differently-abled energy found a way to reach the broken part in everyone you met. You saw that somewhere deep inside we're all just a little disabled.

Thank you for the love-filled lessons you allowed us to see. I've tried to the best of my ability to give credence to your voice in the way I imagine you would have wanted. It seems uncanny to me, still, as if from birth you silently called out to release the ink of my heart on paper, enabling me to write from my soul, where all your lessons had been stored.

Today I finished your story—the final letting go. Love and grief will always fight for the greater space in my heart. Most days love wins. On the days that grief wins I pull out your black and white bandana and I look up to the heavens at all the broken little pieces that light up the sky, and love fills my eyes.

I realize once again what I've known to be true your entire life: without the negative spaces, the lightness would be but a blur. It makes perfect sense.

The irreconcilable colors as you arrived, the sharp against the flat were put in our way so we'd have to excavate our old lives to find the subtle miracles in our new life.

In heaven I imagine laughter so glorious the mountains themselves quiver with resounding joy. When I close my eyes and still my heart long enough, I can hear you laugh. It carries with it the lightness we vowed never to forget.

And I know with great certainty, beyond all that remains unknowable, you would want your life story to end with a good hearty laugh. My Mothers Being nods.

Knock knock . . .

Love you (to the other end of the rainbow and beyond),

Mom

Epilogue

"Enough" is a feast.　　　　　　　　　　　　　　Buddhist proverb

*I*T'S A BEAUTIFUL MARCH MORNING, WITH PROMISES OF spring by the way the birds chirp outside. Sam is standing at the front door. I lean over the banister in the hallway upstairs telling him, "See ya. Have a good day. Love you. Be safe." I say the exact same thing to him every morning, never saying goodbye. It makes me uncomfortable. On the wall behind me is a large, framed photograph of Preston under the banyan tree. After Sam leaves, I turn toward it and blow a kiss to his photo, then tap it lightly and smile. That is my offering to our son, the only one I have to give, and in doing so I offer life to myself.

As parents, we have returned from the frightful place of nothingness. It's been almost thirteen years since he died, six of which I've spent writing this book. When I think of the many layers of my soul that went into writing I'm overcome with gratitude. This book was first written by a young girl who didn't have much of a voice because she was embarrassed by its nasally tone. By a rebellious teenager who couldn't talk back for fear of what might happen, by a frightened young mom who experienced indifference, ignorance and miracles all at once. Then by a grief shocked mom who had to learn a new identity. And though my Mothers Being was as real as she was phantom-like; she was there from the moment I birthed Preston, then again with Samantha—waiting for me to call her up and use her fully and unconditionally. It was through stepping into the many places of me that I learned to fully own the place of us.

I began writing this book with the intention of starting a conversation of listening and understanding. So a parent who had a child with disabilities or health issues could talk with someone who didn't, so a parent who'd lost a child could talk with someone who hadn't. And mostly, so anyone could have a conversation of listening and understanding with someone different from them so we could all be human together. Some stories were hard to tell, but I've always believed that an uncomfortable truth is better than an uncomfortable lie. Life isn't always comfortable and some of the greatest lessons are learned when we're uncomfortable. We are all drenched in lightness. We are lightness. And at some point we are bathed in darkness. We are darkness. To embody both throughout our lifetime is to understand that each human being is filled with disability and ability the same way the sky is lit by both the sun and the moon.

Though I began writing scraps of the book ten years before Preston died, it has been my way of gently tucking him into bed and pulling up the covers, allowing his memory to rest well.

While life hasn't been by our design, it's always been by our own definition. The best we can do is to know how much we don't know and try to map out our life realizing that some plans may get erased along the way. The four of us lived a lifetime of love concentrated within twenty-three years. And you know what happens when something is concentrated—it gets stronger.

We lived our life fully, with the realization that what we had was enough. And in the end our enough was overwhelming and good and true.

The Place of Us was never a physical place but rather a spiritual place. It was every place we were, together and apart. That was the beauty of it.

This is not the end. Just another opening in that great space in between. Thank you for reading our story.

Acknowledgments

*L*IFE IS AN EVERLASTING BENEVOLENT BREATH—INWARD to us, then outward to another. And so it is with my longest, most benevolent breath that I say *Thank you* to the following people.

To my husband, Sam, the love of my life and my source of tender strength, who listened to snippets of the book and offered advice as a whole, who provided a steady stream of cappuccinos and his gentle, wild love and support without fail. You are my 'enough.'

To my daughter, Samantha, my best girlfriend and my light, who fiercely believed in me and made me laugh when I needed to, who I knew before I met how precious she would be. You are my other heart.

To my parents, Joe and Jane Hannigan, who loved Sam, like a son and who we couldn't have survived without (especially the years on South Mountain).

To Julie, who is the best little sister I'm delighted to 'stick together' with.

To Emory and Lorraine, thank you for the gift of your son.

To Miss Steph, Preston's other mother, who loved him unconditionally and who saved our souls and bodies, and lightened our hearts and hands.

To family, friends, mentors and bosses too numerous to mention, who showed their belief in me in tangible ways, you know who you are. Your love and support meant everything.

To Preston's teachers, friends and principal at Myersville Elementary, who went above and beyond in their teaching, openness and humanity.

To Preston's teachers, friends and principal at Rock Creek, who, in the end, he wanted and needed to be with.

To Preston's instructional aides, who cared for him more lovingly and intelligently than we could've ever imagined. You were the right hand to his left.

To Preston's respite caregivers, who so carefully took care of him, also cared for us. Respite is both physically and mentally vital to a full time caregiver's wellness.

To the NICU doctors and nurses at CMC, thank you seems inadequate. Without your diligent care there would be no story to tell.

To all the doctors and nurses, who treated Preston as a person first while first doing no harm, and in an odd way to the ones who didn't. They helped us to become better advocates.

To my beta readers, whose insight was invaluable.

To my editor, MaryAnne Hafen, who showed me that less is more, more or less, and for accepting my made up words and sentences as legal. She was like the best clothing stylist ever, which brought out more of me.

To the WiDo staff, who have guided and supported me.

To all hummingbirds and fireflies that flit around this universe lighting another.

And finally, other than the help of the aforementioned people, I would be remiss to think I wrote this book alone.

I was never alone. With me were spirit guides, angels and God.